Hegel on Pseudo-Philosophy

Also Available from Bloomsbury

Hegel's Grammatical Ontology: Vanishing Words and Hermeneutical Openness in the 'Phenomenology of Spirit,' Jeffrey Reid
Hegel on Possibility: Dialectics, Contradiction, and Modality, Nahum Brown
Hegel, Logic and Speculation, ed. Paolo Diego Bubbio, Alessandro De Cesaris, Maurizio Pagano and Hager Weslati
The Relevance of Hegel's Concept of Philosophy: From Classical German Philosophy to Contemporary Metaphilosophy, ed. Luca Illetterati and Giovanna Miolli

Hegel on Pseudo-Philosophy

Reading the Preface to the Phenomenology of Spirit

Andrew Alexander Davis

BLOOMSBURY ACADEMIC
LONDON • NEW YORK • OXFORD • NEW DELHI • SYDNEY

BLOOMSBURY ACADEMIC
Bloomsbury Publishing Plc
50 Bedford Square, London, WC1B 3DP, UK
1385 Broadway, New York, NY 10018, USA
29 Earlsfort Terrace, Dublin 2, Ireland

BLOOMSBURY, BLOOMSBURY ACADEMIC and the Diana logo are trademarks of
Bloomsbury Publishing Plc

First published in Great Britain 2023
This paperback edition published in 2024

Copyright © Andrew Alexander Davis, 2023

Andrew Alexander Davis has asserted his right under the Copyright, Designs and Patents Act, 1988, to be identified as Author of this work.

For legal purposes the Acknowledgments on p. viii constitute an extension of this copyright page.

Series design by Charlotte Daniels
Cover image: Clonopsis gallica (french stick insect) (© Paul Starosta / Getty Images)

All rights reserved. No part of this publication may be reproduced or transmitted in any form or by any means, electronic or mechanical, including photocopying, recording, or any information storage or retrieval system, without prior permission in writing from the publishers.

Bloomsbury Publishing Plc does not have any control over, or responsibility for, any third-party websites referred to or in this book. All internet addresses given in this book were correct at the time of going to press. The author and publisher regret any inconvenience caused if addresses have changed or sites have ceased to exist, but can accept no responsibility for any such changes.

A catalogue record for this book is available from the British Library.

A catalog record for this book is available from the Library of Congress.

ISBN: HB: 978-1-3503-4775-5
PB: 978-1-3503-4779-3
ePDF: 978-1-3503-4776-2
eBook: 978-1-3503-4777-9

Typeset by Deanta Global Publishing Services, Chennai, India

To find out more about our authors and books visit www.bloomsbury.com and sign up for our newsletters.

Nothing was more natural than that these things should be the other things that they absolutely were not.
—Henry James, "A Turn of the Screw"

Every determination of spirit can be taken . . . as something it negates so that spirit itself is the pure, self-relating light.
—Hegel, *Vorlesungen vol. 13*

. . . everything that is not God consumed with intellectual fire.
—W. B. Yeats, "Blood and the Moon"

For my parents, Dennis and Nancy Davis
ἔστι δ' ἡ μὲν πρὸς γονεῖς φιλία τέκνοις, καὶ ἀνθρώποις πρὸς θεούς, ὡς πρὸς ἀγαθὸν καὶ ὑπερέχον: εὖ γὰρ πεποιήκασι τὰ μέγιστα: τοῦ γὰρ εἶναι καὶ τραφῆναι αἴτιοι, καὶ γενομένοις τοῦ παιδευθῆναι.
—*Aristotle,* Nicomachean Ethics *1162a5*

Contents

Acknowledgments	viii
Texts and Editions	ix
Introduction	1
1 Philosophy Is Not Explanation (§1–3, 48)	19
2 Philosophy Is Not Edification (§6–11, 14, 19, 55, 66)	41
3 Philosophy Is Not Formalism (§12–16, 50–53)	65
4 Philosophy Is Not Phenomenology (§26–37)	85
5 Philosophy Is Not Mathematical (§42–46)	119
6 Philosophy Is Not Propositional (§22–23, 38–41, 47–66)	131
7 Philosophy Is Not Personal (§67–72)	151
Conclusion: Notes toward Negation	169
Appendix: Hegel's 1807 Preface, Summary by Paragraph	175
Notes	199
Bibliography	208
Index	212

Acknowledgments

This book evolved out of a lecture I gave at St. John's College in 2015. I want to thank Peter Kalkavage for the invitation as well as the students and tutors who participated in a lively discussion afterward. I want to thank the members and attendees of the biennial Hegel Society of North America conferences, without which my study of Hegel would be much poorer. I want to thank my friends Mark Anderson, Peter Kuryla, and Raoni Padui for discussing the general project and the manuscript itself with me on many occasions. I want to thank my students for their candor when I teach Hegel, especially Michael Agrella, who read and commented on the manuscript. I want to thank the anonymous readers at Bloomsbury for their valuable comments and Liza Thompson and Lucy Russell for editorial guidance. I want to thank my parents and siblings for their long-standing support. Finally, I want to thank Jessica Blagys for life beyond words.

Texts and Editions

There are currently seven English-language translations of the preface to the *Phenomenology of Spirit:* five as part of complete translations of Hegel's book (Baillie 1910, Miller 1977, Pinkard 2018, Inwood 2018, Fuss and Dobbins 2019) and two as standalone translations of the preface with commentary (Kaufmann 1965 and Yovel 2005). The existing translations are accurate enough, though none reliably captures the nuances that make a difference to my reading. I therefore provide my own translations throughout. I cite Hegel's books and lectures in the Suhrkamp *Taschenbuch Wissenschaft* edition of Hegel's *Werke* [W volume: page]. The Suhrkamp *Werke* text of the preface varies only slightly from that of the Meiner critical edition, the *Gesammelte Werke,* and is more readily available to readers at much lower cost. Occasionally, an argument depends on precise wording and the critical edition contains an important textual variant. In these cases, I cite the critical edition as well [GW volume:page]. Citations from the *Phenomenology* are followed by the paragraph number [§], which allows the reader to find the passage in the English translation of choice.

Introduction

How This Book Began

A few years ago, I read Hegel's seven prefaces back to back. I began with the long preface to *The Phenomenology of Spirit* (1807), followed by the two mid-length prefaces to *The Science of Logic* (1816, 1831), the preface to *The Philosophy of Right* (1820), and finally the three short prefaces to the *Encyclopedia* (1817, 1827, and 1830). What I observed was an astonishing amount of continuity.

The prefaces are best understood as a genre unto themselves. There are allusions to the topic at hand in each of them, be it phenomenology, logic, or political philosophy, but a significant portion of each preface concerns another issue that they all argue in common. This common issue is *how to recognize and guard against pseudo-philosophy*.

On noticing this common thread between the prefaces, it struck me that focusing on the issue of pseudo-philosophy would be particularly beneficial to an interpretation of the 1807 preface which, because of its length, tone, and diversity of topics has proven difficult to piece together as a whole text with a single purpose. As H. S. Harris observed, "We all expect that we may come to comprehend almost any part of the book sooner, or better, than we shall ever comprehend the Preface" (Harris 1997, 34).

What Is Pseudo-philosophy?

By pseudo-philosophy, I mean to describe methods that appear philosophical but fall short of the actual practice of philosophy. I choose the term to underscore that Hegel is not simply critiquing rival positions *within* philosophy as is often assumed, but exposing methodological tendencies that abandon the task that unites the philosophical tradition from Thales to the present. It should be noted that "pseudo-philosophy" is not Hegel's term. Hegel himself refers to these tendencies as "forms [of thought] that, in their familiarity, are an obstacle to philosophical knowing" (W3:22, §16). I take this to mean that these forms of thought are familiar to us as philosophy, but are actually obstacles to it. While I prefer to work with Hegel's own words wherever possible and am reluctant to introduce a term to the text, I hope "pseudo-philosophy" captures both the familiarity and the obstruction present in these forms of thought. More, I intend the word to hint at the way that familiarity itself is the obstacle: precisely the things we assume to be philosophical can prove, for that very reason, to be obstacles to genuine inquiry.

Because the pseudo-philosophical tendencies Hegel highlights are associated with texts from accepted philosophers (Kant, Fichte, Schelling, etc.), readers have assumed that any insinuation of pseudo-philosophy is either polemical hyperbole or else unjust criticism. As a result, the critical force of Hegel's prefaces is often dismissed or diminished. There is, however, another possibility. Hegel's critique is sincere and defensible and does not concern Kant's work or Schelling's work *as a whole* but only certain tendencies found there, problematic tendencies that were often exacerbated in the work of their followers and students. Instead of carrying on the genuine aim of philosophy to think freely, to begin their inquiry again without presuppositions, these followers often assumed the truth of a principle or dogma from their teachers and then applied it to all manner of content. Noticing this, Hegel directs some critical energy toward the formulations in his contemporaries' work that had become gateways to dogmatism and skepticism.

Hegel's prefaces have some kinship with the Platonic dialogues that expose sophistry and eristic while only hinting at the shape of philosophy proper. As addressed in Plato's work, sophistry is not just another point of view within philosophy but a different practice with different ends (*Meno* 75a ff., *Sophist* 264b–268d). Aristotle later observes that philosophy is turned toward being and sophistry is turned in the opposite direction toward non-being (*Met.* 1004b19 ff.). As contraries, philosophy and sophistry are easily confused. Philosophy and sophistry seem similar in their ability to tackle abstract questions and contents, but they take those questions up in a different spirit and for a different purpose.

To this day, sophistry is often confused with philosophy. The issue of mistaken identity is important enough to Hegel that he spins out fifty-plus pages on it in his first preface, making it the longest preface to any work in the philosophical canon. It is important enough to him that he keeps addressing it in every preface to every edition of every book he publishes. It is important enough to him that it forces him to overcome his often stated aversion to prefaces.

As we will see, Hegel identifies several pseudo-philosophical tendencies in the work of his contemporaries: a tendency to explain rather than present, a tendency to edify rather than seek insight, a tendency toward rigid formalism rather than organic development, a tendency toward mathematical demonstration rather than the observation of purposive activity, a tendency toward propositional atomism rather than linguistic holism, and a tendency to view thinking as the work of individuals rather than communities. By exposing these tendencies, Hegel's first preface goes some way toward describing how philosophy has been and should be practiced, but mostly in a negative sense. Hegel will insist that an adequate understanding of philosophy emerges only from engagement with the concrete contents of philosophy itself (e.g., being, quantity, syllogism, density, organism, soul, right, freedom, and God) and thus cannot be described in advance.

Shifting the Focus

Hegel's critique of pseudo-philosophy has not gotten the attention it deserves. Scholars typically approach the 1807 preface to the *Phenomenology of Spirit* as a general introduction to Hegel's method, as if the critical remarks were just a way to put his own philosophical practice in relief.

Yet Hegel argues that all genuine philosophical thinking articulates itself slowly and laboriously through practice. Whatever sketches and hints he gives about philosophy in the prefaces must be taken with this rather large grain of salt. Still, because Hegel's major works are long and difficult, it is natural to look for some hints about what we might learn if we commit to studying them. Hegel himself realizes this and writes the 1807 preface with this in mind, as he himself notes (W3:22, §16). Yet because of strong convictions about the need for full engagement with the actual content of philosophy, Hegel's positive remarks about method in the preface often point toward their own deficiency (W3:47, §48).

Though Hegel discusses his own philosophical practice in the preface, any evaluation of these remarks would depend on familiarity with the specific movements of the determinate contents of his systematic presentations (e.g., how finitude relates to infinity or how mechanism relates to teleology). By contrast, Hegel's critical remarks about pseudo-philosophy are more self-sufficient. These remarks do not require the same demonstration through a systematic engagement with the specific contents of philosophy. The deficiencies in these pseudo-philosophical approaches can be seen by simply comparing what they claim to want with how they go about getting it. For example, pseudo-philosophical approaches claim to want an account of the whole, yet they methodologically exclude certain parts or aspects of that whole from consideration. This mismatch between the stated aims of philosophy and the limitations of pseudo-philosophical methods can be assessed without detailed knowledge of the actual contents of philosophy.

Given these considerations, my hypothesis is that the prevailing approach to the 1807 preface has things backward: Hegel's primary concern is not with the positive task of accounting for his own practice but with the negative task of exposing pseudo-philosophy. Because the positive task, such as it is present in the preface, depends on and derives its determinate character from the negative task, Hegel's critique of pseudo-philosophy takes precedence and gives us guidance on how to interpret the roughly sketched positive claims. Just as shifting the relationship of foreground and background transforms a photograph, this change of focus alters our reading experience.

The Contemporary Relevance of Hegel's Prefaces

In each of his seven prefaces, Hegel claims to address the current cultural context for his book. This seems, in his eyes, to be a chief purpose of a preface. In advance of the public judging his book, Hegel judges what state philosophy is in at the moment. This discussion is often taken by scholars to be historical in nature and to require a careful dissection of Hegel's possible references to his contemporaries (Fichte, Schelling, Reinhold, Jacobi, Fries, etc.). This, perhaps unintentionally, suggests that the prefaces are primarily *of historical interest.*

When we consider all the prefaces together, however, we see that despite the passage of over two decades, the cultural concerns Hegel observes are largely the same. Knowing is taken up in two distinct and incompatible registers. On the one hand, knowledge is pursued as *abstract reflection* and, on the other hand, knowledge is pursued as *immediate feeling*.[1] The former kind of knowing is led and governed by the natural sciences. The latter kind of knowing is understood alternately as religious faith, as common sense, or as artistic genius. While the salient representatives of each camp change between 1807 and 1831, the epistemic camps themselves remain entrenched.

Despite their heterogeneity, both abstract reflection and immediate feeling approach knowing as a kind of *certainty*. The former certainty derives its apodictic surety from completely *impersonal* mechanical necessity, a strict chain of efficient causation. The latter certainty derives its apodictic surety from the complete exclusion of all mechanical necessity, from its unassailably *personal* character as a feeling that cannot be known to anyone else. We will see these two forms of certainty at the root of the various forms of pseudo-philosophy in the 1807 preface. Hegel calls the opposition of abstract reflection and immediate feeling the "primary knot [*hauptsächlichste Knoten*]" in which modern attitudes toward knowledge have become entangled (W3:20, §14).

This opposition within epistemic culture that Hegel observes did not just stay constant from 1807 to 1831. It is still with us. We continue to struggle for an alternative to the opposition between abstract reflection and immediate feeling. We continue to mistake certainty for truth and continue to complain that in the absence of certainty we are left in a vacuum of relativism, even as our daily life and behavior attest to countless complex habits, values, norms, motives, reasons, purposes, goals, and commitments. Ironically, had Hegel's own intervention in the epistemic "knot" of modernity been more successful, we would have less need to go back and read his work for clues as to how we might untangle the knot ourselves.

Reading the Preface to the *Phenomenology*

Hegel's preface to the *Phenomenology of Spirit* combines some of his most accessible prose with some of his most obscure. Not surprisingly, it has inspired both enthusiastic eulogy and dismissal bordering on contempt.[2] Some insist it is the key to understanding Hegel (perhaps because it ranges so widely and leaves so much room for interpretation), while others consider it hastily composed juvenilia (probably for the same reason). There are several worthwhile discussions of the 1807 preface in print and they address many important questions, particularly those concerning Hegel's intellectual context.[3] However, they leave key stylistic and structural questions unexplored.

Many scholars read this preface as if its audience were philosophy professors and as if the value of philosophy could be presumed, making the question not *if* philosophy has value but *which* philosophical approach is best. They thus consider it a defense of Hegel's approach to philosophy and an introduction to his system specifically.[4] If we attend more closely to Hegel's tone, however, he is engaging a more fundamental problem. His imagined reader has doubts about philosophy itself, not just doubts about Hegel's philosophical merit. More, Hegel thinks his imagined reader is right to have these more thoroughgoing doubts. Philosophy has been debased, and the way to restore confidence in it begins in acknowledging this.[5]

The 1807 preface offers a rich, sustained discussion of the problems associated with many of our customary ways of reading and writing philosophy. Consider some results from the preface's various arguments: (1) philosophy cannot be communicated in a preface; (2) philosophy must be presented in a way that is necessary (not haphazard); (3) philosophy should not be confused with edifying discourse; (4) philosophy should not be confused with formalism; (5) philosophy cannot have a preset method but should be presented in a way that allows the content to produce its own form spontaneously; (6) philosophy should not be presented in a style that imitates mathematical proof; (7) philosophy should not be written (or read) as if individual sentences had atomic truth value; (8) philosophy should not be confused with argumentative rationalization [*Räsonieren*]; (9) philosophical writing must be read again and again because it employs an unfamiliar style; (10) philosophy should be presented in a way that is so complete that anyone (not just an intuitive genius) can learn the relation of its parts to each other; (11) philosophy does not conform to the uncritical prejudices of common sense; (12) philosophy is not the work of single individuals and should not be presented as if it were.[6] Surveying this list of conclusions, it strikes me that their overriding concern is not with the *content* of philosophy (the nature of being, the limits of knowledge, how we determine ethical norms, etc.) but the *form* philosophy takes to express any of its contents.

The 1807 preface asks: How can philosophical thinking be presented in writing without becoming rigid and dogmatic, on the one hand, or loose and capricious, on the other?[7] The dominance of abstract reflection and immediate feeling as modes of knowledge have guided us toward two unsatisfying forms of presentation: the dogmatic and the skeptical. To find the proper form for a philosophical inquiry, we must first liberate ourselves from these prejudices.

For millennia, thinkers have struggled to discover the best written form for expressing philosophical inquiry. We have tried hymn, dialogue, myth, treatise, disputation, commentary, meditation, geometrical demonstration, novel, poem, discourse, essay, and critique, to name a few. The insight that animates Hegel's 1807 preface is that we cannot decide *in advance* on any particular presentational form for philosophy. Philosophical content, Hegel argues, will discover a structure or form on its own. If this is true, the prevailing opinion that Hegel presents his own method up front in this preface is problematic.

Philosophy as a Science

It was Kant who clearly posed the problem that would define the task of philosophy in Germany for decades: how can philosophy become a science [*Wissenschaft*]? Much has been written on this question and Hegel's work has often been interpreted through it. Yet this way of phrasing things, which Hegel himself adopts as early as the fifth paragraph of the preface to the *Phenomenology of Spirit*, can be misleading.

In the spirit of Bacon and Descartes, Kant suggested that to become a science, philosophy must try a *new* method. Many modern philosophers favored methodological revolution because they looked at the history of philosophy skeptically. To them, it appeared to be a stalemate of the sort Kant represents so well in the antinomies of pure reason. Equally valid arguments seemed to support mutually exclusive ontologies. It seemed that philosophers had argued as cogently for the eternity of the world as they had for its beginning in creation. In response to this supposed deadlock, Kant recommended turning philosophy on its head: instead of asking about whether our concepts conform to objects, we should ask if objects conform to our concepts (CPR B xvi). Kant took this to be a novel approach that promised novel results.

When we approach Hegel's work as an answer to Kant's question, we may already expect a novel solution like Kant's. What is Hegel's new move? And here we are usually told: the dialectic. A dialectical method, rigorously applied, will allow philosophy to become a science. But this response, while not completely false, misrepresents matters substantially.

For Hegel, dialectical movement that posits and sublates differences is not a new method applied to thinking. Rather, it is just how thinking works on its own without assistance. Thinking is naturally and inherently dialectical. One sign of this is that when we begin thinking through an issue, we often stake out two opposed conceptual extremes in order to identify a bounded field or terrain of thinking (being and non-being, great and small, finitude and infinity, matter and spirit, etc.). This tendency of thinking is so strong that we often turn ideas that are not even logically opposed into conceptual extremes (e.g., capitalism and socialism). We also find that as soon as the contraries are available and the field of inquiry is defined, the differences begin to interact and point us toward new thoughts. Without any training in "dialectical method," Heraclitus and Aristotle and Descartes and many others have gradually refined the nature of their inquiry by positing, negating, and sublating opposed thoughts.

Hegel does not believe thinking needs correction, and, as a result, he does not view the history of philosophy skeptically. In fact, philosophy does not need to *reinvent* itself at all but rather to *recover* itself. Philosophy must become *fully* the activity that it has been all along in a *partial* way. And so the road to philosophical science must pass through whatever was genuinely philosophical in the works of all philosophers worthy of the name: Plato, Aristotle, and Descartes, of course, but also Anaxagoras, Epicurus, and Leibniz. For Hegel, philosophy must become a *recollective* science. It would be strange if the activity of philosophy had, until Kant, simply failed to be genuinely philosophical because it was turned in the wrong direction.

Hegel is concerned that, in the Kantian quest to set philosophy on properly scientific footing, philosophers have been copying the methods of recognized sciences like anatomy or geometry. The problem here is that, both historically and conceptually, all of the recognized sciences developed out of the activity we call "philosophy" and are thus subordinate to it in the sense that they depend on it for their genesis. The word "science" and the activity that it names can and should be traced to the inquiries ancient Greek philosophers made about "episteme." In this light, Kant's question is less about finding a new method (the focus of so much early modern philosophy) and more about recovering the bigger picture of where science came from and where it is going. For Hegel, "science" must be reconceived broadly to include the whole history of philosophy rather than limited to the narrow range of experimental methods associated with the new science. The meteoric rise of mathematical physics and the mechanical sciences in the seventeenth century obscured the long and patient gestation of ideas that led to it. Hegel saw philosophers busily imitating these new sciences without an appreciation for how their adopted methods sometimes limited and distorted the broader nature of philosophical inquiry. Modern philosophers with their novel methods were forbidding concrete discussion of traditional philosophical subjects, such as final purposes or teleology (W3:26, §22). Modern philosophers were shrinking the expansive human endeavor to know into the narrow shape of the latest fruit it had produced.[8]

At the same time, parallel to this worrying scientization of philosophy, Hegel saw a backlash against scientized philosophy from primarily religious camps. Here immediate knowledge and faith and conscience and genius were to lead to new philosophical presentations that hoped to avoid the deadlock in the history of philosophy by consulting our deepest intuitions which sat below the problematic questions and distinctions. These two tendencies, for scientization and against it, thus came to take up the entire discursive space of philosophy at the opening of the nineteenth century. The Kantian quest to make philosophy a science had descended into a brawl between those who borrowed their method from the natural sciences and those who thoughtlessly borrowed their method from religious discourse. This brawl kicked up so much dust that it became difficult to make out what was philosophical and what was not.

It is precisely here that Hegel's 1807 preface intervenes, hoping to give us a sense of how to tell real gold from false. Hegel realizes that Kant's question misled people because of the narrow way that they interpreted the word "science" [*Wissenschaft*]. He aimed to give the word a more expansive register by recollecting the historical usage whereby "science" was synonymous with philosophy which was synonymous with accounting for knowledge or knowing knowing. But to accomplish this, Hegel had to first fight his way through the pseudo-philosophical tendencies into which post-Kantian philosophy had devolved. It might seem that Hegel is just attacking rival views to assert his own here, but he means to do something quite different. He works to reveal something about the essence of philosophy, all genuine philosophy, and not just his own project, by highlighting the ways that pseudo-philosophy fails to do justice to philosophical content.

Allow me to illustrate this with an example. Hegel's prefaces contain significant claims that should help us separate the philosophical spirit of Spinoza's work from the formalistic presentation of his *Ethics*. Hegel's concern is that without such a separation, we will lose the valuable effort of Spinoza's thought altogether and fail to grasp how philosophical thinking has developed and reached its current state through the work of Spinoza (and many others). Among his peers, Hegel saw Spinoza-enthusiasts and Spinoza-detractors and the two groups completely missed their common ground. The enthusiasts were right that Spinoza was a genius, the "pivot point" of modern philosophy, and the detractors were right, Spinoza's geometrical method was rigid and, taken alone, led to mechanism and atheism, that is, to an overly narrow view of philosophy's scope and content. Spinoza's work has dueling tendencies whereby it is both a catalyst for and a limitation on thinking. A study of pseudo-philosophy of the sort Hegel undertakes in his 1807 preface reveals both why Spinoza's formalistic presentation appeals to us and why it limits us and how it can be corrected. Loosed from the distracting novelty of their formalistic edifice, key concepts in Spinoza's work reveal their place in a continuous line of developing thought descending from the first Greek philosophers. In grasping this continuous act of thinking, we will be grasping philosophy not as a heap of isolated viewpoints that cannot be brought to common ground but as a single activity, as the universal *science* of thinking itself.

We should pause here because it is just this sort of talk that gets Hegel into trouble with his audiences. To offer "the universal science of thinking itself" sounds both exceedingly arrogant and tremendously boring. Yet it should be noted that this reaction is itself founded on a prejudice, namely the prejudice that each person has an individual "point of view" or "position" and that philosophy is not a single activity at all but a hodge-podge of individual views. If we begin from the assumption that philosophy has no single essence and actually consists of individually distinct philosophies, independent viewpoints that must do battle with each other, then searching for a single essence of philosophy in all past philosophies will appear as *just another viewpoint*. Worse, it will appear as a hegemonic attempt to silence the diversity of viewpoints by asserting itself as the supreme one that incorporates all others. This is one of the most popular ways of dismissing Hegel's work. Notice that the premise of this interpretation of philosophy's history is similar to the intuition that grounds empiricism: a plurality of particulars are real and the universals that gather them up into kinds are convenient fictions.

By contrast, if we grant instead that philosophy might name a single activity that is imperfectly expressed by any individual thinker (including Hegel), then our concern is for what this or that work reveals about the common essence of philosophy. Whatever our inclination, it will only be by studying the history of philosophy that we actualize and demonstrate its truth. To even test the plausibility of Hegel's presentation of philosophy as a single enterprise, a universal science of thinking, we must first be able to recognize the tell-tale signs of pseudo-philosophy so that their failures and limitations do not get imputed to philosophy proper.

The Unity of Form and Content in Philosophy

I have suggested that Hegel's preface to the *Phenomenology of Spirit* is more concerned with determining what philosophy is not than it is with determining what it is. I am not, of course, claiming that there are no positive remarks about what philosophy is within the preface. I am claiming rather that these positive remarks remain very general and can hardly be considered a good guide to "Hegel's method" or a good introduction to the nature and content of the system of science (this is what Hegel calls his career-spanning work to gather up and develop the contents of philosophy in a systematic way).

Reading books about Hegel, one might easily conclude that Hegel has a method and that this method is called "dialectic" or "speculative dialectic."[9] If this is so, why does Hegel insist that philosophy cannot have a special method over and above its content? In each of the prefaces to his four published books, Hegel notes that the *distinguishing feature* of philosophy is that its "content" is inseparable from its "form" (W3:47, W5:16, W7:13, W8:11). In other words, the method of philosophy is inseparable from the subject matter of philosophy. Method cannot be isolated and discussed on its own. Philosophy is thinking (form) about thinking (content) (W7:27). As we reveal more of the content, we reveal more of the method. This indicates that Hegel *has no specialized method*. Though this is still not widely accepted, I am not alone in arguing this.[10]

As Hegel discusses it, dialectical movement through determinate negation is not a method, not something we *apply* to thinking to make it work in a different way than it normally does. Rather, "the nature of thinking itself is the dialectic . . ." (W8:55, Enz §11). By contrast, Bacon and Descartes explicitly formulate new methodological rules for the would-be philosopher to follow because they argue that the human mind, left to its own course, leads into error.[11] Hegel's work continues to be important and difficult for us today because it challenges the basic orthodoxy of modern philosophy that thinking must be corrected. For Hegel, we take thinking *as it is*, though not in a piecemeal way, but *as a whole*.[12]

This is part of why Hegel's work attempts to gather up and study every major expression of thinking from algebra to zoology, from arguments for God's existence to the history of painting. Hegel purposely includes the study of modes of thinking that have fallen out of favor and which are considered riddled with error like alchemy, animal sacrifice, or phrenology and seeks to uncover the rational impulse from which they spring so as to connect up the whole history of thought's self-expression. Hegel is interested in such disparate topics not because he is a megalomaniac who needs to mouth off on every topic under the sun but because they are all *ways of thinking*. Because philosophy is thinking about thinking, Hegel takes seriously that he himself has to think about all the kinds of thinking that there are. But since methods are ways of thinking which direct us toward certain things rather than others, no single, specialized method can lead through *all* the ways of thinking. This may indicate why Hegel foregrounds negation as a methodologically neutral catalyst for the self-unfolding content of philosophical thinking. Negation does not need to be invented or added into thinking by the philosopher; it is already there. It does not need to be learned from a preface but a preface might issue reminders about it.

Anatomy and history can adopt artificial forms or pre-established methods to meet various practical ends but philosophy, as the search for truth or *the knowing of knowing itself*, is not satisfied with being useful.[13] Philosophy's aim is more total and more fundamental. Those who seek to pin overweening ambition on Hegel might thus be directed toward the scale of ambition inherent in the long-standing task of philosophy itself. In other forms of study, we *use* thinking for this or that end. In philosophy, we think about thinking itself and thus philosophy, at least since Plato, has been both lauded and condemned as useless (*Republic* 487d).

If the philosopher does not give thinking a new method, then what the philosopher "adds" is only the *manner of presentation* for the contents of philosophy. The individual thinker is responsible not for correcting thinking itself but, Hegel would argue, for finding out how we can unfold the total contents of thinking in a necessary sequence from a single starting point. Again, this might sound like some peculiar fetish of "Hegelian dialectics" but it also describes the basic structure of any book: to unfold, from the first sentence to the last, a meaningful sequence that at best seems necessary (and at least is not arbitrary) and leaves nothing essential out.

In the first preface to the *Science of Logic*, Hegel refers back to his 1807 preface to the *Phenomenology* and reaffirms something that he suggested there. Hegel writes:

> The essential point is that, in general, we are concerned with a new concept of scientific procedure here. Philosophy, insofar as it should be science, cannot, as I have noted elsewhere [in the preface to the *Phenomenology of Spirit*], borrow its method from a subordinate science, like mathematics; still less can it be left to the categorical assurances of inner intuition or serve rationalizations based on external reflection. By contrast, it can only be the *nature of the content* that *moves* scientific knowing, for it is the innate [*eigene*] reflection of the content that first sets forth and *produces* its *determination*. (W5:16)

Though Hegel refers to the unity of form and content here as a "new concept of scientific procedure," we should take care in how we understand this. Philosophy has already exhibited this form-content unity throughout its history. But it has done so without full awareness. What Hegel adds as "new" is the explicit awareness of what has been implicitly active. This is not a "new method" in the usual sense; it is, if anything, an ancestral practice brought to fresh awareness.

Hegel then calls out three practices that obstruct our access to self-moving content: first, borrowing a method from subordinate sciences, second, leaving method up to immediate assurances, and third, using whatever method best achieves some external aim. By falling into any of these methodological traps, we will find ourselves pursuing pseudo-philosophy. Our inquiry may concern a philosophical content, the essence of God, perhaps, or the concept of quantity, but the inquiry will be conducted in a way that fails to let the content develop itself and so the resulting *presentation* will be pseudo-philosophical even as the content, taken in itself, is legitimately philosophical.

In this passage, Hegel contrasts external reflection [*äußere Reflexion*] with innate reflection [*eigene Reflexion*]. He contrasts thinking as a means to an end with thinking as an end in itself. External reflection offers justifications for some content based on an outside consideration, principle, or rule. Innate reflection allows for the free play of self-justification and self-undermining that belongs to any living, changing, moving, or developing content as it presents itself (and expresses its many sides) in thinking.

Innate reflection, though undertaken by you or I, is not about you or I. It is always about the thought content itself and what it becomes on its own. Philosophy must therefore be presented as an activity for its own sake. We are accustomed to treating sentient beings (or some selection of them that we do not kill, eat, enslave, exploit, or disregard) as autonomous. What prevents us from thinking about philosophical content in the same way? Hegel argues that for philosophy to become a science, for its method to be joined with its content, we must learn to think about every philosophical thought content as *self-moving*.[14] We must learn to think of a syllogism as we think of an organism.[15] Where is it going? What does it want? What is the source of its life and movement? How might this thought be connected in an evolutionary or developmental chain with other thoughts? What kind of life governs them all and governs the transitions between them?

Thinking as an End in Itself

What does the natural self-movement of thinking look like? We might consider the beginning of Hegel's *Science of Logic*. Thinking moves naturally from the thought of being to the thought of nothing.[16] Why? Because the thought of being is so general, so empty of specificity, it seems like nothing determinate at all. This opening movement is not the work of a specialized thing called "Hegel's dialectic" but a widespread experience one can find in, for example, undergraduates encountering ontology for the first time. A student asks: "what is this being thing we are talking about?" and whatever response is given ("whatever is" or "everything" or "whatever allows beings to be") will amount to saying "being" names the most abstract kind of thinking that you can muster. The most abstract thought, of course, is the fullest in one sense (it includes the thinking of every other thought content as *potential*) but it is also the emptiest (it lacks all *actualization* through development and internal differentiation among the thought contents). And so, being seems large in scope but empty, like nothingness. We do not import nothingness here: it emerges on its own, especially in a relatively untrained stream of thought. Notice that the study of ontology appears either absurd or boring to most people: they see more or less immediately that "being" is "nothing," that is, nothing worth exploring or talking about because it is so abstract and empty, so removed from all concrete projects and practical commitments. The absence of interest itself is an example of the thought of being turning into the thought of nothing. If, however, we need the term "being" to do specific work in an argument, we would not be free to simply observe it move into nothingness on its own but would constrain it to follow the terms we lay out for it. Thus a reader with a more determinate task for thought in hand, for example, someone writing a persuasive book defending a metaphysical thesis, would be unable to observe the *flow* of thinking.

This may help us see why Hegel suggests throughout the 1807 preface that philosophy is both natural to us and yet completely unfamiliar. Philosophy is unfamiliar because we are accustomed to approaching thinking as a tool that we can use to get something done, not as an end in itself with its own nature. The thought itself does not usually interest us much as whether the thought gets us closer to what we want. One prevalent example of this occurs when we do not care if our speech is really understood in detail as long as it achieves the desired effect. If the audience laughs, the comic does not usually interrogate them to make sure they understood each part of the joke. Often we are content with the "gist" of someone's speech because we simply need to know what this person wants, not what is ultimately true. When Plato's Socrates asks a question, his interlocutors often think there is some particular response that he has in mind that will impress him. They pay less attention to the question or thought content itself and more to the practical aim of winning a reputation for wisdom. And this focus on the utility of thought makes genuine philosophical inquiry impossible, as the dialogues repeatedly show.

Hegel is well aware that the prejudices leading us to treat thinking as an instrument are strong. The unusual length of the 1807 preface offers an indication of the magnitude of Hegel's anxiety over being misread due to the prejudices he highlights. Hegel keeps adding on caveat after caveat, extending the preface far beyond the normal length. He even ends the preface with a brief account of why, even after all his efforts, he will still be misread. He writes that it is because philosophy must follow the "self-movement of the concept" and that what most people believe is "completely opposed" to this (W3:65–6, §71).[17]

While the "self-movement of the concept" sounds like a specialized "Hegelian" way of thinking, what Hegel means is related to what Plato or Aristotle mean when they discuss philosophy as knowing for its own sake. If we inquire into knowing not to use it but simply to understand how it works, we must allow thinking to show itself to us on its own terms. These "terms" are the self-movement of the concept. Hegel will explicate them in the *Science of Logic*, exploring how the structure of thinking develops toward (and beyond) syllogistic reasoning on its own steam.

Underlying all of this talk about knowing for its own sake and thinking about thinking and unity of form and content is the experience that *thinking has a life of its own*. It does not just do as we command it. If we want to get to know it, we will have to take a more observational approach.

The Obstacles to Philosophy

As we take a closer look at the potential obstacles to philosophy, the things that prevent us from simply sitting back and observing thinking, we notice that they interconnect in important ways. This is the origin of the most maddening stylistic feature of the 1807 preface: that Hegel keeps juggling his themes. I suspect Hegel writes this way because the themes are mutually illuminating. The problem with prefaces helps us see the problem with edification, which helps us see the problem with formalism. This helps us understand the problem with propositions which, in turn, helps us return to the problem with formalism at a deeper level. All of these interconnecting pseudo-philosophical approaches will indirectly point the way toward the thinking we can call genuinely philosophical. This sort of thinking cannot be defined or summarized in a preface. It has no set rules or single method. No one philosopher can claim it or make it his or her own. But we can begin to appreciate free thinking, difficult as it is to describe directly, by looking at the ways that thinking can become unfree.

It is worth stressing that the preface does not concern rival philosophical positions, but rather "forms" of thought that "obstruct philosophical knowing" due to their "familiarity" (W3:22, §16). The 1807 preface is not

Hegel's attempt to distinguish his point of view from other philosophers' views. The second paragraph of the preface addresses this directly, but its force has not been sufficiently felt by Hegel's readers. If form and content are inseparable in a philosophical work, no single expression of philosophy (e.g., Kant's *Critique of Pure Reason* or Spinoza's *Ethics*) can be separated from other expressions of philosophy. Hegel warns us not to simply compare and contrast philosophical works as if they were independent. We often fall into the habit of contrasting Plato and Aristotle or Descartes and Locke or Kant and Hegel. These oppositions clarify boundaries and create a powerful shorthand for academic debates. What they fail to do is sustain inquiry into the essential nature of philosophy insofar as it is one single activity that expresses itself through these different presentations. Our typical way of approaching philosophy in university courses fixes differences instead of making them "fluid," which Hegel argues is the most pressing task of all genuine philosophy in the modern era (W3:37, §33). Hegel writes, "The opinion that holds to the antithesis of true and false . . . grasps the difference between philosophical systems not so much as the progressive development of truth, but rather in the difference it sees only contradiction" (W3:12, §2). This should help us see why Hegel's references remain so general throughout the preface. Hegel is not trying to call out specific philosophers, books, or claims; he is trying to problematize widespread, familiar expectations about how philosophy is best expressed.

I have structured my interpretation of Hegel's preface around the pseudo-philosophical forms of presentation that obstruct philosophical knowing. The first chapter tries to figure out why explanation has no place in philosophy and thus why all prefaces to philosophy should be viewed critically. The second chapter addresses why philosophy derails so easily into edifying discourse, especially with the advent of modernity. The third chapter explores why we confuse formalism and system and thus assume philosophical thinking should be presented in a strict and rigid way rather than in an organic and fluid way. The fourth chapter addresses why a phenomenology of spirit should not be considered philosophy proper but rather a preparation for philosophy. This is the longest chapter and where interested readers will find the most detail concerning how I think through some of the more difficult questions in Hegel interpretation (i.e., what is a concept, what is a self, what is negation, etc.). The fifth chapter explores why philosophy cannot model itself on mathematical demonstration. The sixth chapter examines forms of presentation that foreground individual propositions as bearers of truth and the ways they block us from recognizing the speculative qualities of our own thinking. The final chapter turns to look at why philosophical thinking should not be presented as the work of single individuals. Taken together, these seven chapters account for the major movements in Hegel's great essay on pseudo-philosophy, the 1807 preface to the *Phenomenology of Spirit*.

1

Philosophy Is Not Explanation (§1–3, 48)

Go gather by the humming sea
Some twisted, echo-harbouring shell.
And to its lips thy story tell,
And they thy comforters will be.
—W. B. Yeats, "The Song of the Happy Shepherd"

First Words

The first two words of Hegel's 1807 preface to the *Phenomenology* are "Eine Erklärung" or "an explanation." He will go on to note that he considers prefaces a kind of explanation and will criticize them as such. Yet he does not go into detail here about the word "explanation" and what he understands by it. It is worth observing that the German word preserves an etymological relationship to "klar" or "clear" and thus carries with it the association of explanation and clarification. Clarity might seem an uncontroversial goal, but Hegel will attempt to persuade us it is not. Seeking clarity can be harmful if the matter to be explained is distorted or diminished by being made clear. Much later in the *Phenomenology*, in the chapter entitled "Force and the Understanding" Hegel will explore the futility of trying to clarify things, the futility of *Erklärungen*. Similarly, Hegel will begin the introduction to the book (which follows the preface) by criticizing those who try to avoid error right from the start, seeking an artificial clarity. It is important to know, right from the beginning, that Hegel does not hold clarity to be a philosophical virtue. Indeed, as we will see, Hegel argues that when it comes to philosophy, clear really just means familiar, tautological, or superficial.

This is helpful to keep in mind because Hegel's writing is not "clear." Even his preface, which he freely grants is a kind of "explanation" or "sketch" or "outline," is a layered text, full of qualifications, evasions, false starts, and disavowals. My working hypothesis is that these difficulties are not defects that derive from hasty composition, but Hegel's ways of resisting explanation. In the preface we see Hegel at war with the very idea of writing a preface. On the one hand he wants to use the preface to present some key issues that might help him gain sympathetic readers. On the other hand, he resists his own simplifications and drives the issues into complexity immediately. Hegel does get better at writing succinct prefaces over his career but here, in his first preface, he is clearly struggling with the task for reasons that become obvious as we attend to the arguments of the preface. Because the preface as a whole concerns modernity's infatuation with superficial clarity and the problems that result from it, Hegel's problematization of clarity both in form and content is relevant to any interpretation of it.

In the first sentence of the 1807 preface, Hegel *seems* to privilege not preliminary explanations but final results. And yet, it is not quite so simple. For a preface aims to be *an explanation of results*, as Hegel will soon tell us. Yet genuine results are not something that can be summarized or appreciated apart from the work that it takes to reach them, that is, demonstrations. This is why readers are disappointed if they simply skip to the tantalizingly titled final chapter of Hegel's book "Absolute Knowing." I myself did this when I first acquired the book at twenty years old. The final chapter does little but remind the reader that the result of the book is not a proposition, claim, determinate idea, or conclusion. Instead, the result is a rhythmic movement of thinking that has been learned by repeated practice throughout the book.

Hegel insists that he has no standalone content to explain or clarify. Indeed, he would argue that no philosopher does. In philosophy, form and content cannot be separated and so the content cannot simply be presented in another, clearer form. The form in which the content evolves is the form that belongs to it. Wanting philosophical thinking to give itself up in a simplified preface is like wishing one's life had taken a simpler course to its present shape. In retrospect, a life's present shape is inseparable from the course it has taken. Thinking likewise requires its winding path, its false starts, and dead ends. To simply map a beeline from start to finish misrepresents the activity of thinking and thus brings us no closer to thinking about thinking itself. Clarity and the practice of philosophy are at odds.

For Hegel, philosophical knowledge is performative. Just as Glenn Gould cannot explain how to play Bach but can perform it, Hegel cannot explain how to think but hopes we will stick around for what he knows is a difficult and challenging performance. If one task of this preface is to get us to stay for the performance that follows, Hegel would not help matters by making false promises of a clarity he cannot deliver.

The Preface Begins with Itself

Hegel's preface opens with three dense paragraphs that caution the reader about several problems with prefaces to philosophical works. Some readers have found Hegel's choice to open a preface with a critique of prefaces strange. Yet Hegel often begins not only his books but also his lectures by problematizing the common expectations attached to the textual form or genre he is about to engage. He introduces the *Science of Logic* with critical remarks about what currently passes for logic, opens the aesthetics lectures with criticism of the misleading name "aesthetics," and opens the *Outline of the Philosophy of Right* by specifying how his "outline" is not what one might normally expect from an outline.[1] Even the *Phenomenology*'s own introduction (which follows the preface) begins by considering and critiquing a "natural assumption" the reader might have about how the book will proceed.[2] Hegel often begins an inquiry by considering a widely held misapprehension about how the subject at hand should be presented. To this end, Hegel often discusses the title or some word in the title (e.g., *Logik*, *Aesthetik*, *Grundlinien*, *Vorrede*), signaling that his presentation will differ from what his audience might expect from the title. By countering an expectation, negating an anticipated prejudice, Hegel makes a first step into his subject. This is worth noting: Hegel begins not positively but negatively, not with assertions but with denials.

Hegel calls the text that we aim to study a "*Vorrede*" or preface, but this does not mean that it will match our expectations for that genre. In some respects it will be like other prefaces and in many respects it will not. It is, we can already see, unusually and inappropriately long for a preface. We might ask, then, why Hegel chooses titles that he must disavow. Surely this has led to confusion. Why call this text a preface if he dislikes prefaces?[3] Why call his second book a logic if it is really an ontology or metaphysics? Why call his lectures "Aesthetics" rather than "Philosophy of the Fine Arts" if the latter is closer to the actual content? Each of the titles Hegel chooses is the most common, familiar title for the content. Following what Aristotle calls the "natural road," Hegel chooses to begin with what is more common or familiar and proceed slowly toward what is more true.[4] If Hegel believed we could avoid error altogether, he might approach things in a different manner. He might aim to be as technical and precise as possible with his titles and terminology. This is, for example, how Kant writes, by securing a distinct and carefully bounded domain for each of his terms which are often borrowed from Latin to avoid confusion with everyday language.

Hegel argues already in the second paragraph of the preface (and again in the early paragraphs of the introduction) that we cannot fruitfully avoid error. For one thinker to simply reject a past thinker's work is like a blossom rejecting the bud from which it issued.[5] Not only is error unavoidable, we actually need it. Error is not just occasionally instructive (as common sense holds it to be); rather it is essential to truth because *all determinations are developed by way of negations*. If "the true is the whole" (§20), and each part of the whole taken alone is incomplete or one-sided, then truth itself is composed of nothing but what we call error. The real error is not in the partial claim itself but in the *isolation* of the partial claim from the other claims that complete and support it like the stones of an archway. By engaging so-called errors instead of excluding them, we *situate* each claim with respect to other claims. We are then on the path to a comprehensive picture of where each partial claim stands in relation to the other partial claims that, together, fill it out and complete it. This is why seasoned interpreters of Hegel often point to the *systematic position* of infamous, contested, or confusing claims. No sentence of Hegel's works should be read as an assertion hanging in mid-air. The meaning of a claim depends on *where* it occurs.

Given all this, it should not be surprising that Hegel forgoes the (then common) strategy of coining new terms or borrowing technical terms from Latin. Specialized jargon disconnects the content from daily life and experience. It attempts to exclude errors and prejudices by developing a new and pristine language. By contrast, Hegel borrows most of his central terms from everyday speech (*Begriff, Bewusstsein, Wissen, Denken, Vernunft, Geist*, etc.) confident that the dynamic struggle to unpack their ambiguities will be more revealing than a conflict-free technical jargon invented for a single use.[6] Hegel's use of the word *Vorrede* is no exception. And so all of the sentences we are about to read belong to a preface that chafes against its own task. Only by acknowledging this tension can we begin to see the individual sentences in the right light.

If philosophy is to participate in and recount thinking's struggle for self-articulation, we do ourselves no favors by seeking placid, error-free forms for its expression like prefaces, summaries, definitions, and treatises or, frankly, academic articles and books. Clarity, so often prized in philosophical writing, is counterproductive to the full exercise of philosophical thinking. Clarity covers over philosophy's beginnings, which are found in thinking's struggle, not its repose. In the preface, Hegel mocks the title and notion of Fichte's "sun clear report" because Fichte's title captures the naive hope for error-free clarity (W3:50, §51). Philosophical thinking relies on error, mistake, confusion, impasse. A sign of this is that philosophical thinking is initiated by noticing something strange or incongruous. As Aristotle reminds us, philosophy begins with an impasse.[7] Aristotle suggests further that this is what is meant by Socrates' claim that wonder is the origin of philosophy.[8] The premature appearance of clarity can circumvent an impasse before it is felt and bypass the philosophical struggle altogether, replacing it with an apparently persuasive dogma.

By stirring up confusion about the very idea of a preface right from the start, Hegel shows his commitment to the long and difficult path of natural thinking as opposed to the sanitized course of an artificial substitute for the actual, dynamic act of thinking. This theme will recur throughout the text.

Prefacing Philosophy as an Impasse

Hegel begins not by simply telling us something straightforward about prefaces but by thinking through a problem. The impasse presented in the first paragraph is this: philosophy seems like it is ideally suited to prefaces but also like it is not. Because it values the universal (which includes the particular), philosophy seems well suited to brief, synoptic statements like prefaces. Indeed if everything is just the expression of a single true idea (as Hegel himself says of the history of philosophy), then by grasping this one idea (the infinite, the good, being, God, etc.), we could skip right to the end. In fact, all the complicated work of argumentation that leads to the result could obscure the clarity of the result and just confuse things.

On the other hand, because philosophical results supposedly arise from necessary demonstrations, the conclusions do not seem separable from the body of the work. A philosophical conclusion cannot be fairly summarized in a preface any more than a mathematical result could be known without its demonstration. At issue here is whether truth is immediate and self-evident, or comes by way of mediations, that is, if truth must appear *through* something untrue.

The back-and-forth movement of the first paragraph structures this impasse by bringing out the opposing sides that together block the road forward. If the solution to an impasse is always some distinction that is not made by the opposing sides, Hegel invites us right from the start to wonder what distinction might arbitrate this conflict.[9] We will not catch sight of this arbitrating distinction until §17 and a still better view comes in §20–2. Both sides (truth is immediate and truth is always mediated) fail to recognize a third possibility that truth, like a living being, is *self-mediating*.¹⁰

For now, we might appreciate that Hegel does not just dump a claim like "substance must be grasped and expressed as subject" in our laps at the start. Hegel does not begin by asserting that mediation has been understood only as alienation and that we need to see that mediation can also be grasped as self-relation. While this distinction between mediation as alienation and mediation as self-development will eventually lead us out of the problem of prefacing philosophy, it does us no good if we do not realize that we have a problem in the first place. Hegel's first task in the preface is to attune the reader to feel the force of the problem with philosophy as it is currently understood. Given the current, popular understanding of what philosophy is and how it works, it is not clear why a preface to a book of philosophy could not effectively replace the book itself. This should be alarming.

Hegel begins with the preface-problem because it is a reflexive beginning: he begins by talking about what he is supposedly beginning. Further, it foreshadows the other problems he will soon discuss. We should be able to see the absurdity of replacing a rich, complex argument with a mere summary. This should help us see the problem with several other ways of replacing the hard work of philosophy with mere "anticipations" of the absolute (cf. §23) preparing us for critical encounters with edification, formalism, phenomenology, mathematical precision, propositional truth, common sense, and genius. By talking about the title and expectations it brings, he already begins to unfold the thematic thread of the whole.

Construction versus Recollection

The preface begins with three paragraphs that distance the practice of philosophy from the sort of premature judgment encouraged by prefaces. Without telling us what philosophy is, Hegel comments on what it cannot be. It cannot be something easily communicated in a preface. Prefaces are valued because they are concise, direct, and immediate. Hegel's preface has none of these virtues. If anything, it is the opposite: expansive, indirect, and labored. Hegel's performative preface brings the struggle and confusion of philosophy into the usually placid fields of the preface. If prefaces usually aim for clarity, Hegel's preface makes war on clarity in its form and its content.

Hegel's preface will go on to argue that truth cannot be known directly or in an immediate way. It is therefore not surprising that the beginning of the preface is such a hesitant affair full of self-criticism. The immediate beginning should cast doubt on immediate beginnings. Hegel may seem defensive for opening with a round of polemics against philosophical prefaces. But by refusing to begin by telling us what the book is about, Hegel does indeed hint at how this book will be different from other philosophical books and thus gives us some clue about the book.

This much should be clear from the opening: this book will not be a defense of immediacy or clarity in philosophy. That is a philosophically rich indication. Hegel's book begins by indirectly announcing that the system of science will not continue the modern philosopher's characteristic search for a simple, indubitable beginning of knowledge.[11] This procedure (which, for convenience, we may call "foundationalism") leads to viewing knowledge as a *construction*, an artifice built up bit by bit from simple parts.[12] Hegel, we will see, turns us away from construction and toward recollection, gathering up what knowing has actually been (including its mistakes and misleads) rather than constructing an artificially simplified stand-in for it. This theme (recollection vs. construction) re-appears throughout the preface.

The preface begins with itself because all knowing must begin where it is. Knowing is a matter of looking around and taking stock, letting the current situation lead us back, step by step, to its sources. When we try to speed this process along, we lose touch with truth entirely, since truth is not in any part by itself but in the whole or in a great chain of recollections that reveals each seemingly independent element as a moment in a more comprehensive ongoing activity. If analytic acumen is the preeminent virtue of the early modern philosopher, patience is the virtue of philosophy in a Hegelian key.

The Broad Reach of the Preface Critique

After the third paragraph, the 1807 preface turns from the reflexive criticism of prefaces and seems to leave it behind. Soon we are discussing a "system of science" and "formalism" and the nature of "substance" and "subject" without casting a backward glance to the problem of prefaces. This has led many interpreters to consider the opening paragraphs less important than what follows, as if they were a coy rhetorical play that Hegel quickly drops. Any reader searching for a direct description of Hegel's proposed philosophical project will ignore the opening and jump to the fifth paragraph. But even here the reader encounters more indirection, another detour that will be the topic of our next chapter.

Still refusing to see the writing on the wall, one might jump to the seventeenth paragraph, where Hegel famously describes "his insight" that "the true" must be grasped and expressed not only as "substance" but as "subject." Hegel follows this with dense discussions of negation and mediation that will strike many readers as more philosophical than the preface critique of §1–3 or the explorations of the current stage of Geist in §6–16. Yet if the reader has failed to see how the opening of the preface already *performs* what these later paragraphs *describe*, the insight will fall flat. Hegel is not trying to give us a disembodied category called "negativity." He tries to teach us how to think with the negative.

Hegel's critical appraisal of prefaces prefigures his main themes in important ways. In the two later paragraphs where Hegel mentions prefaces again, he connects the critique of prefaces to the critique of formalism (§48) and the critique of common sense (§70). Both of these are major strands of the preface that weave through multiple paragraphs from the beginning to the end. By associating the critique of prefaces with these major concerns, Hegel invites us to consider it as an ongoing issue. Prefaces, formalism, and common sense are all connected within this preface as popular substitutes for the hard work of philosophy proper, the patient self-examination of thinking that takes nothing for granted and leans on no extra-philosophical foundation or starting point.[13]

With a little imagination, the shadow of the preface-critique stretches further to the concerns Hegel expresses about immediate knowing, substance ontology, propositions, mathematical knowing, and more. The expectation that a preface could offer clearer understanding than a whole book (because it is more direct and concise) exhibits the same allergy to step-by-step mediation that we witness in these other approaches. These approaches *anticipate* the absolute instead of patiently recollecting it.[14] We are all prone to this sort of lazy, anticipatory thinking and this is one reason why Hegel's books are good (if not delicious) medicine. These books are good for us precisely because they often seem so tedious.

As Hegel will argue, philosophy appears tedious to common sense. New readers often find the nit-picky, circular conversations in the Platonic dialogues infuriating while seasoned readers take delight in them. In truth, it is common sense that is tedious. Without conceptual necessity, common sense can only produce "aggregates" or lists of one thing after another with no pervading reason or purpose. Rhetorical orations pile up points in favor of their conclusion but lack necessary connection between parts. The rhetorical whole lacks any purpose other than persuasion itself. By contrast, we can be said to value philosophy when fresh collections of incidental particulars seem tedious and patient strings of conceptual necessities seem exciting. This is the sign we have turned from a view of knowledge as a collection of things thought to knowledge as the dynamic activity of thinking itself. If the preface critique can be understood broadly as a critique of lazy anticipation and a defense of patient recollection, then it is a natural place to begin a defense of philosophy.

What is remarkable about Hegel's defense of philosophy here is that it is made largely to readers who consider themselves philosophical but who, according to the arguments of the preface, are not philosophers but rather dogmatists, formalists, subjectivists, and skeptics. It is no wonder that this preface inspires heated criticism or even dismissal. In it Hegel involves himself in the unpopular practice of trying to save philosophy from itself.

The Historical and the Conceptual (§1)

The preface's first paragraph moves back and forth between praise for and criticism of prefaces. Hegel begins the first sentence as if he were going to endorse explanatory philosophical prefaces, but finishes the sentence by criticizing them. Then he turns around again and considers why we might believe philosophical thinking is expressed well by prefaces. Then he pivots again and chastises those who think such things, since they are suggesting that philosophy stands in less need of detail and careful development than a clearly inferior study like anatomy (W3:11, §1). All these concerns are complicated by the fact that we are reading a preface. When Hegel criticizes philosophical prefaces we wonder why he wrote this one, which, looking ahead, we can see is quite long.

If these twists and turns aren't confusing enough, the force of the argument in §1 is rooted in a sense of shame unlikely to be felt by many readers. Readers who see nothing wrong with considering anatomy more scientific and more content-rich than philosophy will not see why the insufficiency of prefaces for the study of anatomy should incline us to believe that we need more than a preface to study philosophy. Since the contemporary reader is likely to be in this position, she may well feel that Hegel's first paragraph is an unconvincing mess.

Hegel's opening salvo against prefaces and other mere "aggregates of information" depends on a distinction between the historical and the conceptual that he raises at the end of the first paragraph. Anatomy books and prefaces address their content in a "historical [*historisch*] and conceptless [*begrifflos*] way" (W3:11, §1). Note that it is possible to treat past events in a concept-rich way and Hegel himself will use the word "*Geschichte*" to designate this rather than

"*Historie.*"¹⁵ Prefaces and certain whole fields of study (like anatomy) approach their content as if each datum were an independent, self-standing fact. This way of proceeding is what Hegel later calls "dogmatism" (W3:41, §40). Dogmatism, of course, is rarely endorsed by anyone and so realizing that Hegel opposes dogmatism brings no insight. The question is, what is meant by dogmatism here?

An account is dogmatic if it is "conceptless." But what does Hegel mean by "concept"? This simple question has proven extremely difficult to answer. Yet if we cannot answer it, Hegel's claim that X is dogmatic while Y is philosophical will prove arbitrary. In a way, all books by and about Hegel are largely about "the concept" because most of Hegel's thinking is thinking in or through the concept. In writing about Hegel, we often rehearse facts about the concept: the concept is the focus of the whole third part of Hegel's *Science of Logic*; it has three moments (the universal, particular and singular), when it is actualized or realized it is called "Idea" [*die Idee*]. But where do we begin if we do not want to presume competence with Hegel's logic, as in this preface we cannot?

Within the 1807 preface, Hegel continually refers to but never defines concept or *Begriff*. Instead, he associates it with a certain way of thinking or working. The concept involves "labor," it is the "cold, developmental necessity of the issue itself," it is "the true self of the object," it is "self-moving," it is "self-like," it has an "immanent rhythm," and it has a "life" of its own.¹⁶ From this, we can glean that "concept" refers not to some lifeless abstraction (like the "concept" of the number three) but to the cause of activity and movement in some thing. Concept is to all intelligible things what soul is to a living thing. Concept is source and cause and purpose; it is the reason why some thing, issue, object, plant, or animal develops one way rather than another. "Concept" names a certain way of approaching the being of beings. If this is true, it would make sense that "the concept" proves difficult to define.

But, the historically astute might object: Kant's first critique freed us from the need to ask about "being" and Hegel, as a post-Kantian, must either follow suit or be viewed as a renegade. These are tangled questions, but even viewed historically it is clear that we never "overcame metaphysics" or liberated philosophy from ontological inquiry. If one looks at our present moment alone, one can see that (1) metaphysical questions have returned to Anglo-American philosophical conversations which traditionally were hostile to them and (2) most working Hegel scholars accept that Hegel addresses ontological concerns without falling into the transcendental realism Kant exposes.¹⁷

Nonetheless, if Hegel addresses the source and cause of beings by way of the "concept," this seems to be a nod in the Kantian direction, if only because it suggests we are talking not about being qua being but being as it is *thought*. For concept is, if nothing else, a word we readily associate with thinking and Hegel knows this. And yet, unlike the transcendental idealist's "appearance," Hegel's "concept" seems to suggest that what thinking thinks expresses what being actually is.

While this is only a beginning, we can say that a concept refers to the grasping in thinking of an activity by which something relates to itself and becomes itself rather than something else. "Concept" names selfhood as thinking. When, in the system of science, we watch some content shift and change from its immediate appearance to some other shape, we are watching a concept at work. We are not imposing the shape change; we are merely observing it and noting the underlying, continuous activity that makes it possible. The *Phenomenology of Spirit*, for example, charts the developments of consciousness [*Bewusstsein*] as it reveals itself to be spirit or Geist. Geist turns out to be the *concept* of consciousness, active in it from the beginning. From the beginning, the activity of Geist (freedom, thinking, self-awareness, restless negativity) could be found in the demands consciousness placed upon itself.

What dogmatic explanations lack, then, is the developmental activity of a self-relating concept. Anatomy operates as if the heart were something on its own without continual reference to the form of life and purposes of the animal in which the heart is found. The activity of life is, we might conjecture, the concept of the heart. Anatomy treats the heart as a machine, looking only at its material and efficient causes. But what Hegel calls the "concept" is typically found in the final causes, and final causes are not considered in the modern science of anatomy. Anatomy is thus called "historical and conceptless" in the first paragraph even though it may accurately report things that are the case concerning subordinate (material and efficient) causes.

When Hegel accuses prefaces and anatomy of being "historical," he does not mean that they only look at the past. Hegel is not criticizing interest in the past at all. Actually, the system of science is largely a gathering up of things past (though not simply as past but rather in their ongoing significance). Hegel means, rather, that the preface writer or anatomist treats her content like a historian might treat a historical fact, as a bare empirical datum without reference to some greater purpose, some self-moving concept. In Hegel's usage, "*historisch*" is usually synonymous with "*empirisch*."[18] As the preface unfolds, Hegel will have much more to say about the historical/empirical as it relates to the "formalism" that has hi-jacked philosophy.[19]

Prefaces (like anatomies and histories) pretend that there are independently justifiable "facts" and "results" but even cursory investigation reveals these so-called facts are not independent but have many causes that account for them and on which they depend both for being-at-all and for being-significant. Our knowing these facts and results likewise depends on knowing their causes and so requires the whole exposition or demonstration that produced them.

Prefaces must be "historical" and "conceptless" because they hope to set the main results of a book off against various competing alternatives. This differentiation is not the slow internal self-differentiation of concepts and conceptual thought but the rapid external determination possible when various limits and boundaries are taken for granted. For example, if we take for granted an opposition between "empiricism" and "rationalism" we can quickly bring Kant's first critique to light as a middle way between them. But this is an extraneous and historical affair, relying on various assumed determinations.

Paragraph one concludes: if philosophy is conducted the way we write prefaces (i.e., conceptlessly), then it is incapable of grasping truth. It would be disastrous for science if as lowly a study as anatomy were to have a more necessary relation between its exposition and its results than philosophy, the queen of the sciences. If we think philosophy is best expressed in prefaces but anatomy actually requires a full exposition to demonstrate its conclusions, we must have lost confidence in the rigor and necessity of the steps of philosophical inquiry. This is exactly what has happened to us, as Hegel will discuss in paragraph 7. Hegel *expects* us to have an impoverished understanding of philosophy. We have lost confidence in the necessity of philosophical thinking and typically present a given philosophical text as one "position" among others, as if it were just the contingent and arbitrary construction of one individual according to the peculiarities of his or her temperament. The alternative would be to see that philosophy is something on its own, apart from this or that expression, and that every expression succeeds or fails by nearing or losing touch with the nature of philosophy itself. Yet this latter view might seem old-fashioned or even mystical to us today. It seems strange to talk about philosophy as if it had a life of its own apart from the private aims and personal projects of individual philosophers. Interestingly, we view natural science as an endeavor with necessity and greater purpose which individual scientists simply serve and help along and this does not seem mystical at all. Hegel sees no reason why we should view natural science as a larger cultural movement and view philosophy as individualistic quibbling. That we do is only the result of a series of prejudices and misunderstandings he will try to address. Nevertheless he expects us to have some inkling that philosophy once was (and still deserves to be) guided by greater necessity than anatomy.

Hegel likely exploits a contrast between anatomy and philosophy here because anatomy considers the lifeless body as a mere thing divisible into parts and philosophy considers the life of the whole embodied soul in its highest vocation: thinking, inquiring, knowing. Most of Hegel's analogies and images in the preface will turn on the distinction between following a living movement and analyzing dead parts. The invocation of anatomy in the first paragraph prepares this theme.

The Blossom and the Bud (§2)

The second paragraph follows up on the contrast with anatomy and the remark that prefaces are expected to explain "the relation" in which the author believes the book stands "to earlier or contemporary treatments of the same object." The first paragraph explores the relationship between a summary of results and the work taken to reach the result within a single work. The second paragraph explores the relationship between different philosophical works, books, or systems. To highlight the difference between how he understands this "relation" between works and how prefaces encourage us to understand it, Hegel again reminds us of the difference between studying the living and studying the dead. It is absurd to think that a blossom "refutes" a bud from which it issues (W3:12, §2). If works of philosophy are understood in living relation to one another, they cannot be apprehended as fixed positions to accept or reject as prefaces invite us to do.

This paragraph gives us a vital clue about something that is widely misunderstood. In the image of the bud and the blossom, Hegel suggests that the kind of necessity we should expect in the history of philosophy is not absolute necessity but conditional necessity or developmental necessity. The bud is not absolutely necessary in itself but necessary only for the blossom to be. Each stage of Geist that Hegel will discuss is not absolutely necessary but necessary conditionally, that is, on account of what comes next that it makes possible. If we take Hegel to be saying that the history of philosophy could not, logically, be otherwise than it is, we can find many reasons to the contrary. But if we apprehend conditional necessity properly, this worry vanishes.

When readers complain of transition problems (e.g., between consciousness and self-consciousness) they demand that the first stage require exactly *this* second stage to follow it and not another. Subjected to this requirement, none of the transitions in Hegel's books can be fully adequate. Indeed, it is misleading to suggest that there are "transitions" in these books at all. They are not transitions but developments. "Transition" suggests an alteration between two independent states. "Development" reminds us that each stage is partial and part of an ongoing movement. A thing develops into itself, but it transitions into something else. Since each stage is developing, the meaning and sense of the stage do not come from itself but from this purposive movement. The collapse of a stage is not a loss at all; it is a recovery of the ongoing movement from a false appearance of an independent state.

Hegel will give us explicit cause to link his thinking to Aristotle's thinking about nature in paragraph 22. There, he calls reason "purposive activity" and compares Aristotle's account of nature as purposive activity to his own account of "subject" as purposive activity (W3:26, §22). A brief glance at Aristotle's thinking about nature can help us better grasp conditional necessity. When we say that it is necessary that the ax be made of iron, we mean only that it must be made of hard stuff like iron. It could have been bronze, but here it happens to be iron and so here, the iron was necessary conditionally on account of its hardness. The history of philosophy is a unified development that can have a single name because it has one aim, one purpose and so can be grasped as a developmental sequence in relation to this purpose. Surely the stages could have been different in many details as long as they served the same purpose in the development. We see manifold variation in flower buds and yet they all *function* as buds. In our world, as it happens, stoicism came about as a way that human beings attempted to reach self-knowledge. This is neither absolutely necessary nor is it arbitrary. Stoicism is not really something in itself. It is a stage of growth in the movement we call "philosophy." Stoicism, insofar as it can be grasped as something, is not arbitrary; it fulfills a distinct role in the growth of philosophy. But it is not independently necessary either. The discrete names of stages of philosophy give a false appearance of independence to them. In truth, they are all just modifications of the same one activity of philosophy.

The second paragraph's analogy between philosophical views and flowering trees manages to make two points at once. The image suggests that different positions in the history of philosophy are more interconnected than we typically think and also, more controversially, that this history must be purposively oriented. The two claims rely on one another. It is only by glimpsing a common purpose that we will be able to see the works of Heraclitus, Epictetus, Anselm, and Hobbes as a continuous growth rather than as fundamentally separate views that have been lumped together by subjective caprice. Some students of philosophy try to study this or that philosopher. Hegel reminds us that we can only ever study philosophy, the whole, and individual works and views can neither be simply accepted nor can they be simply rejected as such. The appearance of individuality here is an illusion, an illusion propagated in large part by prefaces and the anticipatory thinking common to them.

The second paragraph lodges its criticism of prefaces on the same grounds as the first: prefatory explanations ignore the self-justifying necessity of philosophical presentations. By seeking to justify the presentation externally (in the preface), the author suggests that the presentation requires external justification and thus that it lacks internal necessity. The perception that external justification is helpful follows from a false assumption that philosophy is a loose gathering of distinct positions rather than a unified activity with diverse expressions.

The Sache Selbst (§3)

In paragraph three, the arguments of paragraphs one and two are combined. Together, a preface's two tasks (a statement of results and a differentiation of one view from another) substitute the real work of philosophy. When we have the results and the differences, we can easily believe we have gotten hold of the essence of a philosophical work. To better see the problem here, we might consider how we teach philosophy in universities. If I were to teach Kant's *Critique of Pure Reason*, for example, I would most likely guide students toward (1) the major claims that result from the work of the book and (2) how Kant differs from Descartes, Hume, and Berkeley. But this is not philosophical thinking; it is reportage. It has its place, of course, but Hegel's point is that we confuse reports about philosophy with the work of philosophy itself. Too often, we survey and map the terrain of philosophy rather than losing ourselves in the movement of thinking, the actual activity of philosophy.

The preference for explanation in philosophy is a way of evading the hard work of thinking, the challenge of working with the *"Sache selbst"* (literally "the issue itself," i.e. the genuine concern of philosophy). As we will come to see throughout the preface, the real issue we moderns avoid thinking through is self-relation, self-movement, or more generally, selfing activity. Hegel will often call this selfing activity, somewhat unhelpfully, "Subject" [Subjekt], which he will then gloss as "negativity" [Negativität]. Both of these words have been stumbling blocks for Hegel's readers. "Subject" suggests subjectivism and "negativity" suggests a barren logical operation. But both words should point toward self-motion, the power that something has to determine itself for itself (as opposed to being determined by outside forces). The "self-moving concept" is, Hegel recognizes, a focus that is likely to be misunderstood (see §71). Self-motion is central to Aristotle's *Physics* which, it can be argued, misled the sciences for centuries before the scientific revolutions of modernity corrected it. Our natural sciences have given up on the idea of self-motion as unprovable and thus cannot provide accounts of self-moving activities like "life" and "soul" and "consciousness," which are the very things we most want to know.

The concern here can be better elaborated if we see the problem with prefaces embedded within a more fundamental problem that Hegel associates with "*Erklärung*" (explanation or, more literally, clarification). "*Erklärung*" is, we might recall, the very first word of the preface and is brought back in paragraph three as the thing prefaces give us instead of the "*Sache selbst*."

Against Explanation

A typical preface tries to provide "eine *Erklärung*" or an explanation of the book's contents. Hegel notes (in §3) that prefaces are problematic because the author tries to explain the content of the book from the outside instead of "forgetting" or losing herself in the content, the *Sache selbst*. Hegel does not explicitly discuss "explanation" at length in the preface but he does explore the word in more depth elsewhere.

In "Force and the Understanding," Hegel notes that explanations [*Erklärungen*] are tautological. An explanation of lightning explains the event by saying it is an instance of the law of electricity and justifies the law of electricity by saying that it is what explains an event of lightning (W3:124; §154). An explanation does not unfold from attention to the movement of the content; rather it is applied top-down. Explanation does not provide satisfaction by deepening our understanding of nature. Instead, Hegel says, it satisfies us for another reason:

> The reason why explaining affords so much self-satisfaction is just because in it consciousness is, so to speak, communing directly with itself, enjoying only itself; although it seems to be busy with something else, it is in fact occupied only with itself. (W3:133; §163)

Hegel treats explanations as subjective satisfactions. Explanations are not discoveries; they are translations. The satisfaction afforded by a "good" explanation is the satisfaction of aligning two accounts that were previously considered to be separate. *Explanation satisfies us because it translates something that seems foreign into familiar language.* If I am familiar with electrical charge, I am satisfied by the explanation of lightning in terms of electrical charge. Explanation is not dialectical: it does not force us out of our comfort zone or negate our familiar assumptions. In fact, it does just the opposite. Because Hegel has reason to believe that thinking works by negation, by disorientation and alienation, he views explanation as a problematic procedure which gives the appearance of thinking where no thinking (no dialectical transformation of a content from within) is taking place.

Teachers witness the danger of explanation all the time. What a teacher often provides for students are translations of strange texts into terms they already understand, a process which bypasses the challenge of the material altogether. This transaction has the potential to satisfy both parties because it gives the appearance of change and growth when actually the challenging content is just being reduced to an already available content.

A typical preface is a good example of the tautology of explanation. A preface takes the unfamiliar content of the book and translates it into a familiar language that is considered the property of the general reading public. Prefaces, Hegel tells us, should explain why the author "wrote the book" and how the book relates to other books past or present "on the same subject" (W3:11, §1). The author is expected to take the work and relate it to his personal biography and to the other books that have already been published. Both procedures translate hard-won insights into the language of prevailing prejudices about philosophy. If, for example, most readers view philosophy as a contest between empiricism and rationalism, a preface must situate the work in relation to those terms, even if both are discovered to be misleading within the work itself.

The generally accepted opinion is that a preface should appeal to a broad audience and make philosophical thinking more accessible. But Hegel argues it does just the opposite. Prefaces substantially obscure philosophy itself and teach us to accept substitutes for it. Prefaces prepare us for dogmatism and formalism, and their externally justified claims, rather than philosophy which is always self-justifying, self-presenting, and has its element in the self-moving concept. Prefaces cannot reach the *Sache selbst* (the content as an end in itself) because they try to explain it (and this treats content as a means or instrument).

Prefaces as Subjective Satisfactions

Explanation does not explore a given content on its own terms, but quickly ties it back to already available terms. Thus it is not surprising that those with ample experience in a certain area are not necessarily good at explaining it. For the experienced, each consideration leads to another and the whole network cannot be severed at will and served up in convenient chunks. Proper appreciation for the subject matter tends to bring with it a dissatisfaction with tidy explanations, since one begins to feel how limited and limiting they are. We seek explanations when we seek "self-satisfaction" instead of the challenge of patient immersion in a disorienting and difficult content.

As explanations and thus as subjective satisfactions, prefaces do not and cannot adequately condense philosophical content; they rather summarize an author's intention. But what the author thinks he has done is unimportant when our concern is with what thinking has actually been done in the book. The author's intention may be close or it may be far from what the book actually presents but since we cannot know how close or far until we engage the content for its own sake, such assurances provide no help up front.

If anything, a statement of intention proves a substantial obstacle or distraction in philosophy. Instead of focusing on the argument itself, we will be looking to see if the argument serves Kant's or Locke's stated intention. We might consider how the lack of prefaces or biographical and historical material allows the reader to engage a Platonic dialogue more directly and *philosophically*. Unless one reads them to confirm an orthodoxy (e.g., a doctrine of the forms), one is always at sea in these dialogues, suspended in the content with no easy summary or intention available. Plato himself is conspicuously absent as a character. Platonic dialogues often begin *in medias res* and often end in aporia or myth. This forces the reader to take each turn of the conversation as it comes and not subordinate them all to a claim that can be stated upfront. This lack of context forces the reader to be at work thinking. This feeling of being at sea is what Hegel calls "forgetting" ourselves in the issue, content, or matter itself, the "*Sache selbst*":

> Instead of grappling with the *Sache*, this sort of procedure [prefacing] is always already beyond it; instead of lingering with the *Sache* and forgetting itself in it, this sort of knowing always gropes after some Other but stays much more with itself than it ever [stays with] the *Sache* or gives itself over to it. (W3:13, §3)

The key insight here is that when we seek explanations of philosophical works like prefaces, we believe that we are getting something different, something other than we already had, but in fact this procedure can only tell us what we already know. It is because we are deceived about what is going on here that we do not seek to remedy it. We believe explanations advance or expand our knowledge when they merely pass the buck to some explanatory term we already accept. In Kantian terms, we think explanations involve synthetic judgments but they are merely analytic. No new path for thinking has been forged.

From Explanation to Presentation [*Darstellung*]

What we cannot represent/imagine [vorstellen], we can and must perform [darstellen].[20]

—Friedrich Schlegel

Instead of giving an external explanation [*Erklärung*] of knowing, Hegel's systematic work (i.e., not his prefaces) aims to give an immersive performance or immanent presentation [*Darstellung*] of it. The 1807 preface opens with a critique of prefaces because they are extraneous. Hegel then avoids using the word "explanation" to describe his own book (though he will use the word to describe the book's preface), preferring instead to call the *Phenomenology of Spirit* a "*Darstellung*" (e.g., W3:22, 38, 55, 72, 79). Hegel's *Phenomenology* is not a "*Kritik*" or an "*Entwurf*" or an "*Erklärung*" but a "*Darstellung*" of phenomenal knowing. In the preface, we learn that the "authentic presentation" of philosophy is a "speculative presentation" or a presentation that presents dialectical movement itself as the central subject matter, as opposed to those works that concern fixed propositions, finite objects, or categories (W3:61, §65).

Hegel's first advertisement for his book offers a telling contrast between presentation and explanation. Here, Hegel describes the *Phenomenology* as a presentation and his preface as an explanation:

This volume presents [darstellt] knowing becoming knowing [das werdende Wissen]. The phenomenology of spirit should step in the place of psychological explanations [Erklärungen] or abstract considerations of the foundation of knowing. . . . In the preface, the author explains [erklärt] himself about what seems to him to be the need of philosophy at its present standpoint: further about the presumptiveness and nuisance of philosophical formulas that are currently devaluing philosophy, and about what belongs generally to philosophy and to the study of philosophy. (W3:593)

The presentation here is of *das werdende Wissen* as it presents itself. It should replace "psychological explanations" of *Wissen* made from outside. Presentation, in Hegel's usage, is always immanent. Presentation is self-presentation. It is not the author's presentation but the content's self-presentation. An explanation, as we saw, turns out to be a catalog of the author's prejudices. Presentation assumes nothing about the content and allows every important expression of that content a chance to present itself. The author's work, then, is to help guide the reader through those expressions.

In the presentation, Hegel makes no mention of himself as author or his own view. This is only discussed in the preface to the book and even there is it minimized and problematized (see §17 and 72). This suggests something about how we should read the book as presentation and the preface as explanation. We should not expect the private views of the author in the rest of the book and, conversely, we should not expect the preface to be a self-justifying presentation. In short, it is a serious hermeneutic error to read the preface and the book in the same way.

Hegel writes:

> The inner necessity that knowing be science [*daß das Wissen Wissenschaft sei*] lies in its nature, and a satisfactory explanation of this can only be the presentation of philosophy itself. (W3:14, §5)

This compact expression illuminates the relationship between the *Phenomenology* and its preface. The sentence relates four terms: knowing [*Wissen*], science [*Wissenschaft*], explanation [*Erklärung*], and presentation [*Darstellung*]. We could rephrase Hegel's sentence as follows: just as private knowing must become collective knowing, the explanation of knowing from the outside must become an immanent presentation of knowing.

The *Phenomenology of Spirit* should help us to transform our naive assumptions about the proper content of philosophy. Before reading it, we are likely to think that philosophy concerns reasonings about subjects and objects and their relations. After reading it, we should recognize that the division between subject and object is untenable and that both are moments in *movements* which turn out to be the true content of philosophy. Subject and object are not basic, fundamental terms. Hegel captures this inversion in a memorable image: philosophy asks natural consciousness to "walk on its head" (W3:29, §26).

To put this in standard Hegelese: subjects and objects are only moments in a movement that generates and also sublates them. This does not mean individual persons are disregarded by Hegel in favor of some vague, impersonal absolute entity. This means, rather, that the personhood of persons is to be understood, ontologically, as doing, as activity, as self-movement [*Selbstbewegung*], rather than as some passive substance or static essence. The "I" is not some persisting thing or substance, but is only its activity of relating itself to itself (through actions like sensing, digesting, thinking, etc.). If subjects are what they do and so-called objects are only objects in and for some kind of doing, then the subject-object relation is subordinate to the activities that require them as moments. We see both "I" and "other" emerge as problematic terms in the course of the *Phenomenology*, because they fixate on moments of a single selfing activity that involves both I-ness (self identity) and other-ness (self difference) in reciprocal interchange. I realize this language may not be very illuminating to new readers and ask for their patience as we gradually work with Hegel's new way of exploring the subject-object relation, which will be the major theme of Chapter 4.

Because the *Phenomenology* is an immersive presentation it will not be persuasive for the reader who prefers external explanations. This preference may appear as an inability to see a difference between explanation and presentation. Hegel writes the preface precisely to address this reader. We need to be prepared for the system of science by the *Phenomenology* that addresses natural consciousness, but we likely need to be prepared for the *Phenomenology* by a preface that addresses our desire for explanations (which would subvert the work of the *Phenomenology* before it even gets going).

Transforming the Desire for Explanations

As we have seen, Hegel argues that prefaces are typically explanations of the books they preface. In all likelihood, the reader picked up Hegel's book seeking an explanation of "Hegel's viewpoint," not an immersive encounter with philosophy, reason, or thinking itself in which Hegel himself aimed to disappear.

Prefaces keep us supplied with pre-philosophical understandings of the external differences between *philosophies* and thus prevent us from grasping the unity of *philosophy* as an activity that underlies them. We use prefaces, textbooks, and other external discussions to keep our Descartes separate from our Locke and both separate from our Aristotle. But if philosophy is *one selfsame activity* and these are all examples of it, we run the constant risk of losing the integrity and unity of philosophy by discussing it in this external way. If we begin to think that these partitioning explanations are philosophy itself, we will lose any hope of ever practicing it. Instead of providing an easier entry into philosophy, a preface can actually bar the way altogether. A preface often teaches us how to categorize works of philosophy, not how to think philosophically.

In this light, the first important transformation required in order to practice philosophy is a transformation in desire. The reader must undergo a change from desiring explanations to desiring presentations. Hegel's 1807 preface hopes to persuade us to give up our desire for prefaces to philosophy and seek out complete presentations of thinking's expressions, a system of science. Hegel's preface employs a variety of means to effect this transformation of desire. He shames us for wanting easy answers, he jokes and jabs at the different character types that fall afoul of philosophical thinking while claiming to practice it, and he invites curiosity by offering riddle-like suggestions about the true nature of philosophy.

Choosing to read Hegel's system of science is not a matter of being convinced in advance that Hegel's "method" or results are true when compared to those of other philosophers. It is rather a matter of accepting that philosophy can offer no advance assurances and that any assurances offered on its behalf in this way are perhaps interesting but philosophically irrelevant. Hegel's preface does not promise an understanding of philosophy; rather it attacks our faith in promises when it comes to philosophy. Hegel's preface does this by exploring what philosophy is not, what it cannot possibly be if it is to answer to our human need for a transparent, rational community (see §69). When Hegel takes away our other options, we are expected to turn toward the self-presentation of philosophy in earnest.

2

Philosophy Is Not Edification (§6–11, 14, 19, 55, 66)

What's dying but a second wind?

—W. B. Yeats, "Tom O'Roughley"

The Present Moment as Argument

After expressing concern about prefaces to philosophy, Hegel tells us how philosophy ought to be presented, namely, as a system of science (§5). This seems to be an important turning point, the moment when Hegel will finally tell us what his work is all about. But Hegel does not then define his terms "system" or "science" or say what this system will contain. There is no mention of logic, nature, and Geist—the three parts of the system. Instead, he tells us that we can better understand a system of science only by recognizing that "now is the time" for it to appear (W3:14, §5). Hegel refuses to define system of science, but instead aims to situate it temporally, historically, culturally. We will gradually learn that this sort of dynamic contextualization within a larger movement is what Hegel typically presents instead of definitions. The new reader, however, likely finds this irksome, as it appears to be yet another *detour*.

From §5 to §16, we turn to study the current conditions, the intellectual culture in which philosophy as science is incubating and will grow. Here, as elsewhere, Hegel specifies his subject matter indirectly, by way of an opposition or contrast. In fact, what Hegel goes on to describe as the condition for a system of science is a culture that seems *opposed* to both "system" and "science." We have reached a cultural stage that approaches "the absolute" as something that can only be "felt or intuited" and therefore not *known* (W3:15, §6).

It is surprising that Hegel finds so much promise in such a simple and even naive proposal. It is surprising that the quest for knowledge of the absolute begins by recognizing the value of the position that holds such knowledge to be impossible. Why does Hegel see so much promise in the immediate knowing position? To answer this question, we need some background on the absolute on the one hand and knowledge on the other.

What is the absolute? To be absolute is to be independent, self-sufficient, whole. Here, ontological independence is meant. If the being in question does not rely on any other being in order to be what it is, then it is ontologically independent or absolute. We are concerned with the absolute wherever we are concerned with God, Being itself, human freedom, as well as truth, beauty, and the good. In other words, when our discussions turn toward fundamental questions of metaphysics, theology, ethics, political philosophy, and aesthetics, the absolute (and whether anything absolute can be known) is at issue.

The central problem here is that knowledge seems to take place discursively or bit by bit, but the absolute cannot be cut up into bits for any such bits would no longer be absolute themselves but would be dependent on the whole from which they were derived (or even the method by which they were derived). Take, for example, the fact that by 1807 and continuing to this day, it is generally believed (by philosophers and non-philosophers alike) that it is impossible to prove God's existence. If God can be known at all, we suspect that an immediate *feeling* will get us closer to an experience of God's truth than proofs that proceed by dividing God's absolute unity up into various predicates, properties, or qualities. Likewise, we suspect the gut *feeling* for what is right and wrong will be more effective in an ethical dilemma than knowledge of systems of morality. We suspect that the *feeling* imparted by an artwork will be closer to its truth than any analysis of it. The hope in all of these cases is to catch the absolute whole in an immediate feeling before it gets split up by reflection. For this reason, it is generally believed that there can be no science of the absolute.

While this emphasis on immediate feeling may seem simplistic or even regressive, it appears only at a very late stage of human cultural development when rigorous sciences have become so widespread and so thorough that we begin to encounter their limits. Hegel will agree with this current stage that we have reached the limits of *a certain understanding of science*. Our sciences, which are based in discursive analysis (breaking things into simple parts, knowing each part individually, and then adding them together), cannot tackle metaphysics, religion, ethics, or aesthetics. Here Hegel more or less agrees with the prevailing opinion. But Hegel insists that science has an older, deeper meaning to recover. Hegel does not view science as beginning with Galileo and Descartes. Science in the wider sense has been around since the early Greek thinkers. Hegel's gambit is that if we can recollect the whole development of science, we may be able to see a way forward for actual *knowledge* of the absolute rather than just intuitions or feelings about it.

Our modern sciences have another feature that limits them from approaching the absolute. Regardless of what topic one undertakes to study rigorously or scientifically, one approaches the topic as an *object* that is to be known by a *subject*. Modern sciences have made tremendous progress by studying the world as if it were a collection of objects to be isolated and analyzed by a separate observer. Yet this epistemic progress has come at a price, namely that we conceive ourselves as knowers (subjects) to be fundamentally different in kind from the things we know (objects). This assumption is easy to observe in Descartes' *Meditations on First Philosophy*, where the task of grounding scientific knowledge leads Descartes to propose that there are two fundamentally different kinds of substance or being, namely objects (*res extensa* or extended things) and subjects (*res cogitans* or thinking things). By treating object questions as requiring different approaches and rules than subject questions, we separate so-called objective phenomena from so-called subjective phenomena. This has had a monumental impact on our current ways of thinking about thinking.

The subject-object split also breaks with our pre-reflective experience of the world as one whole. Our pre-reflective grasp of the world does not divide things up according to subject and object. To grow up in a modern, postscientific culture, therefore means that we have both an obscure feeling for our unified prescientific experience at the same time as we have knowledge of the duality of the world according to the subject-object paradigm. Because knowledge of the absolute aims at knowledge of the unified whole that includes everything, it seems to require a nonanalytic (or holistic) approach, and thus it seems therefore to call on our *feeling* for the prescientific unity of the world.

In this context, the turn toward immediate feeling that Hegel notices in the post-Enlightenment culture offers a hopeful sign. It is now possible to recognize a need for unity and wholeness, to demand more from the sciences that otherwise leave us with a fragmented world. The earnestness of this aim to move beyond the subject-object split (present in the turn toward immediate feeling) is crucial for Hegel's efforts even if the strategy of returning to feeling proves problematic. Hegel sees that if philosophy is to be a science, our attitude toward science (and therefore knowledge) must be transformed. This transformation will never occur as long as we accept a split world of matter/thought, body/mind, phenomena/noumena, freedom/determinism. The first step, then, is to admit that we have a problem.

The view that insists "the absolute" must be "felt or intuited" is the first moment within modern philosophy to fully recognize the subject-object split as a problem, as *the* problem of modernity. Even if it goes about solving this problem in the wrong way, the fact that it has caught sight of the real problem is crucial. Because Hegel is so critical of feeling-based approaches to the absolute, the reader can easily lose sight of the vital role they play in preparing the ground for a system of science by rejecting dualism. Later, in his *Encyclopedia*, Hegel will make the reliance of speculative science on this negation of discursive analysis through pure feeling even more explicit.[1]

Introducing Edification

The current culture feels itself to be beyond knowledge when it comes to the absolute. As a result, we look to philosophy not for knowledge or "insight" (which we suspect to be out of reach) but for "edification" (W3:16, §7). This may seem harmless enough, but Hegel soon writes, "philosophy must guard itself from the desire to be edifying" (W3:17, §9). Edification will remain a central theme throughout the 1807 preface. It is mentioned by name in paragraphs 7, 9, 19, 55, and 66. More, edification is an implied danger throughout Hegel's discussions of prefaces, faith, immediate knowing, common sense, genius, and inspiration.

Edification [*Erbaulichkeit*], in German as in English, has a religious and moral connotation. Edification provides not knowledge but noble opinion, high-minded sentiment. As much as we like to claim philosophy seeks knowledge or truth, a closer look reveals philosophy is more often treated as an edifying discourse. The prevailing attitude, then as now, is that philosophy concerns unanswerable questions that nevertheless may confer some mysterious dignity on those who ask them. On this view, philosophy is supposed to improve our character in a nebulous way, as would attending a sermon or doing volunteer work. Edification trades in language that produces the *feeling* of goodness, righteousness, justice, serenity, wisdom, and so on. Because pseudo-philosophy as edification aims to produce feelings rather than reasons, it prefers lofty rhetoric to close study. Just as sophistry cannot be separated from philosophy if one cannot see a difference between power and truth, edification cannot be distinguished from philosophy if one cannot see a difference between inspiration and wisdom.

In the section from §5–16, Hegel has a double task. On the one hand, he must show us that this prevailing attitude toward philosophy, that is, treating it as edification, is unsatisfactory. On the other hand, he must also show that this attitude has something right, something that points the way toward a system of science, a proper grasp of philosophical thinking. Our treatment of edification will therefore be dialectical; it will negate edification in such a way that it points toward another way of thinking about thinking. Without grasping what edification gets right, we will simply return to the empirical sciences without recognizing the need for a different interpretation of the role of science and philosophy.

Hegel indicates the task ahead:

> Geist shows itself so impoverished that, like a wanderer in the desert craves a simple drink of water, it appears to long for the meager feeling of the divine in general for its refreshment. By this [meager feeling] that now satisfies Geist, we can measure the extent of its loss. (W3:17, §8)

There are several things to note in this passage. First, craving the bare feeling of the divine is still better than taking the attitude which does not look to the divine at all. Yet if we sit with it, it becomes clear how much this bare feeling is lacking. This should spark the need to "measure the extent" of our loss. This, in fact, is what a system of science proposes to do. The system of science is not acquisitive. It does not offer us new secrets for a better life or a better world. It does not construct a new and yet unknown science, knowledge, or technique. It is a recollective exercise; it "measures the extent" of our loss. In doing so, the system allows us to come to know ourselves not as we would like to be but as we actually are. We are defined not by what we have but by what we lose, by what we negate.

In treating philosophy as mere edification rather than as the positive acquisition of practically actionable truths, our current age comes close to realizing the real truth about philosophy: it is not practical. But instead of being less-than-practical, it is more-than-practical: it is foundationless, restlessly self-critical thinking about thinking. When this pure act of self-knowing knowing is compared with past models of knowledge as a storehouse of valuable goods, it appears empty, devoid of content and meaning. This means that we have already caught a glimpse of the pure act of negation at the center of a system of science and mistaken it for nihilism. Mistaking negativity for nihilism, we feel that our only hope, going forward, is to turn philosophy toward edifying discourses.

By talking loosely about the divine and the beautiful, we hope to distract attention from the yawning abyss opening in our self-awareness. We have not yet recognized how negation is positive. We have not yet learned how to put dynamic activities in the place of the fixed representations we have lost, and so philosophy seems to be without content. Indeed, if we only recognize finite determinations, philosophy has no content at all and is purely negative. Yet if we learn to recognize the infinite or self-relating activities that thread through our finite determinations, making and unmaking them, then philosophy can be said to have a content. Within the preface, we can offer no verdict on any of this. Instead, we can learn to feel the insufficiency of treating philosophy as edification.

Hegel's account of the "current stage" of culture is a condemnation of our collective loss of confidence in the transformative power of philosophical thinking. This is a loss of confidence in the power of recollection and contemplation and in knowing for knowing's sake (as opposed to for some practical end). But it is more than that. Hegel shows that we are aware of the loss incurred by turning philosophy into mere edification even as we do it. This awareness (and the suffering it causes us) suggests that a "qualitative leap" is forthcoming even though we may resist it (W3:18, §11). The hard lesson here is that a culture must die to be re-born and this means we must suffer the limitations of our current epistemic outlook *completely*.

Hegel was wrong to suggest that such a recognition was imminently forthcoming. We today are still coming to terms with the limitations of analytic empiricism. To choose just one example: environmental degradation reminds us that we need more comprehensive and holistic approaches to knowledge. Though philosophers have explored countless postempirical epistemological models since Hegel, the culture at large remains rooted in empiricist prejudices. If the discovery of philosophy as a science is possible, it lies ahead of us still.

Complacency

We confuse the "enthusiasm and haziness" of edifying rhetoric with philosophical thinking because we have learned to expect very little from philosophy and thus to be satisfied by very little. It is this "complacency" [*Genügsamkeit*] that opens the door for this species of pseudo-philosophy. Looking back, we can note that complacency was also at the root of the desire for an explanation in the form of a preface. It was because we did not expect philosophy to be more rigorous than anatomy that we expect and accept extraneous assurances and summaries.

We have reached a stage in the history of philosophy where we think we have seen enough to know what philosophy is before we even study it. Before cracking the books, we have heard the rumors: philosophy is a form of bullshitting.

Descartes captures this well with his opinion of philosophy as a young man: "philosophy provides the means of speaking plausibly about all things and of making oneself admired by the less learned" (AT IV 6).

Philosophy has sunk to the position of empty rhetoric because it has been "cultivated for many centuries by the most excellent minds . . . nevertheless, there is still nothing in it about which there is not some dispute" (AT IV 8). Descartes compares this perennial dispute with the steady progress and clear evidences of mathematics and concludes that philosophy must be set on a similar foundation if it is to have any hope of similar success. Francis Bacon, Descartes, and Kant all appeal to this reasoning (the history of philosophy is endless dispute without consensus) and use it to justify the attempt of radically new methods in philosophy. The suggestion is that the old methods failed and we need to try something different.

How are we to feel now that these modern revolutionaries have met the same fate as their ancient and medieval forebears? We are left with the same cynicism about the past but without their revolutionary hope for the future. After all, we have now seen enough calls for a new method in philosophy to be on our guard. Hegel knows this all too well. While it is tempting to read this preface as another version of the modern call for a revolutionary method, that would be a mistake. Hegel does not think we need a new method; he thinks we need to try harder to understand the commonality in the methods we already have. Where previous moderns emphasized discontinuity with the ancient and medieval traditions of philosophy, Hegel emphasizes the need for continuity with them. What commentators call "Hegel's dialectic" is not a signature method so much as a lowest common denominator that Hegel notices in all thinking. Because it is a natural feature of thinking's activity, it can be found in all philosophical thinking from Heraclitus, who Hegel recognizes as a master of dialectical reversals, to Socrates, the Stoics, Anselm, Descartes, Kant, and so on. Instead of differentiating Hegel from his forebears, the dialectical action of thinking should bring them together into a common activity.

Hegel does not need to use his preface to announce "his new method," since speculative dialectic is neither new nor specifically Hegel's, nor even a method, given that it occurs naturally in thinking and has done so since the beginning of philosophy. Hegel's task is not to persuade us to try a new method, but to recognize the prejudices which are keeping us from allowing philosophical thinking its full exercise. He is not trying to set thinking on the right track but to set it free to follow its own inner necessity. Of course, we are likely to meet such talk with a measure of world-weary cynicism.

What I am describing as cynicism, Hegel calls "Genügsamkeit," complacency or self-satisfaction. The root of this complacency, Hegel suggests, is a disdain for "determinateness" in philosophy. Determinateness and "empirical wealth" have become the province of the natural sciences. Natural science has helped us uncover more fine differences in the world. There are 350 known species of parrots alone.

Philosophy, on the other hand, is assumed to be not determinate but abstract, to concern not precision but generalization. Hegel grants that many see it this way, but he denies that philosophy abstracts and generalizes and insists it requires determinateness just as much as the sciences. In the short, witty essay "Who Thinks Abstractly?" Hegel takes up the example of a murderer being led to execution. A woman remarks that he is handsome. To this comment there is general moral outrage: how can she call a murderer handsome? At that moment, he is treated as nothing but a murderer. This is abstract thinking, according to Hegel, and it is the property of common sense, not philosophy. "This is abstract thinking: to see nothing in the murderer except the abstract fact that he is a murderer, and with this simple quality cancel out everything else of the human essence in him" (W2:578). Reason and philosophy should allow us to see past the label "murderer" and see the complexity of a human being. This is why reason wants to know "why" he is a murderer, how he became a murderer, and so on. Rational thinking gives developmental accounts of things, while abstract thinking avoids giving accounts by giving labels.

Hegel notes that one kind of abstraction despises the murderer while another, Christian abstraction, responds with abstract sentimentality, decking the gallows with roses and likening the gallows to the cross. This too is an abstraction from the actual situation of complex, determinate qualities coexisting alongside each other. This is the abstraction of edification.

The Lure of Edification

What makes edification so appealing? Hegel connects the desire for edification with "shrouding the earthly manifold of existence and thought in a mist" (W3:16, §9). The sheer difficulty of thinking the complexity of human nature, thinking through our history and destiny, makes edification preferable. We prefer to repeat noble-sounding phrases about human beings, invoking freedom and justice, to actually studying ourselves.

Philosophy is often criticized by the general public as "abstract," with no interest in the "real world." Philosophy is thus confused with edification, as if it involved pontificating about universals with no real concern for particulars. This contrasts it with *Bildung*, which requires the "concrete and rich wealth of determinations" (W3:14, §4). *Bildung* describes learning through mediation, catching sight of the whole in the particular, while edification claims to offer an immediate vision of the naked truth itself. As we see in §23, edification names the sort of writing or speaking that trades in grand proverbs like "God is love" without working out exactly how this idea expresses itself in "the earthly manifold of existence and thought."

In §8, Hegel further develops how we got into our current predicament where we look to philosophy for edification rather than insight. Hegel describes his own time as experiencing a powerful backlash against the prevailing frame of mind that privileges business and private affairs. As self-aware lovers of learning, human beings naturally chafe against the epistemic emptiness of a life spent in pursuit of private economic stability. But in rejecting the practical and mundane, Hegel's peers replace it with a vague longing for something higher. Even though this spiritual longing is devoid of content, Hegel reads its arrival as a good sign. It suggests that, with the right approach, we could tap into our larger selves again, re-awakening interest in ontological, cosmological, and theological content.

We are aware that we cannot just leave the realms of the absolute, the realms of autonomous self-expression (art, religion, and philosophy) behind to focus on business. Yet we find it hard to accept any of the old contents that are traditionally associated with art, religion, and philosophy. Religion is really the pivot here, since art and philosophy had, for a long time, worked in tandem with Christian theology. The rise of Protestantism was necessary to liberate self-aware individuals from dogmatic authority, but it also entailed a steady loss of content as the Christian religion was reduced to a form that could be felt and experienced by all: immediate faith or the witness of the spirit/heart. In brief, we overthrew dogmas without anything to put in their place.

This is where a system of science comes in. We cannot accept dogmas any longer. But our intellectual lives do need content. How can we get rich content without getting the rigid framework or arbitrary principles that usually come along with it? We must find a way to allow content to generate itself. In the next chapter we begin to address the challenge of self-generating content by exploring how a system of science can overcome empty formalism and rigid dogmatism.

Re-discovering Content

In order to step out from under the shadow of edification, philosophy must have determinate content. The question, of course, is what this content is and where it will be found. Psychology and physics seem to have usurped a great deal of the content of philosophy.

One way of re-acquiring content is as the handmaiden to science, as the logical positivists suggested. This would allow philosophy access to determinate content, but the content would never be philosophy's own content; it would remain the property of the sciences and would be understood according to all the conditions set in place by those sciences.

Another way of retrieving determinate content is by resuming the mantle of "queen of the sciences" and by incorporating natural scientific discovery within a greater ontologically grounded whole. Whether materialist or idealist, the need for an ontology would at least make philosophical thinking essential to scientific discovery. Yet after Kant's critical philosophy, this sort of approach appears dogmatic. Moreover, it seems unlikely the natural sciences would ever seek out ontological grounding and so philosophy would most likely be a queen without a country.

Hegel's proposal is that philosophy can integrate content through *recollection*. This allows philosophy to avoid putting itself in a position where it is either serving or commanding the natural sciences. In recollection, the moment of action has passed and whatever relations are discovered between contents pertain to the knowledge of knowledge, not to actionable aspects in the specific domains of the contents themselves. In other words, philosophy can leverage the history of natural scientific thinking (along with all other kinds of thinking) to better account for the activity of thinking itself. This means that philosophy will have determinate content, but the content will be serving a different end than it did in the hands of the scientist. In philosophical recollection, determinate contents within a specific domain like cell biology or particle physics are related as movements of knowing, not as actionable or manipulatable beings. All the contents of philosophy (whether recollected from natural sciences, history, mathematics, religion, art, etc.) are relevant only insofar as they help us know knowing. We do not recollect them in order to then take part in the specific domains from which they are borrowed. This allows philosophy to have content and thus to pursue an investigation of thinking not on abstract and vague terms but in very concrete terms. Yet because the goal is to know knowing, not to intervene in specific domains of beings, philosophy remains free in relation to its content. In this way, philosophy has determinacy but it also has autonomy.

Philosophical recollection thus need not already have an ontological principle on hand in advance to organize its content. It can simply follow as the content develops over time, as one scientific discovery follows another for the scientists themselves. And yet the whole pursuit might be *ontologically oriented* if to know knowing is to know being. The outcome of philosophical recollection will depend on whether there is some insuperable divide between subject and object (transcendental idealism) or whether thinking and being prove to be one (absolute idealism). What matters now is that either of these would be an ontologically meaningful outcome without having presupposed a specific ontology to get the recollection off the ground.

From Edification to Recollection

As the context for his own book, Hegel gives a portrait not so much of a period in time but of a *kind of thinking*. The "current stage reached by self-conscious Geist" is a kind of thinking. It is a thinking that feels itself "beyond" everything (W3:15; §7). It has reached the height of civilization, learned everything there is to learn, and found no satisfaction in it. But note carefully: despite this melodramatic feeling of loss, late modern life is as stable as it has ever been. We complain about the loss of meaning but meaning and purpose are everywhere in our institutions, technologies, laws, arts, and sciences. We need only recollect it.

Geist is now conscious of having already tried out and gone beyond all the available certainties: certainty in universal thought, certainty in God, certainty in God-man reconciliation, and certainty in self-reflection (W3:15; §7). As a result, we have become uncertain and crave the former security of belief in something, anything and so we turn to edification. But Geist, Hegel reports, has not only passed through and beyond all of these possible ways of grounding itself in the world but, importantly, it is also "conscious of this loss."

The stage Geist has reached is, it seems, the end of the line, not a historical moment but the end of history. This gloomy scenario seems like a strange setting for Hegel's monument to absolute knowing. But this beyond-it-all end time, Hegel soon reminds us, is a beginning, a "birth time" (W3:18, §11). The end of *trying* to know is the beginning of *actual* knowing. Only when we have given up entirely on knowledge as *acquisition* can we turn to knowing as *recollection*. The importance of the shift from an acquisitive account of knowledge to a recollective one is hard to overstate if we are to be sympathetic to a system of science.

And yet, we do not want to recollect. Because the past only reminds us of what we have lost, we turn away from all of these rich contents, our past lives. In turning away from Geist's former lives, we turn away from ourselves, from knowing ourselves. Self-knowledge demands facing and assessing an uncomfortable loss. This is why we have given up on knowledge as a goal for philosophy and turned it into edification. We demand not knowledge (actually restoring knowing to itself) but a "feeling" of restoration achieved by "repressing" [*unterdrücken*] knowledge of the loss (W3:16, §7). We want to cheat, to find restoration by forgetting rupture. At the current stage, knowledge would only be knowledge of how we are broken, empty, uncertain. Recollection could only tell the story of a great loss. As a result, Geist no longer wants "to know what it is" (W3:15, §7).

We have reached a cynical stage where we openly disregard all content in philosophy before we even find out what it is. Assuming truth must, if it exists, be absolute, we assume it could never be found in finite or conditioned contents. And we are right to be skeptical about the old ways of organizing contents. Content organized by structures and principles we decide in advance can only follow along the lines we set for it. We bury the bone and dig it back up again, achieving nothing. Hegel will soon reveal the game-changing discovery that content can be self-mediating, that it organize itself, in §17–22. In the meantime, Hegel takes some time to explore our relationship to determinate content and how we have come to despise it.

The Knot (§14)

Why is now, this moment, the time for a system of science to emerge? When Hegel describes the "current stage reached by Geist" as one of conflict between the knowledge of finitude and a feeling for the infinite, he is describing both a historical situation and a conceptual one. Just as the historical rise of the new science led to a religious and poetic backlash (romanticism and its satellites), empirical knowledge implies the necessary existence of a non-empirical correlate. Kant makes this explicit, arguing that the concept of appearance (the object of empirical knowledge) implies the concept of the thing in itself (the unknowable source of the appearance).

The cultural situation of a system of science is therefore one that is caught in the conflict between empirical accounts of truth as objective and religious-artistic accounts of truth as subjective. Hegel calls this opposition "the foremost knot" of our current scientific culture (W3:20, §14). Some readers are quick to assess this stage as one limited to Hegel's historical context or to Germany in the first decade of the nineteenth century. This is often done by connecting Hegel's comments about immediate knowing with the writings of Jacobi and Schleiermacher. Whatever its historical roots, this attitude is still with us. While much has changed, we have not resolved the "foremost knot" that Hegel describes here. Now, as then, religious believers tend to describe God's existence as something felt but never known. Perhaps even more revealing, scientific atheists that turn their thoughts to "the absolute" conclude the same thing: the beauty of an ever-expanding universe may be *felt* when we look into the starry sky but we cannot *know* that the universe is coherent, beautiful, purposive, whole. The crucial point is that we consider individual particulars within the whole to be knowable in limited, human-constructed contexts but consider the actual or natural whole itself to be beyond the reach of knowledge. Thus the whole becomes an object of personal feeling, not articulate or demonstrable knowledge. This leaves science without a governing source, like a body without a head. To merely assert by feeling that God exists or that nature is a beautiful whole brings us no closer to addressing the lack within the domains of knowledge.

Hegel's strategy for addressing the "knot" of scientific culture is to catch us off guard by insisting that science has just barely begun. We tend to think that the dream of a comprehensive science that can tackle all aspects of human life lies *behind us* and that the failure of the Enlightenment was the failure of this comprehensive scientific outlook in general. After this, we accepted, following Kant, that the aims of the natural sciences should be more modest and practical. The "hard" sciences may yield many new conveniences, but are not expected to provide us with self-knowledge. Even today it is a minority view that neuroscience will help us solve moral problems or provide substantial ethical insight. Continued belief in free human agency renders any account of "hard-wiring" unable to explain human behavior. The fact that we accept this separation between scientific knowledge (or determinism) and ethical insight (or freedom) is one small sign that we have given up on the possibility of a science of metaphysics or knowledge of the governing source of the whole.

Against this presupposition, Hegel argues that what the early modern Europeans called "the new science"—an empirical, experimental natural science rooted in mathematical physics—is not the true science. To this day, we use the word "science" to refer almost exclusively to the new science. Hegel wants to reclaim the word and inflect it with a different meaning. The new science's failure to account for religious and artistic truth is not proof that religion and art are beyond the reach of thorough, systematic articulation (i.e., science conceived more broadly). It is merely proof that science is now "in its beginning stages" and has not yet gathered the power of expression to tackle such rich and complex realms of human experience (W3:20, §14). What we took to be the end of science was really just the beginning.

When Hegel uses the word "science," what he means is usually closer to what we mean by "systematic philosophy." The reader might believe that the words could simply be swapped and the awkward use of "science" could just be dropped altogether. Sometimes interpreters tell us that the German word *Wissenschaft* is much richer than the English word "science" because it includes the humanities. But this merely evades the real issue. Our discomfort with a "science" of metaphysics reveals the problem Hegel means to address here. If the whole point of Hegel's work, like Kant's before him, is to transform philosophy into a science, this also entails transforming science into philosophy. It is not a matter of shrinking philosophy to fit the narrow confines of mathematical physics, but of allowing a dialogue between philosophy and science to transform both parties.

Our discomfort with Hegel's use of the word "science" is therefore a necessary part of the process by which philosophy becomes a science. Asking Hegel to use another word because it makes more immediate sense to us amounts to asking Hegel to ignore the central epistemological problem of modernity. If we do not reclaim the word "science" to include *all knowledge* we will never heal the rift between the calculable parts and the incalculable whole. A great deal of edifying pseudo-insight can be acquired quickly through the strategic redefinition of terms. Recollecting the whole legacy of science that moderns prefer to forget— the legacy that includes the work of thinkers like Moses, Homer, Heraclitus, Ptolemy, Augustine, Spinoza and many more—is hard work.

The Rebirth of Reason

Hegel's preface positions the post-Enlightenment resurgence of religious faith as a hinge between reductive materialism and a more robust and content-rich philosophical account of nature and culture (i.e., a system of science). The preface thus presents itself as bearing witness to a rebirth of reason through the rise of immediate knowing. In this stage, philosophy is necessarily treated as a merely edifying discourse because truth and knowledge are still considered to be the territory of analytic understanding and its empirical data. Hegel takes for granted Kant's distinction between *Verstand* (understanding) as a power of knowing finite parts and *Vernunft* (reason) as the power of knowing wholes.

Philosophy, if it is to be grounded in reason at all, must content itself for the time being with *immediate reason* or with intuition and feeling. If we do not learn how to start with reason as a feeling and work toward more mediated, articulated insights, we will remain stuck with the boundaries of the understanding as the boundaries of knowledge. Eventually, Hegel projects, reason will reclaim its rightful place governing the understanding and its empirical wealth, allowing us both an account of the whole (which is now merely a feeling) and a capacity to articulate and differentiate particular contents within it (which are now taken up without relation to the whole).

At the same time, this way of representing a system of philosophical science as combining the best of both worlds (empirical and spiritual) misses how the system demands that we give up the security of both of our former attitudes. Hegel is often presented as the philosopher of the both-and, the philosopher who incorporates and appropriates everything. But this misses how we can only include both sides of an opposition by breaking them out of the limitations that oppose them. By opposing one another, natural science and religion (or empiricism and immediate knowing) actually re-enforce their own identities; they give each other sharp limits and clear territories of operation. While they threaten each other in their rhetoric, they prove respectful of the boundary that separates them. Without this boundary to protect them, we find that many of our modern prejudices, customs, and familiar forms of thought will be threatened. While a system of science appears to value empirical content much more than immediate knowing does, it transforms the meaning and function of the empirical. For example, a system of science will subordinate mathematical physics to teleological physics. Immediate knowing chastises but ultimately allows mathematical physics to operate unchanged with respect to causal accounts of motion. Similarly, the empiricist rejects religious claims that impinge on empirical territory (e.g., creationism) but ultimately allows religious tradition to continue in many areas without any emendation (e.g., ethical norms). By contrast, a system of science will transform how the religious tradition and empirical science are understood. Both will contribute to philosophy instead of having their own turf they defend from each other.

It should be easy to see, then, why Hegel's system of science is often criticized from both sides. In empirical claims it is not determinate enough, in non-empirical claims, too determinate. As long as we accept the partitioning of human experience into these camps, the system of science must appear extravagant or even absurd. This is why the 1807 preface performs such a valuable function. It helps us catch sight of our prejudices that keep this partition in place.

From Immediacy to Self-mediation

In §7–14 we are trying to understand why immediate knowing could possibly be a compelling viewpoint when it lacks all determinate content. What do we gain from the claim that the absolute can only be felt? How is this possibly an outlook worthy of educated, late modern peoples? On the face of it, this view seems naive in the extreme and empiricism that preceded it, however reductive, must be preferable.

To reclaim reason we must first pass through a stage where reason is taken up as immediate knowing, as a mere feeling for the whole. This stage brings with it the constant danger of devolving into mere edification. Just as there is "empty breadth" (the endless catalogs of particulars kept by empirical sciences that never amount to a whole) there is also "empty depth" (inspired feelings that cannot be developed or shared) (W3:17, §10).

Empiricism is unable to account for the whole by means of external mediation and transitive causes. The critique of modern empiricism actually entails a rediscovery of self-mediation and self-motion. This insight is concealed from immediate knowing because it views itself as the opposite of empiricism. Immediate knowing *rejects* empiricism, finitude, and thus knowledge and science when it should seek instead to *revise* empiricism's account of causes.

To understand why Hegel draws the conclusion that a system of science will inevitably arise from the position he calls "immediate knowing," we need to see how the modern debate over mediation fails to consider that mediations must ultimately be rooted in an act of self-mediation. Hegel writes:

> This abhorrence [of mediation] actually arises from an unfamiliarity with the nature of mediation and of absolute knowing itself. For mediation is nothing other than the self-moving self-sameness, of reflection into itself, the moment of for-itself-ness, the I, pure negativity, or reduced to its pure abstraction, *simple becoming*. (W3:25, §21)

These crucial sentences are easily misunderstood. At first glance they appear like vague jargon. Hegel does not seem to make the "nature of mediation" much clearer by noting that it is the same thing as a long list of things that do not seem to be the same as each other. What is Hegel's strategy here? First, we should note that Hegel has written in this way before. Paragraph 18 is essentially a long list indicating that substance is the same as subject and subject is the same as many of the terms in the quote above. Similar whirlwind statements of the speculative identity of seemingly different thoughts can be found sprinkled throughout the preface. In each case, Hegel's strategy is to upset the boundaries we draw between so-called subjects and so-called objects. If the sentence is confusing, disconcerting, this is a sign that we are grasping enough of the meaning of the individual terms to find the *mere assertion* of their identity troubling. More, Hegel would argue that we should find this mere assertion of speculative truth unsatisfactory. We must work very hard to see these identities. In fact, the whole of the *Science of Logic* is required. Why, then, is Hegel strategically inserting these mere assertions of speculative identity into this preface?

To invite deeper study of immediate knowing, all we can do at this point is *assert* that there is a third way, neither immediacy nor external mediation but self-mediation. To this end, Hegel here indicates that the process of becoming itself is self-moving. Divine self-sameness is not absent from the constant change we witness in supposedly finite things. To demonstrate this, we must take the supposedly finite things, each by each, and show how any claim about them makes implicit reference to their selfhood, a capacity to self-relate. Because it is impossible to run through all the finite things, we must content ourselves with a systematic presentation of their major kinds (the logical, the natural, and the *geistig*). The system of science will offer precisely this. In this way, it will take seriously the empiricist's interest in finitude and limitation while also honoring the immediatist's insistence that the highest truth is purely self-involved.

The immediatist, of course, goes further to insist that the divine is so self-involved that it cannot enter into the finite at all. That would be a reasonable hypothesis if the structure of thinking, the whole moving natural world, and the entirety of human history, habit, and endeavor did not loudly contradict it. To the extent that the world is meaningful, it somehow allows for the recognition of identity in difference, constancy in perpetual change.

In the earlier quotation, "the I" and "becoming" are said to have the same nature as each other and mediation. This undermines the customary distinction between subjective (the I) and objective (becoming) by referring both to a neutral ground that is neither subjective nor objective (mediation). This is not a synthesis of the subjective and objective but an excavation beneath their opposition and a recollection of an ancient idea (self-motion) in a modern context.

Immediate knowing does not recognize itself as mediated and thus it does not recognize that there can be a transition from finite or externally determined content to infinite or self-determining content. The mere existence of immediate knowing is itself a testament to this transition because it emerges out of the finite limits of empiricism. Immediate knowing presumes that finite content can only lead to more finite content. According to it, there is no way to make a qualitative leap from the kind of content that relies on something outside it to a completely unlimited content. The belief in this impossibility is precisely what allows highly educated late modern people to expect nothing more than edification from philosophical discourses.

Passage beyond immediate knowing (and thus treating philosophy as edification) begins with the recognition that we do not need an *unlimited* content to escape from the reductive limitations of empiricism. A content *that limits itself* would be sufficient; such a content would not be externally determined but it would also present temporary determinations or limits according to which it could be known. Such a content would be continually pushing its own boundaries and revising its own limits; it would be knowable according to its limits but never reduced to them. The comprehensive presentation of this sort of self-limiting and self-overcoming content is the task of a system of science.

Negativity not Nihilism

Hegel sees that the "current standpoint" is not nihilistic, but negative. Geist has not fallen away from itself at all; it has found itself as *neither this nor that* stage it has passed. Geist is now seen as the activity that moves through stages of culture without ever resting in them. This ongoing activity of restless negation is obscured by the hunt for a foundational unit of selfhood like body, ego, community, or law. It is in despairing of such a foundation that we come closest to seeing ourselves as Geist, as pure, restless negativity. And so the present moment of despair promises a new insight. All we have to do is learn to see the restlessness as a virtue rather than a vice.

Hegel's insight is easily stated: knowing can know itself if it recollects its past shapes and comes to observe the movement of negativity operative in them as their formative cause. Because selfhood is negativity, knowing can eventually stop identifying with the partial selves along the way (body, soul, ego, mind, law, community, state, language) and come to identify with pure selfhood itself, the underlying rhythm of the activity of negation. But saying this is not the same as demonstrating it. In fact merely stating it makes it sound as if we are discussing another determinate shape, another fixed foundation for knowing. This illusory impression can only be undone by a presentation of a system of science. The insight into negativity is of no use without immersing oneself in the entire development of past shapes up to the discovery that no shape will satisfy Geist, that Geist must be not a *shape* but the activity of *shaping* itself. This insight is achieved by watching shape turn over into shape until no shapes remain. But this is the current standpoint reached by Geist: it is beyond everything, no shape remains! The impossibility of any further addition is the sign we can recollect from the end rather than the middle. We must follow the entire presentation to grasp the truth of the claim that Geist is "absolutely restless."[2] Hence the current standpoint shows us the possibility and consequently the necessity of a system of science.

We will return to negativity and its significance for the form and content of philosophy again and again. For now, we need to see the relationship between this insight about negativity and the present "stage" where Geist stands. It should be plain that Hegel's discussion of the "current standpoint" is not historical. Hegel does not give us historical context as an external aid to understanding his private point of view. For this reason, an intellectual history of German Idealism is actually an impediment to grasping Hegel's insight which exceeds his person and his time. One sign of this is that the moment where Hegel seems to give us historical content is actually a picture of emptiness, of pure negation, the "loss of all substantial life." If that is supposed to be a specific description of Jena in 1807, Hegel really is the terrible writer he is rumored to be. It could be a description of any time, seen from a certain angle. And indeed it is. We today come to this despairing crossroads again and again, like a recurring nightmare. Each time our sympathy for progress and innovation wins out, it is followed by a round of self-doubt and, often, self-destruction. We have been perpetually re-living the death of modernity for at least two centuries, only to watch its ambitions rise from the ashes.

The Owl of Minerva

In this current stage of Geist Hegel finds a condition essential to the appearance of the system of science. If we were not so hopeless, so ready to give up on knowledge and turn to feeling, Hegel would not be able to justify the claim that knowing has reached an upper limit and is thus ready to turn back toward recollection. If the acquisitive pursuit of knowledge were still functioning as intended, Hegel could not justify a perspective that declares it dead and ready for thorough recollection. The failure to know this or that must be seen as a success for knowing as such. What we produce in studying the current stage of Geist is not a foundation or a single principle but knowledge of knowing as presentation and recollection to replace our notion of knowledge as acquisition and explanation.

Toward the end of his 1820 preface to the *Philosophy of Right*, Hegel indicates the character of philosophy with his most memorable image of memory:

> When philosophy paints its grey within grey, then the shape of life has grown old and with the grey in grey it is not made young again but it is known; the owl of minerva begins her flight only at the first stirring of twilight. (W7:28)

Philosophy is not exciting, not young, not colorful. Philosophy is the old age of culture—it is the final fruit. We cannot think comprehensively about content that is underway, content that is still thriving and growing. The sign that a content is ready for philosophy is that it has "grown old," that we have wearied of it and consider ourselves "beyond" it. Exciting new thoughts that break new ground and shake things up belong to the formation of a "shape of life" not to its philosophical recollection. Philosophy is not revolutionary. The perspective of the philosopher is that of the author of *Ecclesiastes*. To turn to thinking, to the infinite concept, we must first encounter futility of knowing finite things *as finite*. For Hegel, philosophy has everything in common with religion except that it is willing to do what religion cannot: to part with images and the imagination and lose itself in the concept, in pure thought.

The owl of minerva flies at dusk: wisdom is only possible after the day is done, after events are settled, "when the shape of life has grown old." Wisdom is not invention; it is recollection. But in order to recollect the whole, the whole must be present, available. But if the whole is already here, why do we need philosophy? Philosophy, with its colorless concepts, leads us through the whole "step by step" which, Socrates tells Meno, is how one should recollect (Meno 82e–83a). Philosophy gathers up life for thinking in such a way that it is thinkable. Philosophy demonstrates the unity of being and thinking by thinking through what is (not what will be or could be or should be). Philosophy gathers; it does not produce. Wisdom is for its own sake, not for some practical use.

The owl of minerva image reminds us that philosophy is by its very nature "beyond it all" just as the current stage of Geist from the 1807 preface feels itself to be. The difference between the rediscovery of philosophy as a system of science and the nihilism of post-Enlightenment Geist has to do with how each views and values thinking. To the current stage of Geist, thinking is idle, mere thought as opposed to real life. It is this opposition between living and thinking that must be overcome.

Being at an End

Many readers struggle with Hegel's declarations that art or history or some other activity is "at an end." By making declarations of this kind, Hegel is issuing a challenge, but not exactly the challenge that we might think. We can now see that if the issue we are considering is not "at an end," then philosophy could not take it up as a *recollected* content. If philosophy does not have concrete, determinate contents, then it will sink into edification. Being at an end is another way of talking about recollection, which is the solution to the very pressing problem of philosophical thought devolving into mere edification.

Recollection, as a contemplative or theoretical activity, does not need live or ongoing contents that it can effect, manipulate or change. It needs content that has matured, taken determinate shapes in succession and revealed a developmental arc and an underlying rhythm of activity. By knowing such activities that govern development, knowing comes closer to recognizing itself as a developmental activity.

If we feel that Hegel's aim "to bring philosophy closer to the form of science" so it can "set aside the name of *love* of *knowing* and be *actual knowing*" is arrogant, we might consider how it follows naturally from grasping philosophy as rational recollection (W3:14, §3). First, "what philosophy concerns is something concrete and strictly present" (W8:200, Enz §94Zu). We can only live and work and think in the actual present. Even the past must be brought into relation to the present in thought. Second, "the owl of minerva begins her flight only at the first stirring of twilight" (W7:28). If the present is to offer a philosophical standpoint on something, that thing must have reached maturity. The tell-tale sign of reaching this maturity (the completion of development) is decline, twilight. Something that has developed, completed, and is in decline cannot be revived, but it can be known. Growing things, young things, cannot be known except by way of adult exemplars. Both the first claim and second claim are variations on a more basic claim: "the true is the whole" (W3:24, §20). Truth can only be seen from the standpoint of wholeness, completion, because all dependent things or parts point toward some whole, something absolute, as their context. For Hegel, as for Aristotle, *energeia* has priority over *dynamis* (*Metaphysics* Θ).

From these considerations, a simple but powerful imperative follows: philosophy must begin at the end in the present. It is not just Hegel who thinks at the end and recollects. He was not simply lucky enough to live at the one time this is possible. All of us are always living at the end of whatever we can think through thoroughly, whatever we can properly recollect.

We may choose to think of this in regulative terms as Kant might: we think *as if* we are at an end. Yet notice that the regulative necessarily becomes constitutive once we actually manage to recollect the whole development of something. If philosophical recollection can grasp the activity at work in all the stages of development, then the *as if* end has proven to be an *actual* end. A system of science will transform our regulative teleology into constitutive purpose by completing itself, by knowing the activity called "knowing" itself.

It is well known that Hegel declared that "art is according to its highest determination a thing of the past" (W13:25). Notice that it is not just art that Hegel says is at an end but everything he studies. Aristotle follows the same principle, remarking, for example, that "when tragedy had gone through many changes, it came to rest, since it had hold of its nature" (*Poetics* 1449a14–16). The fact that tragedy reached a mature form is what makes it possible to give a philosophical account of it in the *Poetics*.

Philosophy, if it is to be a science of absolutes, can only study from the end. We cannot recollect a whole that is not yet actual, that is still undergoing meaningful development as we speak. We can only postulate or posit or *assert* an as yet incomplete whole; we cannot *present* it because it has not presented itself. As we will see in the next chapter, beginning at the end is necessary if we are to avoid imposing outside form onto the content; that is what Hegel calls "formalism." Partial explanations are always possible and may result in practically useful results but these are not philosophical if the true is the whole. Consider how natural scientific investigations can discover some useful feature of a material or process without fully understanding its consequences, such as its impact on the climate or on other organs in the body besides those targeted. Philosophy cannot accept that sort of partial but useful information as knowledge.

Hegel asks us to look at the system of science as a whole as the sole justification for his commitment to the present, actual, rational, purposive, completed, and whole. No argument can justify the procedure, he insists; only the *presentation* as a whole can justify that our commitment to wholeness was not misplaced (W3:22–3, §17–18). The shift from explanation to presentation sets the expectation that we will believe the whole only when we see the whole present itself. That is how we come to believe we know a person's character, or the true nature of tragedy or of democracy. Why should it be any different for philosophy?

Just as Hegel notices that poetry's cultural importance is superseded by prose and art's importance generally is superseded by religion and then philosophy, philosophy's own cultural significance is on the decline. In this decline, Hegel sees the seed for a recollective system of science, *a philosophy of philosophy*.

We saw that the "current stage of Geist" is characterized by epistemic nihilism. Everything has been done and known and lies in the dust. Yet unlike the end of poetry or oligarchy or slavery, the end of philosophy is the beginning of philosophy. The end of philosophy as quest is the beginning of philosophy as science, as knowing whole. The end of philosophy as explanation of the world is the beginning of philosophy as presentation of itself. Philosophy is unique among Geist's activities. Only philosophy can pass beyond its body and survive its own death. "The life of Geist is not the life that shies from death and keeps itself untouched by devastation, but the life that endures death and sustains itself in death" (W3:36, §19). Philosophy's trademark reflexivity allows it to enter into a unique relationship to its own decline and death.

If this talk of decline and death seems metaphorical and the reader is wondering what it might mean for the way philosophy takes up its content, consider again how philosophy has a different relationship to the content of natural science than the individual sciences do. Philosophy does not seek to aid scientists by interpreting or elaborating or clarifying or even systematizing contents, experiments, and results. It uses the content generated by the natural sciences for its own purposes, its own project, which is to bring the activity of thinking to self-knowledge or to know knowing. Because of this, philosophy's appropriation of such contents will appear useless when contrasted with the many practical applications of natural scientific discoveries. In philosophy the content has entered into an afterlife where, like Homer's ghosts, it can no longer effect the world causally or practically. But while this is a miserable state for Homer's action-oriented heroes, Socrates suggests that a philosopher might rejoice in such an afterlife where he could converse with the dead and pursue inquiry without a body, that is, without the distraction of practical interests (*Apology* 41b). The point here is not to make spooky speculations about the afterlife but to affirm the value of purely contemplative activity *in this life*. In the epistemic nihilism of post-Enlightenment Europe that treats philosophy as edifying talk about unknowable things, Hegel sees the ideal conditions for embracing philosophy as recollective contemplation for its own sake.

3

Philosophy Is Not Formalism (§12–16, 50–53)

The wrong of unshapely things is a wrong too great to be told.
—W. B. Yeats, "The Lover Tells of the Rose in His Heart"

The Importance of Formalism in the Preface

Of all the pseudo-philosophical attitudes that Hegel considers in the 1807 preface, none is more important to address than what he calls "formalism." The word "*Formalismus*" appears only once in the *Phenomenology* proper, but it appears repeatedly throughout the preface. Two of Hegel's eighteen section headings in the table of contents directly concern "objections to formalism" (III and XIII). Much of the latter half of the preface is concerned with prejudices that either support or lead to formalism.[1] The critique of formalism is thus the organizing axis on which this otherwise unwieldy preface spins.

Because Hegel's attack on formalism comes to focus directly on Schelling's students (W3:49–50, §51), it is often read as an attack on Schelling himself. Schelling himself took it that way. Because Schelling had been Hegel's closest philosophical collaborator up to this point, he considered the critique a betrayal and it led to an end in communication between the two of them.[2] This falling-out is such a dramatic biographical episode that it can easily distract us from the wider scope of formalism critique. In what follows, I aim to reconstruct the many other concerns it entails.

Within the preface, Hegel explicitly discusses formalism in paragraphs 12 through 16 and again in paragraphs 50 through 52. The first discussion of formalism creates a bridge between the preface's crucial moments: the "current standpoint" of Geist and the revelation of Hegel's "insight" that substance is subject or that being is self-mediating (which Hegel, in a choice destined to frustrate many readers, calls "absolute negativity"). The discussion of formalism should set up the need for a self-mediating account of self-mediating contents, that is, an immanent system of science. It should accomplish this by pointing out the problems with merely external or formalistic mediations. The objections to formalism, then, indicate the need for a new theory of mediation.

The second discussion of formalism toward the end of the preface goes into greater detail about the style or "manner" of formalism and focuses attention on the abuse of "triplicity" in Kant's critiques and in the post-Kantian *Naturphilosophie* (a school associated with Schelling's students). A return to formalism at this point highlights how the concept's self-mediation exhibits triplicity but differs from formalistic triplicity.

We might approach the two discussions of formalism as bookends: one introduces a system of science and the other warns about a possible misunderstanding once it is introduced. The need to return to formalism indicates that without careful attention to the nature or "manner" of formalism, it is easy to mistake the system of science for formalism. This has been done many times and is a frequent culprit behind uncharitable readings of Hegel's work.

The OED connects seventeenth- and eighteenth-century usage of the word "system" with animal bodies (i.e., organic systems) but this is no longer the primary connotation of the word. In the time since Hegel wrote, the word "system" is increasingly used for nonorganic systems such as bureaucracies and computer networks. As a result, "system" has come to mean for us what *"Formalismus"* meant to Hegel: a collection of contents arranged according to rules external to the contents themselves. Thus the problem of distinguishing genuine system from formalistic aggregates has only become more difficult in our own day as philosophy has steadily distanced itself from any confidence in genuinely comprehensive and self-developing (i.e., systematic) thinking.

What Is Formalism?

What, then, is formalism? In Hegel's writings, "formalism" indicates that the form of thinking is *"äusserlich"* or "external" to the content of thinking.[3] Instead of allowing the content to suggest its own form, formalistic thinking applies a form found elsewhere. Formalism handles its material in an "external way" and gives only a "dull appearance of difference" (W3:21, §15). For example, using mathematics to describe human action is a recognizable formalism because the form (discrete numbers) and content (continuous action) are heterogeneous, indifferent to one another, or incommensurable. Human action does not, in any natural way, enumerate itself. We might notice in this example that a quantitative approach to human action typically assumes that the content is otherwise unintelligible without the application of this external form. The content is presumed to be incapable of self-presentation and thus stands in need of something external, something added, something constructed. Formalism is often adopted as a response to skepticism.

This, then, is a central question of the 1807 preface: can contents present themselves? If they cannot, all knowing will be by means of formalisms or constructions and Hegel's complaints about formalism, however true, will not point toward a nonformalistic approach. Formalism seeks a way to link up various fields of knowing (or sciences) through one formula. For example, if we can discuss magnetism as attraction and friendship as attraction, we can relate physics and ethics on this common ground. What Hegel will propose is that "negativity" can function like this sort of common denominator without being rigid or formulaic. Negativity can allow contents to interrelate while also unpacking themselves according to their own activity.

As we follow Hegel's discussions of formalism, it is helpful to remember that many thinkers do not discuss formalism because all thinking is formalistic for them; to them, every act of thinking involves the imposition of some foreign form onto the content. As we will see in the next chapter, this has led to a widespread concern among modern philosophers that all mediation is distortion. This is further related to the modern prejudice that all motion is caused by some external cause, and there is no such thing as genuine self-motion.

The preface suggests that the only way to avoid formalism is to take content seriously and be guided by the content toward the sort of treatment that would be *natural* to it. But this means we must be patient and allow content to change and develop slowly. We treat seemingly nonliving contents like "being" or "judgment" or "dependent self-consciousness" as growing and changing over time in concert with a concept as if it were a soul, a source of self-motion. Hegel's books are long because they allow the subject matter to run through its possibilities one by one without jumping to the conclusion. Formalism can reach results much more quickly than speculative dialectic. This is a chief reason why it is tempting. If a formalistic assemblage is long, it is long in the manner of a list. The essence or principle is given up front and the rest serves only to illustrate it.

The system of science will have no such principle, formula, or essence to give up front. It is based not on a *thought* but on a *concept*. This is an important difference to grasp but Hegel does not dwell on it and it is easy to miss. Hegel discusses the difference between thoughts and concepts in a Wastebook aphorism and in paragraphs 33 and 34.

Thoughts, he remarks, are "valid through themselves," while "concepts [*Begriffe*] must be made comprehensible [*begreiflich*]" (W2:557–8). Thoughts are immediate and the concept is not just mediated but is mediation itself. The concept is synonymous with the activity of making itself comprehensible through thoughts without fixing on this or that thought. It is not some one content, but what spurs movement in and between contents. Just as life is not the heart but what both generates and makes use of the heart, the concept both generates and uses thoughts to make itself comprehensible. We will deal with this difference between thought and concept in greater detail in Chapter 4. For now it is sufficient to remark that formalism keeps us focused on fixed thoughts and thus resists the discovery of the *activity of thinking* that moves through these thoughts, that is, the concept. The system of science is merely the self-presentation of thinking's activity, not an outside characterization of it following a single foundation or driving principle.

We cannot yet tackle the question of how thinking can present itself, which will be the work of the next chapter. At this point we can only open ourselves to the possibility of such a self-presenting content. If we entertain this hypothesis, we can get critical distance from philosophical formalisms. This critique of formalism will then further motivate the desire to find a self-presenting knowing.

Some Examples of Formalism

Before we grapple with Hegel's critique of formalism in the preface, we might familiarize ourselves with examples from Hegel's lectures on the history of philosophy. This will help us to avoid the common mistake of thinking that accusations of formalism in the preface are just polemics against Schelling or his students.

Among ancient philosophers, Hegel chiefly accuses the Stoics of formalism (W19:272). He has in mind the stoic principle that things have no reality except in thought and judgment or in Hamlet's phrase "there is nothing either good or bad, but thinking makes it so" (Hamlet II.2). The death of a loved one, for example, is neither good nor bad, joyous or sad in itself, but only in our judgment (Seneca, *Letters* I.9). This is a sort of ur-formalism because it denies the independent value of content altogether. For the stoic, the judgment *applied* to the content is everything, while the content itself is nothing.

In a similar spirit, Hegel identifies the medieval nominalists as "formalists" (W19:572, 574). Nominalists, by insisting universals are only names, separate form and content. They insist that the form we impose on content through language does not reflect the always particular reality of things. As with the Stoics, the form (universal names) is considered independent of the content (particular beings).

With the Reformation, Protestants accused scholastic philosophy of formalism (W20:54). The implication here is that the form (knowledge) is alien to the content (faith). This line of attack is also taken up by early modern thinkers. Hobbes, for example, accuses the schoolmen of "insignificant speech," because the content of scholastic discourse (inconceivable religious truths) is incommensurate with the form (coherent, logical argument) (Leviathan I.i).

A more colorful example of formalism can be seen in the decadence of French society before the revolution. For Hegel, the French society, government, and official religion at this time is an example of "the most monstrous formalism and death" (W20:295). The formal principles of religion espoused have no relationship to the actual content of life as lived decadently. Talk of morality and justice had become divorced from social reality. Here we can see that an accusation of formalism is an accusation of hypocrisy. Because the content is disregarded and the form is considered sovereign, a formalist's words never match his deeds. His actions disclose what is actually true; his meaning always turns out to be something other than he meant to mean. The content gets its revenge on those who ignore it. We might think of the stoic, telling himself that he is indifferent to death but finding himself crying over a friend's passing just the same, betrayed by his own body.

Among modern thinkers, Hegel finds Schelling's students to be the worst formalists but also criticizes Descartes, Kant, and Fichte for formalism. Hegel finds two significant examples of formalism in Kant's critiques. The first is Kant's derivation of the understanding's categories from the modes of judgment classified in logic textbooks. Kant imports the fourfold categories (quantity, quality, relation, and modality) ready-made from logic into his transcendental psychology (W20:345–6, Enz §42). Kant does not derive the categories from observation of the understanding's own activity. The logical form is simply imposed, top-down, on the psychological content. Kant's categorical imperative is perhaps the clearest example of formalism available. Here a "purely formal" external rule is applied everywhere in the exact same way to diverse content. This supposedly results in a systematic ethics but actually creates a formalistic ethics that has no sensitivity to the variety of ethical contents (W20:366, cf. Enz

§ 54 and PR §135R). This can be seen in Kant's absolute position against lying, for example, which ignores all differences between particular situations wherein lying might be found ethical for a variety of reasons.

The common element in all these examples of formalism is that thinking does not "forget itself in its content" (W3:18, §10). Form and content are estranged from one another, and the result is a kind of violence, forcing content to fit fixed and supposedly infallible formulas. In place of this violent motion or force, speculative science follows natural and spiritual self-motion, changes initiated immanently within the content itself. This is easily said, but the question is, whether it can be adequately shown that philosophical content is truly self-mediating and self-unfolding.

The Principle Is Not the Completion (§12–13)

The third section title from Hegel's outline of the preface hints at the chief problem with formalism: "The principle is not the completion, objections to formalism." Formalism thinks of the form as separable from content and as true on its own *even without the content*. Thus the principle or formula alone is taken as the completion and the rest is just details.

Hegel first turns to discuss formalism by noting that science is only in its beginning stages and has not yet attained *Wirklichkeit* (W3:19, §12). *Wirklichkeit* is usually translated as "actuality" though this English word indicates only a portion of its range. The word is related to *wirken* (to function, operate, or act on something) and *Wirkung* (an effect, force, or action). Both of these derive from the root *wirk-* which, like our word "work," stems from the same Indo-European root we see in the ancient Greek *ergon* [work]. This is the root from which Aristotle forms the word most vital to understanding the being of being: *energeia* [to be at work or to be active]. Aristotle concludes (after considering many available options) that to be is to act or to do, to perform one's being or one's self in an ongoing way.[4] The importance of Aristotle's ontological insight for Hegel's thinking cannot be overstated. The entirety of the preface offers a defense of this insight in modern terms, for example, "substance is subject."[5] *Energeia* is the word that is translated into Latin as *actualitas*. By maintaining a connection to *wirken* and *Wirkung*, *Wirklichkeit* preserves the sense that "actuality" is only actual by being active and effective. *Wirklichkeit* preserves the relationship between being and activity present in *energeia*.

Something is *wirklich* not just by existing (as the English "actual" suggests) but by being at work. A mover, for example, is a cause of motion in the moved. Thus the mover, but not the moved, has *Wirklichkeit*, or effective actuality. Both "exist" but only the mover is active or actual. Only the mover is or has *formative* being. The mover is governing the meaning or significance of the event of the motion while the moved is merely along for the ride. Being is here more properly attributed to what governs meaning, not to what is passively present. If the same body is said to be mover and moved, it is *wirklich* as mover but not as moved.

This simple claim that *Wissenschaft* has not yet attained *Wirklichkeit* is central to the argument of the preface. Hegel claims it is "essential not to let this out of our attention" (W3:19, §12). But it is not obvious to most observers that "science" is not yet "actual." We might look to the natural sciences and all the powers they offer as proof that science is very much actual. Every day we learn how to use natural resources for human ends. But use or power is not proof of knowledge. Hegel will soon discuss how our early-stage science is fractured into two opposed factions: the practical-empirical and the rational-mystical. The tension between religion and science that persists today is a sign of the incompleteness of *Wissenschaft*, a sign we lack true, unified, actualized science. Hegel's demand here is not strange or exorbitant. He expects the ways in which we attribute truth to form one whole. Our talk of different kinds of truth proceeds as if discussing natural laws and human choice or discussing biological life and the life of God were incompatible. We say this but we live in one world. The fracturing of truth is a clear sign that science or knowing needs to mature, develop, and resolve this conflict.

Knowing has not yet come to know itself and thus does not constitute one whole. Knowing, up to this point in Geist's long development, has been the moved but not the mover, the object but not the explicit subject of human inquiry and study. Knowing has not yet proved itself to have effective actuality; it has not yet actively produced itself for itself. The natural sciences we tout as the real progress or even final victory of human knowing are, for all their penetrating observations, painfully lacking in this sort of self-awareness. Their astonishing utility is not, then, what Hegel means by science or actuality or truth.

By presuming that mathematical physics has achieved transparency and has demonstrated itself as the home of truth, we post-Hegelians have failed to heed Hegel's warning not to confuse the beginning of science with its completion or not to confuse philosophy and formalism. The natural sciences without a system of science are formalistic applications of models to contents without attention to the nature of the content itself. The natural sciences are thought to have reached insight when they can manipulate a content, when they have power over it. But if the content is to have *Wirklichkeit* or actuality, it must be the mover or the cause, not simply the moved, the transformed.

All the problems of formalism we will explore have a root cause: the formalist takes the principle for the completion. This closes off our search for development and completion since we take ourselves to have already finished the job. The formalist thus confuses possibility and actuality. To one who, like Hegel, has studied Aristotle, this confuses *kinesis* and *energeia*; it confuses movement toward something, with a matured, abiding activity that keeps itself in the same state.

Now we can better see why the principle is taken to be the completion. Our sense of what counts as completion has been impoverished. Formalism has come to dominate philosophy because we have misunderstood the nature of actuality and wholeness. If we do not know how to look for and recognize wholeness or self-completion, we will conclude that the only wholes available to thinking are formal, constructed, and subjective. Then the chief question is which principle or formula best arranges all the desired contents under it.

Formalism Gives Idealism a Bad Name (§15–16)

In paragraph 15, the work of philosophy is, broadly conceived, to "present" the "Idea," i.e. the unity of thinking and being. Philosophy should show that the rational distinctions we make in dialogue with ourselves and one another are the distinctions that being itself makes. In its most naive formulation this demand is described as a matter of matching up a thought in the mind with a fact in the world. As thinking develops it recognizes that "thoughts" and "facts" are not stable or independent or permanent, but moments in the joint movement of two activities: thinking and being.

It is vital to recognize that Hegel works to undermine the fixedness or finitude of both thoughts and facts. Because the *Phenomenology* dissolves the independent value of phenomena, perceived entities, readers unfamiliar with the whole system of science can conclude that Hegel means to show that reality is "in the mind." This seems to fit with what we call idealism. But the goal is not to show how everything is in the mind. The system of science will explode the very notion of "mind" as a container with items called thoughts and show this "thing" to be nothing but an activity. No immediate position, whether it favors thinking or being, will be accepted. Thinking and being must both be led back to a common activity of self-relating. We will follow out this line of reasoning in the next few chapters.

The chief problem with formalism is that it appears to meet the need of philosophy (the demand of reason to bring together thinking with being) but it does not. Formalisms offer pretended unities of being and thinking. Formalism leaves the Idea in its "beginning" because "development" for it is not development at all but merely the repetition of the same unchanging formula applied to new contents which are not generated from each other but imported from elsewhere. The "differentiations" formalism makes within the Idea are "already provided"; they are, typically, familiar differences already established by the empirical or natural sciences (W3:21, §15).

Formalism acquires content from one place and form from another. The form and content thus remain outside one another and indifferent to one another. Under these conditions, philosophy cannot evolve because its content does not belong to it. When philosophy finds itself talking about magnetism and polarity and electricity as if these were basic ontological principles (rather than products of a separate process of natural scientific experimentation), it has clearly fallen into formalism. This is exactly what some of Schelling's students did, mixing scientific talk of polarity with talk of mythological talk of love and strife as if mentioning them together unified the ancient and modern ages of the world, unifying being and thinking. Trying to artificially unify natural science and religion by talking about thinking in terms of polarity and love, the Romantic formalist assembles a Frankenstein's monster, neither philosophy nor religion nor natural science. In doing so, this sort of formalist gives the "Idea," the unity of being and thinking, a bad name.

Back to Formalism (§50–1)

In the first treatment of formalism within the preface, Hegel hints at the monstrous assemblages of formalism to introduce the opposite: a self-producing system of science. But he does not discuss the most egregious formalisms in detail here. He only briefly refers to the formula "A = A" as an empty formal excuse to blend all kinds of contents carelessly together. This gives some indication that Hegel has in mind to accuse recent German philosophy of formalism.[6] After we are further acquainted with the system of science, the preface returns to formalism and exposes its worst incarnations with examples.

In paragraph 50, Hegel returns to formalism, noting that he has remarked generally about it (in §12–16) but will now look more closely at its *Manier*, its manner or style (W 3:48, §50). First, we might ask why Hegel returns to formalism at this point. Between paragraphs 17 and 50, Hegel has worked to expose several pseudo-philosophies that, by implication, steadily reveal the necessity for self-mediation that allows for the presentation of a system that is not formalistic (§17–26, 47–9). He has worked to indicate the role of the *Phenomenology of Spirit* in preparing readers for such a nonformalistic system (§27–39). Along with these two key considerations, Hegel has also differentiated philosophical truth from historical and mathematical truth which lead to formalism (§40–6).

One sign that we are practicing philosophy is that we move in circles, we return to our beginnings again and again, and so "going forward will be a retreat into the ground, to the *original* and *true*" (W5:70). The return to formalism in §50 signals that we must grapple again with philosophical science's doppelgänger now that we have a deeper sense of the nature of their difference. As Socrates returns to the subject of poetry in book X of the *Republic* after the ontological insights of books VI and VII, we now return to formalism after the ontological insights of the intervening paragraphs have intensified our opposition to it. If mediation can be grasped as self-mediation, formalism's external mediation of content by way of an alien, dead form now appears even more problematic, even more ghoulish.

Hegel's return to formalism begins by going back to Kant, who rediscovered the form of truth: "triplicity" (W3:48, §50). We find here one of Hegel's few direct references to a recent philosopher in the *Phenomenology*. Kant is mentioned by name twice, both times in adjectival form: "Kantian triplicity" (W3:48, §50) and "Kantian expression" (W3:543, §617). It is not Kant himself that Hegel invokes but the thoughts associated with his name used as an adjective.

It is worth noting that Hegel refers to Kant's "rediscovery" of triplicity, indicating that it is a form native to thinking and present to philosophy from its beginnings which had disappeared. What is this rediscovery of triplicity Hegel refers to? Kant saw that philosophy should not be forced to choose between conditioned experience (empiricism) and unconditioned reason (rationalism), but should seek a *third power* to bridge them or reconcile them. Kant pursues such bridges throughout his work. Kant's schema bridges between sense and understanding, moral action bridges between the conditioned (determinism) and the unconditioned (freedom), and reflective judgment bridges between determinate cognition and unconditioned reason. Kant groped toward triplicity, toward a conceptual figure of reconciliation, but did not grasp the three parts as moments in a *single* movement, but rather as independent aspects, associated with distinct faculties. Kant froze and dissected thinking. Kant did not comprehend what he had rediscovered "by instinct" and offered only a "lifeless" schema in place of what Hegel calls the "self-movement of the concept." Kant's triplicity assumes the separation of the three aspects, while Hegel's account of triadic form emphasizes the interdependence and fluidity of the three moments. So fluid is Hegel's triad that the moments have no official names but go by different titles in different places: abstract immediacy, mediation, and concrete immediacy or the in-itself, the for-itself, and the in-and-for-itself, or the universal, particular, and singular, and so on. It is not the individual identity of the moments that matters but the *function* they serve in a larger movement.

Perhaps surprisingly, Hegel credits the post-Kantian formalists with advancing triplicity beyond Kant's lifeless schema. Kant was not conscious of the triadic nature of his work; he did not explicitly align his method with triplicity. After Kant, however, the triadic form becomes standard. Each new philosophical system proclaims some new way of reconciling determinism and freedom, conditioned and unconditioned, nature and spirit. Each new system proclaims some new formula that can mediate empirical content and pure, rational content by means of a third thing (e.g., the deed, feeling, intellectual intuition, the artwork, etc.). The most recent and most egregious formalism, *Naturphilosophie*, settles on quasi-scientific notions like polarity as their mediating third. Hegel does not mention names here because this would narrow and obscure the greater point about formalism that is at stake. For those curious about the intellectual history here, however, I will note: by comparing his account in the history of philosophy lectures with his account here in paragraphs 50 and 51, it is clear enough that Hegel is considering the recent work of Schelling's students like Wagner, Ritter, Oken, and Görres (see W20:442–453). Fortunately, these names mean nothing to most of us now and we can see Hegel's point not as a limited historical critique, but as an enduring philosophical insight. The point is that we should beware philosophical "construction," the top-down combining of empirical and non-empirical contents (W3:49, §51).

Consider one claim of *Naturphilosophie*, that "understanding is electricity." Hegel protests to the "violence" of imposing the arbitrary form of "electricity" on "understanding" (W3:49, §51).[7] While the *Naturphilosophen* may have wanted to invigorate the empirical with speculative considerations, they actually deadened truly speculative content with their empirical associations. Electricity is not a higher form that can make sense of the understanding's place in the cosmos. Kant, at least, would have been horrified by the claim that "understanding is electricity," since one of these terms describes a transcendental faculty of knowledge and the other an empirical object or appearance. In this sense, Hegel recognizes Kant's superiority. But, at the same time, the extravagant formalism of *Naturphilosophie* attempts to resolve the incompatible aspects of the empirical and the rational that Kant leaves unreconciled. Kant's proposed solution is merely *regulative* (we treat things *as if* they belong to a unified whole), while *Naturphilosophie* at least attempts some kind of *constitutive* solution (to demonstrate the *actuality* of the unified whole).

Romantic formalism and Hegel's system of science both aim to find the proper way to treat the world of experience *as a unified whole*, that is, not split it up into a scientific-natural world of phenomena and a moral-spiritual world of noumena. Formalism and the system of science aim to present spirit together with nature, to unify thinking and being. German Idealist *Naturphilosophie* thus has an admirable aim. These thinkers did not want to yield the empirical world over into the hands of a narrowly mathematical physics that never reflects on its own ontology. They did not want to simply cede the territory of experience to natural science and keep only the shadowy realm of unprovable regulative reasonings for philosophy. They aimed to reclaim the empirical by means of more philosophical, more conceptual accounts of fundamental scientific principles like polarity, matter, electricity, magnetism and gravity. But they did this not through insight into thinking, but by treating these principles as flexible forms that could treat both empirical and rational content. This lands them in the absurdity of treating effects of thinking (empirical principles) like causes of thinking. These formalists were fighting for the dignity and importance of philosophical thinking, but they ended up making thinking seem more arbitrary and philosophy look more ridiculous. Instead of unifying thinking and being, the formalistic approach of *Naturphilosophie* produces only a "thoughtless mixture" of materialism and idealism. The result is, Hegel suggests, worse and more arbitrary than the one-sided approaches of Locke or Kant (W20:452). This formalism is nothing but a "drunken brainstorm."[8] Formalism can go no further than this. Form and content are in the most arbitrary and violent relation possible. Even so, this failure points the way forward.

We live in an age that privileges empirical content so much that we will find the bias always against speculative thinking. The examples of formalism teach us that this bias cannot be overcome quickly. It must be steadily developed, bit by bit. The empirical itself must be shown to ground itself in the speculative. The incompleteness of one-sidedly empirical thinking must be shown again and again. This is what Hegel means for his books to do: not to launch us into the speculative stratosphere where understanding and electricity are unified, but to allow the solid empirical content we take for granted to eat away at itself, revealing a speculative core. By foregrounding the difficulties of turning toward speculative thinking in an age that privileges empirical content, formalism sharpens the demand for another approach.

Formalism and the Denial of Self-Motion

We cannot create a new super science that incorporates religion, transcendental idealism and physics by subordinating them all to a single formula. If anything, the attempt to do this (Romantic *Naturphilosophie*) looks dated, like renaissance alchemy. But we cannot simply return to a Kantian model where we keep these domains separate either. What we require is not a system that blends fixed fields by submitting external resemblances to single dominating schema but a system that allows the differences between the fields of knowledge to negate themselves and thus steadily work their way back to a common ground, their common "inner life and self-movement" (W3:49, §51). This common ground will be intelligible and conceptual, not fodder for sensation or poetic imagination. We will not be able to draw a picture of the inner life common to all categories in the *Science of Logic*, nor to all the shapes of consciousness in the *Phenomenology*. Attempting to *represent* the system of science in pictures (e.g. a diagram of interlocking pyramids) misses the point of conceptual thinking and tries to turn it into a sort of formalism.

Hegel argues that what formalists call "construction" is just the application of superficial analogies. To say "understanding is electricity" *seems* speculative, like a recognition of the deep unity of a transcendental activity and an empirical one that bridges the gap between determinate experience and pure thinking. But what is intended is not a conceptual insight into a common activity, but rather a generic *representation* of opposition. Just as electricity requires poles, understanding requires contraries. The understanding's contraries have been reduced poles, rather than electricity's poles being raised up to contrariety. The formalist ultimately privileges sensation and sensory analogies and picture thinking. He would even happily draw a picture of this pole structure he is talking about. This is really no different from the superficial analogies cultivated by the alchemist, a sort of thinking that is very friendly to complicated charts and visual representations of relationships (e.g., between sulfur and soul). This formalism appears speculative to common sense but is just the opposite. It reduces the intelligible to the visible instead of seeking the intelligible sources that govern what we sense.

Instead of Formalism's superficial pictorial analogies, we should aim to bring out "the inner life and self-movement" of the content. Self-movement [*Selbstbewegung*] is the defining feature of speculative content in Hegel's preface. Hegel announces a challenge by choosing this word because the modern natural sciences do not recognize self-movement as legitimate. As Hobbes puts it, "That when a thing lies still, unless somewhat else stir it, it will lie still for ever, is a truth that no man doubts of" (Leviathan I.2). For Hobbes, all motion is initiated from outside the thing moved. This is in direct contrast to Aristotle's *Physics* (II.1). Modern philosophers generally consider rest primary and motion derivative or secondary. I explore in the next chapter how in response to the rise of formalism in modern philosophy, Hegel revives a roughly Aristotelian ontology where motion is primary to rest, self-motion is the primary kind of motion, and thus purposes (the kinds of causes that govern self-motion) are more primary than transitive, external forces.

Hegel's 1807 preface is crucial because it is this text that should block off our recourse to the alternative ways of making philosophy a science, leaving us with no choice but to try arranging philosophical content by determinate negations. The 1807 preface cannot prove the legitimacy of immanent, self-mediating negations, but it can invite us to question the assumptions we have about thinking and being such that we can become open to the suggestion that thinking and being both necessarily revolve around negation. Without sustained attention to formalism and other pseudo-philosophies, however, this insight into negativity might be seen as another formula, another schema.

If negation occurs naturally within the content we do not need to apply a formula or method to change it or bring it together with other content. Likewise, we do not have to impose movement (force) in our contents if they are self-moving (nature). Hegel argues that form and content are not outside one another (as with formalism) but aspects of the same activity of self-negation. This eliminates the need for a third thing that is indifferent to both already differentiated contents that can mediate them. A self-negating content can grow and change into another content through itself without any external addition. Hegel's interest in such contents is evident throughout the 1807 preface, particularly in his constant comparisons of philosophy and the objects of philosophy to living, growing things.

Modernity and Formalism

If this is all so clear, why is it so difficult for us to avoid formalism? The modern turn from ontology toward epistemology is a breeding ground for formalism.

Here the formalistic approach is not seen as a problem but as an advantage. It is the means by which we will become, in Descartes' fateful phrase, "like masters and possessors of nature" (AT VI 62). In his second preface to the *Critique of Pure Reason*, Kant lauds mathematics and natural science for demanding that content fit an already established form of inquiry. An experiment is designed to show not what the phenomena want to show but what the observer wants to see. In this spirit, Kant praises the natural sciences for cutting themselves loose from nature's "leading strings" (Bxiii). Instead of letting nature speak freely, we must constrain it to answer questions of our own devising, Kant writes, as a judge would do with a witness. If we lose ourselves in the content, as Hegel advises, progress seems slow or nonexistent. If we impose our own form on content, we remain always in control of our endeavor. Such a shift, Kant argues, is what allowed the meteoric rise and exponential progress of the natural sciences. The same revolution is necessary in metaphysics if it is to become a science. Kant therefore proposes that we stop seeking what concepts will fit objects and take the opposite course, seeking out what kinds of objects will fit our concepts. This follows the general advice of Locke's preface to his *Essay Concerning Human Understanding*, where he advises turning to a study of the human understanding first (before we study politics or metaphysics) to discover what objects are "fit" and what objects are "unfit" for our various faculties.

As promising as this may sound, and as influential as this line of epistemology-first thinking has been, it is a breeding ground for formalism. Kant sought a way to free philosophy from the stiff formalism of Wolff's dogmatic metaphysics but only discovered another sort of formalism. Kant's Copernican turn, like all formalism, disregards the movement of content in-and-for-itself and constrains it to speak in the language of a pre-established form (e.g., the categories and forms of intuition). The most obvious nagging reminder of this disregard for content is the inconvenient notion of the *Ding an sich*, the necessary postulate that something unknowable lies behind all appearances. With this postulate we grant that the content *is* something in its own right, but deny that it could ever show itself to us. Yet the only reason content cannot show itself to us is because we have refused to treat such an expression as legitimate due to Kant's revolutionary imitation of scientific experimentalism, which frames the boundaries of intelligibility in advance. The need to raise philosophy to the status of a science guided modern philosophers toward a methodological rigor that turned out to be methodological rigidity.

Kant recognizes the "peculiar fate of reason" to seek knowledge beyond the limits of experience but does not see a way to make positive use of this overreaching. Hegel will note in the introduction to the *Phenomenology* that this overreaching or "going beyond itself" is the basic structure of consciousness (W3:74, §80). What to Kant seemed like a beautiful but ultimately unjustifiable affliction appears to Hegel like the condition for the possibility of learning, development, self-awareness, and, ultimately, knowledge. Aristotle resolves the impasse posed by his predecessors about how things could come into being from nothing by introducing the concept of potency. In a similar way, Hegel resolves the Kantian impasse. What if reason's overreaching is not something that needs external correction and strict discipline and "critique" but rather proves self-correcting if we are patient enough to follow it out? What if the impasse appears because we accept only two categories, truth and error, and are missing a way of talking about becoming-true, which could help us see why contents appear in one way true and in another way false? What if this overreaching is the very way that we learn? In this case we do not make progress by excluding mistakes, but by gathering them up, recollecting what stretches itself and moves through them all. One is reminded of some parents who lock down rebellious teenagers, while others recognize the rebellion as a phase and are not too concerned about it.

Hegel's call to "forget ourselves" in the content entails a willingness to err and see error as instructive. This course is slower, but it is surely more comprehensive. Formalism often goes hand in hand with the "fear of error," which is "fear of the truth" (W3:69–70, §74). If "the true is the whole," then the fear of error proves to be the fear of wholeness (W3:24, §20). The attempt to exclude error is often an unconscious attempt to shelter certain prejudices, themselves errors, that would be exposed by more holistic considerations. Formalism is a sanctuary for ignorance. Preferring control or power over truth, preferring clarity over completeness, preferring utility over wholeness, modern formalism hides the presumptions that it often borrows with little or no examination from the natural sciences.

For example, Kant, following Newton, assumes the truth of mechanism or strict transitive causation for all natural phenomena from the outset of the *Critique of Pure Reason* (Bxxvii). No proof is offered. As a result, Kant argues that without separating phenomena and noumena, we would lose all ability to account for human freedom. But, of course, there is an alternative Kant does not consider, namely that nature is not ultimately mechanistic (even if it appears so in some operations) and that further study of human beings and the natural world might reveal a commonality that resolves the problem without requiring Kant's dualistic intervention. Once established, the only way to then cross the divide between phenomena (mechanical nature) and noumena (human freedom) is to take recourse to formalistic analogies: understanding has its contraries as electricity has its poles. To escape formalism, philosophy must become self-justifying and cannot presume any pre-existing theory as a foundation.

The sections on formalism help us understand why Hegel resists turning his preface into a discourse on method. He writes:

> It may seem necessary to say more in advance about the method of this movement, or science. But the concept [of this movement] is already found in what has been said, and the proper presentation of the concept belongs to logic, or, more, is logic itself. For method is nothing other than the build of the whole, set out in its pure essential being [*reinen Wesenheit*]. (W3:47, §48)

The method of the system of science is coincident with the content of the system of science itself. The conceptual kernal "is already found in what has been said," for example in §18: it is negativity, self-mediation, self-sameness through self-othering, or substance become subject. And yet, this insight is fairly useless and Hegel knows it. Negativity is too general to serve as a useful methodology. In any case it is not negativity in general that drives the development of a system of science, but the *negativity of each specific content*. Philosophical method, because it involves determinate negation (and not indeterminate negation), can never be divorced from its content.

Philosophy of art, philosophy of education, philosophy of science, philosophy of language, philosophy of mind: our use of language attests to the content-driven nature of philosophy. Each of these areas is quite different because the content is different. Though it does seem that there is some common ground such that all of these inquiries can be called "philosophy," that common ground is hardly a common method. Philosophy avoids being formalism by becoming genuine inquiry into the content at hand.

Formalism and the Current Standpoint

Hegel's confidence in the inevitability of a system of science that he has not yet written is rooted in a diagnosis of the present condition of Geist. If the current stage of modern culture is as Hegel describes it, the loss of all "substantial life," this leaves us in search of palliative "edification" rather than diagnostic "insight" (W3:15–16, §7). This makes the reader susceptible to formalism. Formalism gives us the look of philosophical rigor without the effort; it invites us to use a single thought or formula as a skeleton key to the kingdom of the sciences. Because in the modern era there are so many sciences and so much information, a short-cut seems not only sensible but necessary. The alternative to such formalistic systems seems to be a skeptical empiricism, a gathering of information without any hope that it will all fit together into some whole. We can each specialize in a small field, but no one can know how it all fits together. Despairing of any knowledge of the whole, we want comfort (edification), not cure (insight). We have lost confidence in reason (as the organ of philosophy) and rationality (a meaningful or purposive world).

Without proper caution, philosophy that steers away from skepticism will become formalism despite its loud condemnations of formalism (W3:22, §16). But just as the decay and death of the current standpoint holds the promise of birth, the decline of philosophy into abject formalism is a sign that a system of science, a comprehensive recollection of thinking, is on the horizon. Still, we cannot wrest philosophy from the temptation of formalism until it exposes itself as such. As long as formalism can masquerade as a concern for truth, it will draw adherents. Formalism, like any disease, must run its course. Hegel's good news in the preface is that formalism has become so egregious that anyone can see it. Recent philosophy has made philosophy into a laughing stock with talk like "electricity is understanding." And so the time to overthrow formalism has come. The "general contempt" for philosophy we observe in the post-Enlightenment age is actually contempt for formalism (W20:452). The contempt for formalism, though misinterpreted as contempt of philosophy, is actually a demand for the return of genuine philosophy. If formalism plagues us with artificial and extrinsic formulas and arguments, what we demand is the opposite: a natural, immanent approach to thinking.

If we think that things have changed substantially between Hegel's day and our own, we might consider the general reputation of philosophy and reason today. Philosophy is seen as "abstract" thinking, as scholastic ornament, as intellectual onanism. Today, educated people associate the genuine search for knowledge with the natural sciences and their imitators, forgetting entirely the history of these sciences. The natural sciences are part of a long-standing human activity called "philosophy" and can only be understood, can only come to self-consciousness, through a full reckoning with their developmental arc. Human thinking has a broader reach and more governing questions than these new sciences can explore.

Formalism and Being at an End

A system of science is only possible when Geist has reached a mature standpoint, when the content to be recollected has developed fully and even gone into decline, when "a shape of life has grown old" (W7:28). By contrast, formalism can apply its formula without any concern for the developmental stage reached by the content. A formalistic theory of fine art could be undertaken at any time while a philosophical science of art is possible only once an art form has become "a thing of the past." Philosophical science requires this, as we saw in the last chapter, because it is guided by the "inner necessity" or the "purposive activity" of the content which only reveals itself fully when the content has reached mature form and entered into decline, indicating there is no further growth and development left to take place. The content (e.g., art) may continue to exist indefinitely; the point is that it has reached its stable nature, presented its mature form, and has no further meaningful development through self-negation to present. The external nature of formalism makes it content-independent and thus context-independent. The formalist need not consider whether now is the appropriate time to inquire into something, as Hegel does in the 1807 preface. This content independence would be an advantage if the formalistic approach could attain truth. But if the "true is the whole," the very independence of the form from the content is the sign it is perpetually divorced from the form-content whole.[9] Formalism begins from and always dead ends into form-content dualism.

Why is Hegel so confident that the late modern decline of philosophy into formalism is a good sign? Hegel is convinced, as Aristotle says in his opening to the *Metaphysics*, that human beings desire to know. We can rid ourselves of philosophy as much as we can rid ourselves of humanity, of thinking, of Geist. Our nature may be suppressed, perverted, diverted, delayed, but it cannot cease to be as long as we live. Hegel's confidence is not, as so many readers think, in his own solution or his own genius, as if he could single-handedly turn back the tide toward ignorance with a new and brilliant method. Hegel insists that his thinking is not "revolutionary" (W3:47, §48). Hegel's confidence is in Geist itself. This confidence comes from reading through the history of philosophy, from seeing reason emerge again and again despite threats of extinction. Hegel, in going over the history of philosophy more closely than many of his modern predecessors, does not see endless dispute (as Bacon, Descartes, and Kant assert). He sees the activity of knowing steadily seeking fuller expression, greater articulation, better self-recognition.

Hegel's discussion of formalism is a further elaboration on the current standpoint and thus of the system's *negative condition for possibility*. Formalism is necessary for the emergence of a system of science. Without the perfection of formalism to study we cannot be sure that external, acquisitive knowing is destined to frustration. Hegel does not exclude formalistic ways of thinking, but includes them in his books regularly and shows how untenable and self-compromising they are. Indeed, many of the shapes of consciousness featured in the *Phenomenology* are formalistic. Phrenology is a particularly vivid example of the imposition of alien form onto content (W3:257, §340). If we expose formalism as formalism, it cannot continue its pretense of being self-moving knowledge and will naturally indicate a need to address its most salient failure: the need to let the content speak for itself.

But is this possible? If so, how? Everything turns on whether thinking can allow content to transform itself, on whether thinking can "forget itself" in the *Sache selbst*. Opposition to Hegel's books often entails opposition to the possibility of such immanent, self-transformative thinking. But too many readers oppose this before they come to understand either why it is necessary (as we have tried to show in the first three chapters by considering the alternatives to it) or how it is possible (as the next chapter will explore).

4

Philosophy Is Not Phenomenology (§26–37)

I must lie down where all the ladders start
In the foul rag and bone shop of the heart.
—W. B. Yeats, "The Circus Animals' Desertion"

Geist's Appearance: A Paradox

As we approach the middle of Hegel's preface, we encounter a different kind of activity that we might confuse with philosophy. This activity is not, like the others we have looked at, an obstacle to philosophy. On the contrary, it can offer a bridge to speculative thinking if we learn how to use it properly. This activity is called phenomenology.

After completing work on his first book, Hegel chose to retitle it "*Die Phänomenologie des Geistes.*"[1] The word "*Phänomenologie*" seems to have been coined in Germany decades before Hegel's book and was not a common or familiar word.[2] Hegel generally favors common German words over Latin or Greek loan words, so the choice here is striking.[3] The word "*Phänomenologie*" appears only twice within the whole book, once in the preface and once in the concluding chapter (W3:31, §27 and W3:589, §805). Why did Hegel add this new title, replacing the previous title, "Science of the Experience of Consciousness"?[4]

A clue comes when we notice that the new title presents a problem not present in the old title. Phenomenology, even in its earlier usage, is a study of "*Schein*," appearance or illusion.[5] But "Geist" is a word Hegel uses to indicate our truest active self, a freedom to think and to do, to initiate and comprehend. Geist is what we call self-relating, self-determining activity or *agency*. It is a further development of the activities we call "life" and "soul," and unlike these predecessors, it includes the whole range of second natural activities and habits we associate with human beings: forming languages, cities, laws, arts, sciences, and so on. The things Geist accomplishes may be perceived by the senses. But Geist itself is not something that appears. After all, what could freedom or pure self-relation or absolute negativity *look* like?

If Geist is not an appearance, not phenomenal, presenting it according to a study of appearances (a phenomenology) seems doomed to failure. We will never be looking at the real Geist, the true underlying source, but rather at its effects. Hegel thus consciously chooses a title for his book that presents tension between the form (phenomenology) and the content (Geist) of the book. The new title is more confusing and prone to misinterpretation, but it is also alive with the work of negativity: it points beyond itself by initiating its own failure.

Between the two titles ("Science of the Experience of Consciousness" and "Phenomenology of Geist"), we find an inversion of form and content. "Science" is the highest kind of knowing, while "consciousness" is the lowest known (within this book). "Phenomenology" is the lowest kind of knowing, while "Geist" is the highest known. Hegel moves from promising the truth about a lowly subject to promising an incomplete view of the highest subject. In other words, Hegel's new title points toward this book's deficiency and thus toward the whole it presupposes, toward the system of science and speculative philosophy. In pointing toward philosophy, this title indicates that this book is not itself a work of philosophy proper but rather a passage to it.

For Hegel, phenomenology is not, as it will become for Husserl and his followers, a new and improved way of doing philosophy. As we will see, the phenomenological approach lacks philosophy's speculative outlook on difference (i.e., it cannot see beyond differences to the common underlying activity that determines them as differences). The phenomenologist, even as he recognizes one set of phenomenal differences (e.g., colors) as "differences that are not differences," still clings to the familiar difference between ego and object as a foundation. To reach philosophy proper, we must learn to release our hold on this root distinction that produces the whole field of phenomenal knowing. This is difficult work.

Our daily life and discourse seem to depend on the ego-object distinction. As we will see, to look beyond the ego-object difference is to give up desire, to engage a contemplative attitude without one-sided, personal attachments. Art, religion, and philosophy all ask us to seek this "higher" self, this "universal" self. The journey of *Phenomenology* ends when art and religion (in that order) teach Geist the full scope of its self-determining agency, thus opening up the possibility of philosophy, of thinking not about this or that, not in this or that way, but thinking about thinking itself without limits or conditions or presuppositions.

A quick note about presuppositionless thinking, since this is a sticking point for many readers. First, this is not what Hegel claims to practice in the *Phenomenology*, but rather in the *Science of Logic*. Just as Kant noted that though knowledge begins in experience that does not mean that all of its elements are derived from experience (CPR B1), Hegel sees that just because we always *begin* thinking with presuppositions does not mean all thinking *depends on* presuppositions. Presuppositionless thinking is not some kind of brutal starting condition, a high entry bar to keep the rabble out. Hegel opposes both elitism and esotericism in philosophy and equates "science" with "universal intelligibility" (W3:20, §13). Yet so long as knowledge rests on presuppositions, it will not achieve *universal* intelligibility because one presupposition will exclude another and science will be fractured into rival schools with differing presuppositions.

Presuppositionless thinking involves an awareness that genuine philosophy moves not forward but backward, that it does not begin with its ground and move toward a conclusion but rather begins from the conclusions of the history of thought and achieves their ground through patient work. Speculative philosophy systematically recognizes and suspends presuppositions, such that "going forward will be a retreat into the ground, to the *original* and *true*" (W5:70).

As we move through the system, we recover the presuppositionless ground. The ground of being is essence, the ground of essence is concept, the ground of concept is idea, the ground of idea is nature, and the ground of nature is Geist. Geist is the root of all presuppositionlessness because Geist is self-determining activity; that is, it is *free*.

Phenomenology is a study of phenomena or appearances together with the conditions of appearance. Appearances are presentations to an individual consciousness or ego. Thus a phenomenology always *presumes* and explores the distinction between ego and object. Hegel emphasizes this repeatedly in the middle paragraphs from the preface we will soon be discussing. Philosophy proper begins only when we have realized that the ego-object split covers over a deeper truth, that the ground of the activity of thinking is not an individual ego but is what Hegel calls Geist. As we will see, the disparity between the I and its object is just one species of negativity. It is not the be-all and end-all form of negativity. Once this realization is opened up through a phenomenology, we can turn to study the key arenas of negativity in a system of science: thinking (logic), living (nature), and enacting (Geist).

The Paradox Continued: Geist as Negation

> Now because this system of the experience of Geist captures only the *appearance* of Geist, its development into a science of the *true* that is in the *proper form for the true* appears to be merely negative. (W3:39–40, §38)

Of the forms of pseudo-philosophy we examine in the preface, only a phenomenology can lead to speculative thinking. Why? Because unlike formalism or edification or geometrical method, phenomenology is productively self-undermining. In the same way that an optical illusion can reveal how vision functions, a study of conditioned appearances can reveal how to think self-conditioning being. While formalism keeps us treading water intellectually because it cannot turn back and question its formula or first principle, a phenomenology of *Geist* constantly erodes its own foundation, the untenable ego-object split, though it does so unintentionally. Phenomenology offers the intensification of consciousness as a problem that allows consciousness to reach rock bottom and reconsider, from the standpoint of despair, its addiction to the ego-object dichotomy.

If our subject matter were only phenomenal, then a phenomenology might reveal its truth instead of falling into despair. This phenomenology, however, is not ultimately about something determinately individuated and conditioned by an ego-object loop. This phenomenology is supposed to be about Geist. Geist is, at the very least, not my viewpoint or yours, but some kind of activity that is the source of both. Geist is the self-determining act through which these individuated determinations become possible.

Just as the word "human" is supposed to collect up all of our biological forms into one class (male/female, tall/short, dark/light skinned, etc.), "Geist" should collect up our spiritual-cultural forms. Geist is what all self-making, city-making, art-making, and religion-making have in common. When we say that music is a universal language or that all religions express a core truth, we are indicating at least a dim awareness of Geist (here conceived as a unified culture-making power observable across various traditions). But Geist can be approached as a purposive activity only by speculative thinking; it is not a force or a body or even a principle acquired or projected by the appearance-governing powers of sensation, imagination, or understanding. We never sense Geist directly but we see its necessity in the way that what we do sense is involved in perpetual self-negation.

The *Phenomenology* is about the finite viewpoints that *claim* to be infinite Geist but prove to be only small expressions of Geist's total power. Once we hear that the *Phenomenology* details false, incomplete, or one-sided views, we might think we should skip it and dive right into the "correct" view. But here we find a problem to which Hegel gave great attention: the "correct" view of Geist is not a single view at all. It has no definition and can only be grasped as the driving rhythm behind a sequence of one-sided views. We must traverse many limited claims to catch sight the truth that animates them all.

The *Phenomenology* does not take the shortest path to its goal. Aiming to avoid the efficient but barren constructivism or formalism of his modern forebears, Hegel has in mind to let the course of the book follow the meandering course of Geist's gradual appearance in time. Despite this temporal element, the book does not proceed chronologically except within some individual sections. The order of the book is rather determined by the comparative richness or scope of the stage of consciousness examined (Consciousness, Self-Consciousness, Reason, Geist, Absolute Geist [Art, Religion, Philosophy]). Once we have traversed the book, much of it seems redundant or overcomplicated. The *Phenomenology* appears too sprawling when we look back from the insight we gain through it. Yet if we are still in need of education from *Vorstellung* (imagination) to speculative thinking (and most of us are still in need of this), the cumbersome adventure of the *Phenomenology* cannot be shortened. A shorter path, a path that gratifies our intellect in its current form, is a path that fails to frustrate and challenge us to look beyond the fixed markers we use to clarify and simplify the rich diversity of thinking's self-expressions. Aristotle reminds us that every natural being, even the very ugly and the very small, has "something of the wonderful" about it (*Parts of Animals* I.5). Hegel reminds us that every shape of thought, no matter how crude or how one-sided, belongs to the majesty of Geist.

Geist is not grasped directly, but only *via negativa*, through the expressions that spring from but never exhaust its restless activity. Like life, Geist may be thought as a source of appearances, but not as an appearance itself. It is always "behind" what appears. As a result, a phenomenology of Geist must be an exercise in frustration as we try to grasp what does not appear through appearances alone. A similar difficulty challenges readers of Kant's *Critique of Pure Reason*. Kant presents transcendental conditions for experience that, while necessary for experience, are not themselves experienced. In this sense, Kant's book is not about actual appearances at all, except incidentally. It concerns their conditions or source.

Here, however, a distinction is necessary. Though the epistemic attitude of phenomenology is not that of speculative philosophy, the failure to present Geist phenomenally leads necessarily to speculative insight, to a shift in attitude. In this way, a phenomenology of Geist specifically turns out to be valuable to philosophy. Note that had Hegel's *Phenomenology* tackled a subject better suited to phenomenal presentation, it would not have resulted in illuminating failure. It is precisely the conflict between form and content that charges this book with its dynamic energy that leads us to philosophy proper. But this means that we have to read the book from two sides at once. We have to try to grasp Geist phenomenally and we have to be able to recognize how and why this fails. We have to approach the book from the side of innocence and the side of experience. This, and not some accidental reason, accounts for why this is a twofold book.[6]

The Paradox Continued: Experienced Innocence

Hegel invites us to inhabit two different perspectives throughout the book. We will immerse ourselves in the phenomenal presentations and we will also stand back and reflect on their general features and their failures. Typical chapters begin by standing back from the phenomenal viewpoint under consideration, proceed to lose us in the viewpoint itself, and then conclude (after it has collapsed in on itself) by noticing what it was really trying to say or to do. This new insight then becomes the basis for our next experience and the cycle starts again. Hegel typically signals the shift to the bird's eye view, the perspective of experience (sometimes called the "phenomenological observer" by commentators), by using the first-person plural. When he writes that "we see this or that," he is inviting us to occupy the standpoint beyond phenomenology as we work our way through a phenomenology.

This dual-perspective approach proves challenging because the new reader lacks the experience to comprehend the transitional passages that demand broad perspective and the seasoned reader often lacks the naiveté to effectively immerse herself in the given phenomenal stage. The special demand this twofold reading places on us is difficult to meet and results in countless complaints about errors or problems in the book's content or transitions. Often, there is no way to see our way from one phenomenological shape to another without standing back and evaluating what has happened so far. To some, this seems to violate the claim that the presentation will involve immanent negations or necessary transitions. Yet notice that this concern results from identifying too strongly with the moment under consideration. This complaint fails to recognize the way part and whole are reciprocal. We can move back and forth between perspectives because the standpoint of the whole is in fact present, though suppressed, within each part. Often it is only an inarticulate feeling for the whole that moves us on from one shape of consciousness to the next.

We should remember: this book does not *construct* the speculative viewpoint; it *recollects* it. Speculative philosophy is already dormant within us; it is there even when we eat food and eliminate waste. All we need to do is wake it up, or actualize it. All we need to do is recall what we have forgotten. If we view the transitions between moments as episodes of partial recollection (rather than rigorous logical construction), we will be better prepared for the various ways Hegel's book might jog our memory or serve as a reminder. We will not, in this case, be looking for every element of the new shape to be motivated by some corresponding negation in the previous shape. It will be enough if the past shape was negated and we recall the new shape as a compelling correction to the major issue that arose.

The Paradox Continued: Imagination at Its Limits

The tension between the form of Hegel's book (phenomenology) and its subject matter (Geist) produces a dizzying effect. No sooner is an image offered up than it is undermined. The book appears more friendly to the imagination than Hegel's other books, but this is an illusion. It does have more compelling images and concrete examples but the aim of the book is to reduce our attachment to this way of thinking in images. The speculative thinking that we are trying to recollect through the presentation is antagonistic to the ease and comfort of stable images. The overall trajectory of the book, then, makes war on the very thing we might like about it, producing a path that is experienced as a "way of despair" (W3:72, §78). Only a person who has come to value speculative thinking and thus already stands beyond the book's work can appreciate the systematic destruction of the representative understanding's claims to truth. We who still need the book must chafe against it.

The conflict between the imagination and speculative thinking is not new to philosophy. Many philosophers before Hegel have been critical of images and how they can mislead us as we try to follow concepts. Plato's dialogues deserve special mention here because they offer the tradition's most beautiful images and also discuss a sort of thinking that goes beyond all images, dialectic or *noesis*.[7] It is possible for one reader of the dialogues to latch on to an image and for another to see its limitations, yielding an exoteric and esoteric message from the same passage.

Hegel's readers will have a harder time fixing on any of the images presented in the *Phenomenology* as a key to the work because the images are more explicitly undermined and negated. Often the images are not even fully formed before they are already falling apart. This can lead us to wonder why we bother to try to take any stage seriously, since we learn it will soon be gone. Yet if we do not absorb ourselves in the images, we will miss the force of the negation and the work of negativity will start to seem like an imposed method rather than the inner tension found in things themselves. If our aim is insight, it is always better to have loved and lost.

Hegel could have written a book with two messages: an exoteric message in images and an esoteric message in their refutations. Such a book would take more care developing each image in the understanding that some readers would walk away with only the images. But Hegel does not take the Platonic approach. Hegel is opposed to esoteric writing (W3:20, §13). Hegel argues that we are finally at a stage of human cultural development that allows for universal education, forever banishing the esotericism that prepares one education for the vulgar and a separate education for the elite. Because we now have thousands of years of cultural achievement behind us, all the once hidden ideas have been expressed and can be recalled if the student is patient enough. Patience replaces genius and because all of us can learn to be patient (while only some are gifted with genius). This patience-based recollection-education is, in principle if not in practice, open to all.

Interestingly, Hegel's book would have been much easier to read if it tolerated a sort of "vulgar" reading together with an "elite" reading. Plato's works are easier to read because his dialogues make space for simplistic readings. That said, getting a truly speculative reading of Plato or Aristotle is, Hegel reminds us at the end of the preface, just as difficult as reading his work (W3:66, §71). Because Hegel makes it harder to get a basic reading of his work, we often feel like we get nothing at all from reading it.

It is worth considering for a moment one reason it is difficult to read Aristotle. Consider how Aristotle's *Metaphysics* leaves unclear whether a human individual or a duck or an oak is an *ousia* or if only thinking thinking thinking is truly an *ousia*. Aristotle seems to embrace both options in different ways and at different levels. A human person is not actually an unqualifiedly independent being (since she needs food to eat, water to drink, air to breathe, parents as causes of birth, etc.), but she is independent in some respects and enough for some purposes. Above all, since a human being can engage in thinking, in this respect, she can, for a brief time, engage in the autonomous activity of the truly independent *ousia*. At such times, the difference is a difference that is no difference—a key hallmark of speculative thinking. If Aristotle were more rigid about his distinctions (i.e., what exactly is and is not an *ousia*), he would not allow speculative thinking the freedom or fluidity it needs to work with the different developmental stages of a single concept.

Hegel refuses to offer any easy sanctuary for the vulgar understanding, not out of contempt for the multitude but out of an expectation that all readers can eventually rise up to the challenge of a true, imageless, nonphenomenal thinking. If his reader can read at all, she has already learned how to take up thinking where the only cue for sensation is a totally arbitrary and empty one, that is, the word or sign. Literacy is already speculative; words are preserved negations of phenomenal appearances. Speculation seems to be lurking in us, ready to be freed once we lose our attachments to certain guiding images that fix the otherwise dynamic activity of thinking into rigid molds. Hegel believes we moderns are ready to think speculatively. Hegel believes in us. His book would be much easier for us to read if he did not have so much confidence in us.

Why We Need a Phenomenology (§26)

Why not just say what philosophy is and begin doing it straightaway? Why make a long detour through the phenomenological education of Geist before we start the system proper?

Without the *Phenomenology*, Hegel worries natural consciousness may try to assume the speculative standpoint immediately. This will result in ordinary thinking trying to "walk on its head," to contort itself to fit the imagined shape of philosophical knowledge by force or "violence" (W3:30, §26). The opposite of the violent is the natural, what happens on its own without forcing it. Hegel aims to introduce philosophy in a way that allows for its slow, natural development according to inner necessity not external compulsion (which would land us in formalism). Both the 1807 preface and the *Phenomenology* itself have important roles to play in this preparation.

Not only will the forced conversion to philosophy lack conviction (and easily backslide), it will also misapprehend the naturalness of philosophy for human beings as an *unnatural* perversion. Because the reader was forced into philosophy, she will assume philosophy is something assumed from without, not grown from within. Our current way of teaching philosophy in universities as a "discipline" covers over the natural road to philosophy within and presents it as a *techne* or craft acquired from experts. We sometimes push back against this by noting that children's natural curiosity is a form of the philosophical impulse and that we need only recover it. Hegel fights against the tendency to think of philosophy as a particular skill acquired by particular individuals. Hegel writes: "By its very nature, however, philosophy can become universal, for its soil is thinking, the universal, and that is the very thing that makes us all human" (W20:428). Forcing speculative thinking on ordinary understanding too quickly (instead of letting it emerge naturally) will only result in formalism or dogmatism. Hegel seems to view Spinoza as an important test case here. Hegel greatly admires Spinoza, noting in his lectures, "Spinoza is the pivot-point [*Hauptpunkt*] of modern philosophy. Either Spinozism or no philosophy at all" (W20:163-4). Spinoza lays bare the core work of speculative philosophy: to overcome dualism by preparing an account of the continuity of being and thinking. Yet Spinoza, for all his brilliance, tried to articulate speculative truth in true propositions straightaway. Spinoza's *Ethics* begins immediately with the absolute, with infinite substance (i.e., God or nature as a whole) and then proceeds to a series of epistemological and ethical consequences. He thus ignored the need for a gradual education of the reader to the speculative standpoint by way of more familiar views. Spinoza ignored what Aristotle called the "natural road" of inquiry: beginning with what is familiar to us but less knowable in-itself and progressing to what is less familiar to us but more knowable in-itself. Hegel does not want to repeat this mistake.

Early modern thinkers abandoned Aristotle's natural road because it seemed slow and unreliable. They tried to write texts that asserted their most absolute or simple or foundational truths up front. These forceful axiomatic beginnings are precisely the "violence" Hegel mentions in paragraph 26. It is then not surprising to Hegel that Spinoza ends up with a lifeless, deterministic account of the whole. The violence of his method effectively killed the selfhood or subjectness of substance. There is a parallel between the kind of rigid causality used in the axiomatic, geometrical method and the kind of deterministic causality attributed to substance, God or nature.

Hegel insists we consider the possibility that philosophy belongs to us all and that a phenomenology of Geist can demonstrate this. When we look at the other ways we have approached knowledge in the long history of Geist, we find them wanting. Only speculative philosophy will offer the full flowering of the human potency for thinking. It bears repeating that Hegel does not think that his system of science is the only example of speculative philosophy. He recognizes the speculative dimension of many other philosophers' thought in his lectures on the history of philosophy. The system of science is supposed to be not the first instance of truly speculative thinking or the first instance of truly dialectical thinking but the first *complete presentation* of speculative thinking.

On the road to speculative philosophical thinking, we start with phenomenology because at first we are only familiar with Geist as an appearance. We see its work from the outside. Even though we *are* this activity called Geist, we do not yet identify with it. For an analogy, we might consider how young people often view their own country's customs as foreign impositions, as merely external, not yet seeing the way these norms belong to them and shape their habits. The opposition to one's own customs is largely a result of viewing them in a narrow way, associating them with a few popular expressions that one rejects, not with a concept that produces these and other, often opposite, expressions, a deeper concept that is responsible even for one's rejection of the popular expression of the custom. We might consider that Socrates, viewed one way, is a great antagonist to Athenian custom and, in another way, is so deeply Athenian that life elsewhere is unthinkable for him. Experience combined with a recollection of action over time will gradually reveal how deeply internalized the roots of custom are. Likewise, even when we catch sight of Geist, when we have those moments where thinking seems to have us rather than us having it, we do not identify with this. We identify, rather, with more superficial aspects of our personal identity and private interests.

Before a thorough recollection has taken place, we can only imagine Geist in a minor but highly visible role: as individual consciousness. At the end of the *Phenomenology* we will see the deeper roots of consciousness in the more comprehensive activity called thinking. At this point we will have made a transition from the standpoint of common sense to the standpoint of philosophy. How this transition is made is the concern of the middle sections of the preface we will treat in this chapter.

Overview: Phenomenology in the Preface (§26–37)

Though much of the 1807 preface does not directly concern the content of the *Phenomenology of Spirit*, Hegel discusses the work of a phenomenology in relation to a system of science in paragraphs 26 through 37. I make note of the starting and ending cues here because some of the content found between 26 and 37 could seem to fall outside a discussion of the *Phenomenology*. As we will see, these outliers reveal important clues about how to understand a phenomenology in the Hegelian sense.

Beginning in paragraph 26, Hegel notes that nonphilosophical thinking has a right to demand a "ladder" to science or speculative philosophy. A phenomenology of Geist presents this ladder because it shows how ordinary consciousness can, by steadily reflecting on itself alone, reveal itself to be speculative thinking. Nothing need be acquired; rather, certain prejudices must be broken down and certain dormant powers must be awakened.

In paragraph 37, Hegel notes that when, by traversing a phenomenology of Geist, consciousness finally grasps itself as speculative thinking, then what appeared "to happen outside of it . . . is really its own doing" (W3:39, §37). This recalls the opening of paragraph 26, which identifies the "ground" of science or speculative philosophy as "pure self-recognition in absolute otherness" (W3:29, §26). It is important to see that this is not just recognizing self and other as one but also recognizing the mode we call "being" and the mode we call "thinking" as one. The message is not just interpersonal or social but ontological. In the just quoted clause, self-recognition is *Selbsterkennen*. *Erkennen* is a kind of thinking. Otherness is *Anderssein*, literally other being. Being and thinking are thus explicitly opposed and joined in the German text, preparing us for difficult later passages where the unity of being and thinking is explored (especially §54).

This brings us to a crucial point. We often say, "that is just a thought," meaning that something does not exist. This reveals the ordinary attitude we need to transform. For speculative thinking there are no "mere thoughts" any more than there are "mere beings." There are contingent forms of thought and contingent forms of being, and there are necessary thoughts and necessary beings. To assume that all existent things are equally "real" just because they all exist in some way is small minded and corresponds to the assumption that all thoughts are "mere" thoughts even when they express the most profound connections or insights. The common, non-speculative view is that all physical existents are real and all thoughts are unreal, mere shadows of impressions. In place of this view, we must come to learn a strict parallelism of thinking-being where necessary thought is of as much worth as necessary being, and where contingent being is viewed as just as partial and fragile as contingent thought. The upshot is perhaps the most vital Hegelian lesson: all necessity (whether it takes the form of thought or physical existence) is *Wirklich* [real/actual/effective/causal].

The hard part of this lesson is realizing that, if necessary thoughts have more "reality" than we ordinarily give them, accidental existents have less "reality" than we customarily give them. Hegel calls our normal, nonphilosophical attitude "*die gewöhnliche Zärtlichkiet für die Dinge*" or the habitual tenderness for mere things (W6:55, see also W5:276). We prefer things to thoughts, even contingent things or incidental aspects of things. According to this prejudice, a passing sensation on the skin is taken as more vital and significant than an illuminating inference. The paleness of Socrates, if he is present in the room, seems more "real" than the thought he expresses that doing injustice is worse than suffering it. But his paleness is incidental to him and his thinking about justice strikes at the heart of who he is. More, the thought reveals something that organizes many different appearances and governs many different relationships. The paleness teaches us very little about our world. To journey from ordinary thinking to speculative thinking, we must relax our interest in and captivation by contingent existents and appearances. This insight comes on its own and by way of experience if we pay adequate attention to phenomenal knowing and its frustrations.

As Hegel puts it in paragraph 37, speculative philosophy can begin when we grasp that "being" is "self-like [*selbstisch*]" (W3:39, §37). It is worth remarking that "selbstisch" is a neologism. Since Hegel tries to avoid neologisms, his repeated use of the word suggests a thought at the limits of the available language. What truly has being acts as an active source, just as a self is the active source of its various appearances. What truly has being is self-like; it is independent, self-relating, and self-determining as opposed to dependent, other-relating, and externally determined. Searching out the truly independent sources of things is the work of philosophy proper. This work demands that we value "mere" thoughts because many of the most important governing sources of things will never appear to our sensation or imagination.

With the key realization that being is self-like "the phenomenology of Geist is concluded." It is worth noting that, were this preface primarily about the *Phenomenology*, this sentence would signal we are close to the end of the preface. In fact, we are barely halfway through and this should tell us that the 1807 preface has many other concerns besides introducing the book at hand.

We thus have clear textual clues that a discussion of phenomenology begins in 26 and draws to a close in 37. Following this, paragraph 38 offers a transition from phenomenology to the next topic, propositional truth. It begins discussing falsehood in phenomenology and moves to a general discussion of falsehood in the paragraphs that follow. We will explore that discussion of falsehood in the next chapter.

The Problem with the Familiar (§26–31)

The most immediately striking feature of Hegel's account of phenomenology in paragraphs 26–37 is the way it problematizes the familiar [*Bekannte*]. This ties back to the critique of formalism. Formalism is accused of appropriating what is "already familiar" from other investigations instead of patiently discovering its own proper content (W3:21, §15). We can also connect the familiar to the "customary" [*Gewohnheit*] and thus to the "obstacle" [*Hindernis*] to philosophical thinking that the customary and familiar presents (W3:22, §16 and W3:62, §63). We will thus be able to find a common thread in the critique of prefaces, formalism, the account of education in §4 and §28–33, and the later discussion of other obstacles to philosophy.

Even the beginning of the preface is implicated in this concern with the limitations placed on philosophical inquiry by the familiar and the customary. Indeed, it is the *custom* of the preface and our familiarity with it that Hegel problematizes in the opening paragraphs. We think we know what prefaces are for and how to use them. Prefaces in themselves are not the problem here; our customary expectations concerning them are the real problem Hegel means to address. In this sense, there is nothing contradictory about Hegel both writing a preface and criticizing how authors and readers *use* prefaces. The customary usage of prefaces aims to evade the *Sache*, the real issue, and to turn the book into an already available position or talking point when it should help us to "lose" ourselves in the book without a definite plan or agenda (W3:13, §3). Hegel objects not to the practice just as such but to the *expectations* it customarily invites. And so he writes a strange and estranging preface, a preface that causes us to reflect on just how odd the practice of prefacing books (or discussing them from outside beforehand) really is. Hegel uses this external discussion of his book (the preface) to criticize *all external approaches* to philosophy.

The chief problem with the familiar is that we are "no longer interested in it" (W3:35, §30). Growth requires challenge and perplexity and will not seek to know what it presumes to know already. Knowing proceeds by alienation, by distancing us from the familiar and immersing us in what seems different or other. Hegel remarks that familiar representations are the mainstay of mental life in its individuated, particular existence. Knowing and science, by contrast, require the negation of this familiarity and are undertaken not on behalf of the individual, but on behalf of the "activity of the universal self and the interest of thinking" (W3:35, §30). The work of the *Phenomenology* is the defamiliarizing of the familiar that should lead to the discovery of oneself not as an individuated existence but in the interest of thinking itself.

The *Phenomenology of Spirit* can be seen as Hegel's most robust attempt to defamiliarize the familiar. Indeed, it continues to be Hegel's most often read book because its contents are the most familiar to us, even if the way Hegel discusses them is so foreign that it invariably proves frustrating to new readers. When we compare the topics addressed here to those covered in the *Science of Logic*, or even much of what is discussed in the philosophies of nature and Geist, we see that the *Phenomenology* tackles more familiar content. Here we are talking about what it is like to live in a phenomenal world, as opposed to discussing the conceptual underpinnings of that world. We are discussing having objects and desiring recognition. Even when we discuss abstruse scientific topics, we are discussing them insofar as they answer to a need or desire of a conscious subject to know objects, which is our familiar model for truth seeking. In the *Science of Logic*, by contrast, there is no ego at the center of the chapters, no desiring, objectifying power, for it has been replaced by another kind of thinking, namely, speculative thinking.

In §26–37 we explore why we need a phenomenology to defamiliarize the familiar for us and receive some hints about what thinking outside the familiar realm of subject-object dichotomy will be like.

Four Stages of *Bildung* (§28–33)

Hegel invites us to read the *Phenomenology* as a story of formative education, *Bildung*. Yet it is not the education of a single individual at issue here but a universal education of human awareness. This is not a "history of the world" that begins with the first records of human activity and proceeds to the present. It is rather a story that begins with the simplest way of conceptualizing ourselves and our activity and proceeds to progressively richer modes of self-understanding. Broadly, it works through many different layers of the subject-object relation, the many different ways that we have defined ourselves by the way that we have our objects (e.g., observing, explaining, desiring, consuming, recognizing, categorizing, etc.). It ends when the subject-object relation is subverted and we recognize our activity in another register.

The best way to follow the compressed discussion of *Bildung* is to identify its four major moments. These moments correspond to kinds of apprehension, powers of the soul, and thus form something like Hegel's take on the divided line. The first moment is the apprehension of a sensuous existence, the second is the apprehension of a familiar representation, the third is the apprehension of an isolated thought, and the final is the apprehension of a concept. These moments correspond to four basic powers of human apprehension: sensation, imagination, understanding, and reason.

Put this way, the account seems straightforward. Why is Hegel's articulation of it so confusing? The main culprit here is that Hegel tries to avoid making the phenomenology of Geist into a faculty psychology like Kant's critiques. Hegel does not actually think these are distinct faculties or powers at all. These are just different ways that one activity, thinking [*das Denken*], expresses itself. So Hegel writes in a way that both makes and cancels the difference between sensation, imagination, understanding, and reason. He does not exaggerate differences for the sake of clarity because this would undermine the ultimate goal: to see the continuity of thinking that runs through these powers.

It is important to see how deep the concept goes: even sensation has always been oriented toward the concept. Hegel reminds us, at the end of sense certainty, that even animals are idealists because when they eat things, they prove they are not captivated by sensuous objects. Even animals do not treat material things as if their existence were an irrefutable truth. Even among nonhuman animals, the sensation of material objects is directed to the self-relating life the individual animal or, ultimately, the animal species. Existents are just a means to the end of selfing. If by "concept" we mean to describe self-relation, the axis of selfhood on which all other activities turn, then even brute sensation is oriented toward the concept.

When we come to grasp that the proper object of thinking is not a sensible thing, image, or isolated thought but a self-moving self or concept, we have completed the *Bildung* of phenomenology and are ready to do philosophy proper or to start the work of a system of science. Put this way it may sound easy, but this realization is difficult to procure. Hegel wagers that the insight into the concept as the proper content of thinking cannot be had easily or directly. The concept is, after all, not a "thing" like an existent individual, a familiar image, or even an understood, isolated, definite thought. The concept is the selfhood of whatever it is the concept of, but this means it cannot be grasped except by a thorough study of all the ways that being *is*. Apparently epistemological inquiries turn ontological or metaphysical in Hegel's hands because thinking and being are mutually illuminating forms of selfing.

Beginning with sensation, we then develop successive powers of discrimination: imagination [*Vorstellung*], understanding, and finally, reason. We need not view these as separate faculties, as Kant does. We can view them as steadily deepening a single activity we call "thinking." The development can then be viewed less as an acquisition of new powers and more as an activation of thinking's nature.

The process of *Bildung* by which thinking educates itself to become knowing involves three movements between the four powers of thinking outlined earlier. Hegel's emphasis is on these movements rather than the faculties or powers. What is crucial is not the power and its object (sensation/impression, imagination/image, understanding/thought, reason/concept) but the activity of forming images, forming thoughts and forming concepts.

Hegel describes three developmental stages of thinking activity in §30–3. It may be helpful to compare my exposition of these three movements to Hegel's later and rather schematic description of the three movements of thinking (positing, negating, and sublating) in the *Encyclopedia* (see W8:168, Enz §79). There is an initial *gathering* of diverse elements from sensation into the imagination, an "elevation into universality," that forms a stable image from the ebb and flow of sensation, an image that can be named and represented (W3:36, §33). This is followed by a second stage, an *"analysis"* of the imaged or represented content into discrete thoughts in the understanding (W3:35, §32). The final stage involves "freeing" these thoughts "from their fixity" and to bring them into interconnection and "fluidity" through the use of reason (W3:37, §33). The chief culprit for this problematic fixity will turn out to be "the I." We have a limited approach to knowing as the work of some "I," and the *Phenomenology* aims to help us realize this and overcome our attachment to the "I" as the foundation of all knowing.

Ancient and Modern Study (§33, First Half)

Hegel's preface argues that we have the wrong idea about thinking. Because of this, we confuse various forms of sophistry with philosophy, we confuse prejudices with the concept, and we confuse obstacles to truth with the truth itself. The problem with the current attitude toward thinking is summed up in paragraph 33.

Here, Hegel contrasts the ancient task of study with the modern task. The ancients had to transform the sensory world into something thinkable. This amounted to seeing individual, sensed things as expressions of universal kinds, forms, powers, activities, or purposes. But the modern individual "finds the abstract form already prepared" (W3:37, §33). The modern person encounters the world not as a collection of sensory things in need of consistent laws and principles but as already grouped and arranged by inherited thoughts. Failing to recognize this difference between ancient study and modern study, the modern thinker does not grapple with thinking's past as a condition of thinking's present. This means we moderns are constantly in danger of misrepresenting our own thinking to ourselves.

Descartes' opening meditation displays this vividly. Descartes is aware that his schooling has given him an already interpreted world. But he presumes that he can simply set this interpretation aside and start afresh from his experiences. As the meditations progress, Descartes introduces countless thoughts as if they were natural to him, when we can easily show these very thoughts to belong to his cultural inheritance and education, his *Bildung*. For example, the distinction between objective reality and formal reality is by no means a basic intuition. It belongs to the scholastic matrix that Descartes is trying so hard to escape. The blind inheritance thus forms a fixed stopping point for thinking, keeping it from fully reckoning with itself.

The ancient task was to produce the content of philosophy by having consciousness "examine itself explicitly in every aspect of its existence" (W3:37, §33). In Plato's *Meno*, Meno offers several social prejudices as if they could stand as definitions of virtue. Socrates tries to help him examine these "aspects" of particular "existence" to look for an "abstract form." Aristotle too examines plants, animals, weather, stars, and every other aspect of consciousness' particular existence, seeking the purposes that govern and arrange them as they are.

Here it is worth noting that ancient Greeks certainly inherited thoughts just as moderns do. The difference Hegel highlights here concerns the kinds of thoughts. Cultural inheritance before classical philosophy, before science, is more loosely arranged and more imagistic (i.e., *Vorstellung*). From Homer we may learn a certain kind of behavior and call it virtue. We settle on this behavior as a community and re-enforce it through praise and blame. Yet, when challenged, the evidence that we appeal to (Homer's poem) proves indefinite. It does not satisfy the thoroughgoing investigation of thinking. Socrates shows how easily Homer can be turned around and made to say something quite different.[8]

Ancient philosophers inherited locally valid images and turned them into universally valid thoughts. They took their community's peculiar cultural inheritance and analyzed it for forms that retain meaning across cultural boundaries. With mathematics and music showing the way, the earliest phase of philosophy uncovered living universals.

For moderns, these hard-won universals are a thoughtless inheritance. The understanding's thoughts are already embedded in complex relationships of opposition and distinction that we take for granted and would struggle to recollect or uncover. Hegel gives some examples of such thoughts in §31: subject, object, God, nature, understanding, sensibility. There are whole treatises behind the distinctions and principles that we find familiar and ready for use. As we saw with Descartes, we may try to set a thought content aside, only to find it is already part of how we conduct our thinking. Working with undergraduates in philosophy classrooms, one learns just how difficult it can be to call the inheritances of the understanding into question.

Without the ancient, first stage of *Bildung*, human beings would not have codified their images and sensations into thoughts that could transfer beyond cultural boundaries. Consciousness would remain a reaction to particular conditions and would not become an "active universality." This was important work, but for Hegel it is a mistake to assume that modern philosophy has this same task. Our task is not to push local images toward universal thoughts but to take the fixed universal thoughts and render them "fluid" again. In the next section we will explore what this might mean.

Too often we think of the modern age as one of novelty, innovation, construction, or even the domination of nature by human ingenuity. This sort of frontier thinking misreads the actual situation of modernity with its complex history and reliance on traditions and cultural inheritances. On Hegel's account, modernity is not really about originality, individuality, and trailblazing new ideas. Modernity, if it is self-aware, is about patient recollection, about making sense of thousands of years of human endeavor, finding the patterns and rhythms of sense-making that can offer a path through the labyrinth of overwhelming inheritances.

As Hegel remarks in §28, what was once the life's work of a mature, adult intelligence is now a lesson for schoolchildren. What was once at the forefront of mathematical investigation later becomes material for ten-year-olds. We must face this astounding fact squarely. The work of countless generations is with us already, hiding in our most familiar words, images, and thoughts. If we do not learn how to think through it, it will use us, giving rise to pseudo-philosophical formalisms rather than genuine inquiry.

Fluid Thinking (§33, Second Half)

The 33rd paragraph of the preface indicates that the task of *Bildung* (education/cultivation) is always to enliven and invigorate the activity of thinking. This is true of ancient, medieval, or modern *Bildung*. They have the same end but achieve it by different means. By nature thinking is active, but by habit it can easily become passive. Early on in its development in the ancient world, Geist had to work against the fixity of sensuous existences in the imagination, while later it must work against the fixity of principles in the understanding. We moderns need to bring "fixed thoughts into fluidity" (W3:37, §33). This modern task, Hegel notes, is "much harder" than the ancient task.

Bringing fixed thoughts into fluidity is difficult because it demands we give up something even nearer and dearer to us than the familiar stability of sensuous existences. It demands we give up the fixity of the "I" or ego itself as a principle. The inherited thoughts are "mine" and I see them not as a transmission but as the product of my own will. This confusion is what blocks the progress of recollection (which would reintroduce activity and dynamism and fluidity into the landscape of thoughts). What Hegel describes here is something he has been trying to introduce in a variety of ways throughout the preface: the individual ego must yield its pretense to total independence and recognize I-ness as a "moment" in the total movement of thinking as such. The I is not the foundation of thinking. Rather, thinking is the foundation of the I (which is only one species of thinking). Thinking need not be always identified as "mine," identified with an "I." It can also be "your" thought or it can be anonymous; it can be the sort of thinking I identify with this discipline or this institution or this language, and so on. Descartes comes very close to this crucial thought when he considers thinking as indubitable to itself but then immediately interprets this foundation as his own thinking. "I think, I am" as opposed to: "there is thinking, there is being." The "I" is not the preeminent or fundamental kind of selfhood but it presents itself as such. Thus, to make thoughts fluid requires the work of a phenomenology, through which we will learn to see the ego-object disparity as merely one species of negativity among others. This is the topic of §37.

Dissolving the ego-object disparity (the task of modern *Bildung*) is much harder than giving up the individuality of some sensible particular or other in order to see it as a moment in the activity of a universal form (the task of ancient *Bildung*). The ancients had only to show that sensuous immediacy is already mediated. Moderns must show that mediation itself (i.e., the ego-object disparity) is mediated (i.e., by negativity in general). We must learn to see what we consider an ultimate horizon for thought (ego-object consciousness) is only one species within the genus of thinking more broadly conceived. To further expose this difficulty, Hegel compares the "impotent abstract immediacy" of "being" as the condition for sensuous determinations with the "power" of the "I" as a condition for thought determinations (W3:37, §33). Since this is challenging content, we should unpack it a bit more.

Hegel identifies "being" with "abstract immediacy." To apprehend the whole as an abstract immediacy is to apprehend what is called "being." This does not mean that being itself *is* abstract immediacy but that the way of thinking the whole which we associate with the name "being" is of this sort. The "abstract" here refers to a lack of context, an absence of prior reflections which qualify the claim to immediacy. An abstract immediacy is "abstracted" or removed from its surroundings or conditions. Abstract immediacy (as opposed to concrete or achieved immediacy) is a form of bare assertion without any background, context, condition, or qualification. Many thinkers assume that the only form of immediacy possible is necessarily abstract because any form of context would render the content nonimmediate. Hegel, however, argues (as we see in §20–3) that when we show a mediated content to be self-mediating (i.e., the source of its own mediations), then we have identified a content that is both mediated and, in a special sense, immediate (insofar as it is not mediated by anything outside itself but rather by its own self). This special kind of content is not an abstract immediacy but a concrete immediacy.

Any determination presented in the mode of abstract immediacy is easy to counter. We can study the sense-certainty chapter of the *Phenomenology* to encounter several examples of this. In one memorable example that is reminiscent of comments made by both Aristotle and Augustine on time, Hegel picks up on the impossibility of identifying an individual "now." As soon as we identify the now, it has already passed. If we write down, "now it is night" as an attempt to express the immediate truth of pure being, this will be false when we read it later. Any attempt to *express* the truth of immediacy is already mediated. And if immediacy is to be *known* as true, it must be expressed. Thus the immediate appearance of something to the senses is not a stable, reliable truth. This lesson is profound, and it is one taught to us by the earliest philosophers.

So much for the impotence of sensuous immediacy which ancient philosophy had to expose. What is the "power" of the "I" that modern philosophy must overturn? The "I" is already a movement, already a mediating activity. Thus we cannot catch it off guard as easily as we can point out that the "now" (or any sensuous immediacy) is never the same. "I" continues to be "I" even as consciousness changes. Kant's account of the transcendental ego, the "I think" that accompanies every possible representation, is a good expression of the "power" of the "I." The ego can accompany any thought without being unseated or shown to be conditioned by something else. For this reason, Kant considers the transcendental unity of apperception as a condition for any experience whatsoever. Many philosophers to this day agree with Kant. Hegel, however, argues that there is an activity of thinking that proves even more fundamental than the activity of thinking we associate with the "I" that represents things to itself.[9]

The chief task of modern philosophical *Bilding* is to challenge the I-centered accounts of thinking which have risen to prominence and, in doing so, to make thinking "fluid":

> Thoughts become fluid insofar as pure thinking, this inner *immediacy*, recognizes itself as a moment, or insofar as the pure conscience abstracts from itself,— not to be left behind or set to the side,— but [so that] it gives up the fixity of its self-positing [*Sichselbstsetzens*] and also gives up the fixity of the purely concrete, which is the I itself in opposition to different contents, as much as it gives up the fixity of differences, which are posited in the element of pure thinking and participate in the unconditionedness [*Unbedingtheit*] of the I. (W3:37, §33)

Simply put, Hegel here describes how thinking becoming "fluid" (the task of modern philosophy) can be grasped as a sublation of the ego-object disparity. There is much we are lacking at this point because this sublation is a long process; it is what Hegel is trying to do with the *entire* book he called *Phenomenology of Spirit*. Still, this description gives us some clues as to why this sublation (i.e., this negation, internalization, and contextualization of the ego-object framework) is so hard to achieve. In the foregoing quote, Hegel shows the ego to have layers such that giving up one layer will not do unless we give them all up. The work of the ego can be found in self-positing, in the opposition to differentiated content, *and* in the differentiations themselves.

The "I" is a resilient creature. It is a master at negating itself in part without negating itself in full. We should be familiar with this resilience from each time we call some aspect of consciousness into question without questioning the self-positing of consciousness itself. This partial or incomplete negativity works for the ego because the ego itself is a power of negation. Indeed, the ego likes to think of itself as *the* power of negation. Each time I delay gratification, I am exercising the power of the I to negate itself in one respect without giving up "the fixity of its self-positing." I can stretch my interest into the non-actual, into the future, into the possible and make a home there. While I negate the sensuous existences and determinations of the present, this does not undermine the "unconditionedness" of egoity itself. To go further and give up this fixity of self-positing, thus allowing thinking to become fluid, is not to give up this or that desire but to give up the fixed structure of desire itself.

In the previously mentioned quote Hegel is careful to note that giving up fixity here does not amount to leaving the I behind or setting it aside. It is a matter of recognizing the ego *within* Geist, not putting the ego aside to embrace Geist instead. This means that we do not actually give up desire; we re-situate it inside a more comprehensive activity of being-a-self. We give up not the ego but its *fixity*. Hegel addresses this process most directly four paragraphs later in §37.

Consciousness and Negativity (§37)

In paragraph 37, Hegel outlines the role of "the negative" within a phenomenology. The attitude or form of thought that we call consciousness is characterized by an opposition between an "I" and its object. A conscious event is constituted by this tension between I and object.

Hegel writes, "The disparity [*Ungleichheit*] that takes place in consciousness between the I and the substance that is its object, is its difference [*Unterschied*], the *negative* in general" (W3:39, §37). This passage connects up the work of a phenomenology, which concerns consciousness specifically, with the work of a system of science, which concerns negativity in general. Consciousness is, it turns out, just one kind of negativity but in our ordinary and familiar way of thinking we privilege it above all others. We take consciousness or conscious experience to be the proper field of knowledge. When we say "seeing is believing," we mean "consciousness is the field of knowledge." By thinking this way, we fail to recognize the broader landscape of thinking (i.e., Geist) in which individual ego-object consciousness is but one mode.

If all this sounds odd, we might consider that human existence and thinking encompass much more than just conscious events governed by the I-object disparity. We engage in countless involuntary, neither-subjective-nor-objective, subconscious, unconscious, or super-conscious activities. I sleep, breathe, grow, and digest. Even when we turn to the conscious powers of sensing, feeling, imagining, and thinking, we find that we are not aware of being an "I" authoring or overseeing all the changes that occur within them. Something may be present to the eye but in my peripheral vision or present in the imagination but unattended to or present in thought but unrealized. In all these cases, these events are actual, having real effects, but nonconscious.

We move habitually without being conscious of having moved. Absent-minded sensation can even allow moments of complete identification with what is sensed before the consciousness kicks in again reminding me there is an I and, opposed to it, an object. A person may even respond to an event she cannot call to mind as having happened to the "I" she identifies as her own. On the other end of the spectrum, mathematical thinking and conceptual reasoning do not require an operative "I" at all and are, for this reason, often called "abstract," meaning abstract from consciousness or abstract from the ego. When one solves an equation, one might have the apprehension that there was nothing personal or perspectival about it, and one might even have the sense that the problem solved itself within the general field of thinking. Some kinds of thinking may even demand that we relax or give up the ego-pole in order to engage them.

That said, most of us probably give the greatest weight to moments of consciousness and to the ways this ego-object tension carves up and characterizes experience. Without this tension we could not love, get angry, or have ambitions. The I-object duality governs the activities we identify with *desire*. When I want something, I am conscious of lacking it—I am explicitly conscious of a tension, a *disparity* between ego and object. We learn in §167 that desire is synonymous with self-consciousness. Self-consciousness is not outside this I-object tension. Yet it differs from consciousness in that it is aware of the tension and disparity *as its own*, whereas to consciousness (the previous stage) the tension itself remained alien: the disparity with the object simply *happened* to it.

This realization by self-consciousness (that ego, object, and the tension between them all belong to it) opens up the path by which we can eventually recognize the I-object disparity for what it is: one manifestation negativity in general. To make the transition from everyday consciousness to philosophical thinking, we must educate desire. The education of desire is a matter of *learning to see individual desires as a manifestation of thinking's attempt to know itself by testing itself out on the world*. My life, while it is mine, is also situated as one link in a vast chain of human thinking and activity that Hegel calls *Geist*. I could not live the way I do if it were not for countless other individuals and their thoughts and thought-infused actions that came before me and coexist with me. I owe my awareness to causes of which I am not aware. My individual desire for this or that end is situated in a greater drama. When we learn to see desire as one species of thinking, we can grasp consciousness itself as one species of negativity.

A phenomenology of Geist helps us see what happens "behind the back" of consciousness (W3:80, §87). At first the disparity between ego and object appears to be a result of the independent existence of each. On this naive view, the ego is real and the object is real. When the two meet in the single field of consciousness, they clash because ego and object both claim to be the proper substrate for consciousness. The early part of Hegel's *Phenomenology* plays out this conflict as consciousness lists back and forth between ego-idealism and object-realism.

The long course of phenomenological experience shows that ego and object are not independent realities which meet in consciousness. Rather they are mere moments of consciousness itself and *have no prior existence*. Ego and object are ideal, non-actual, transitory phases into which thinking divides itself so as to become a determinate field of consciousness.

Here we reach a central point in Hegel's preface that has received little attention. In §37, just as in §18, 32 and 54, Hegel is describing the conditions that make *self-motion* possible. To move itself, a substance must be able to divide itself from itself internally and yet hold itself together, preserve itself through rupture. This may sound strange but Hegel's account of self-motion is the primary evidence for the fact that being is best understood as absolute negativity. Rejecting ontologies of permanence, Hegel explores the possibilities of an ontology of fluid motion and change that nevertheless allows for order and intelligibility. If some one whole can only exist as itself by negating itself (moving and changing), then to be any kind of self requires a *capacity for internal division*. So consciousness is something because it can develop itself by dividing itself into ego and object. Much of what follows will be devoted to better grasping Hegel's account of self-motion, since this is the beating heart that drives all development from ordinary consciousness through phenomenology to a system of science.

Negativity as Selfhood

Consciousness divides itself into disparate poles because it is active. All activity takes place, Hegel argues, by way of self-relation and all self-relation takes place by way of internal division. Internal division takes place by means of negation. Without this internal division into ego and object, consciousness would remain static. To change, move, develop, and grow, consciousness must relate itself to itself. To do this, it must divide itself from itself. Consciousness must self-other to self-relate, just as we distance ourselves from something to reflect on it (with the ultimate aim of understanding or incorporating or internalizing it). As consciousness, we experience this self-othering self-relation as a disparity between ego and object. Here we should notice that this way of accounting for the disparity shows us that the disparity itself is temporary and should not be a fixed limit for philosophy. There is a kind of thinking that precedes consciousness' division into ego and object and there is a kind of thinking that follows from and supersedes it. What precedes consciousness can be called life and what proceeds from it can be called Geist. Consciousness can be understood as the form of thought that spans between life (a form of thinking and being whose internal divisions of sensation, digestion, locomotion, reproduction, etc. are not conscious and reflective) and Geist (a way of thinking/being wherein internal divisions are not just conscious but are actually perceived as Geist's own doing, that is as self-determining and free).

The ego and the object are productive fictions created within consciousness so that it can develop itself. Once again, this helps us see why phenomenology is not philosophy but can lead to it. Once we notice that consciousness is just another vehicle for self-relation, we are no longer stuck thinking that conscious subjectivity is the ultimate horizon of all human inquiry into thinking and knowledge (something that is a very real danger for Kant and his followers). When we realize that ego and object are just means to an end and the end is self-relation (just as it is for life and for Geist), we can begin to see that consciousness is just one kind of self-relation among many. Negativity characterizes the dynamic movement of all of these kinds of self-relation. For this reason, "negativity" turns out to be richer and more comprehensive than "consciousness." But as long as we are stuck inside consciousness, "negativity" sounds hopelessly abstract by comparison.

Negativity will characterize all events, movements, and activities, even those outside the field we call consciousness. Negativity (i.e., self-othering for the sake of self-sameness) will govern even crystal formation, digestion, and doing mathematics. This indicates that the tension (or negativity) found *within* consciousness is not something for consciousness to stamp out (this is its general impulse as we see throughout the *Phenomenology*), but rather the driving force of consciousness itself. This means that self-knowledge, our explicit aim in the *Phenomenology*, will not be the placid union of I and object (as consciousness supposes) but their *dissolution* into the broader dynamic complexes governed by negativity.

Consciousness, insofar as it aims at the resolution of ego-object tension, aims at its own *dissolution*. By reconfiguring consciousness as one species of negativity, however, we may make room for and preserve consciousness, albeit as a lower form of negativity-realization. This is the basic premise of any phenomenological account of Geist: to locate consciousness' conditioned, phenomenal negativity within Geist's absolute negativity. Practically, this amounts to recognizing thinking in general as broader in scope and power than conscious-thinking or ego-thinking.

This gives us a new perspective on several claims Hegel has made in the preface. Hegel's insistence that we overcome or look past our personal, private interests as we read philosophy is not just an author's plea for a fair hearing. It is rooted in an ontological insight that our personal ego-self is not our deepest or most comprehensive self. It bears repeating that Hegel does not think he discovered this ontological insight but rather that he has recovered it from a tradition in which it is always present but not always explicit. We hint at Hegel's insight whenever we talk about submitting our judgment to "reason" or "argument" rather than subjective judgment. The tradition of philosophy continually looks toward a transpersonal, universal thinking. As Heraclitus supposedly wrote, listen not to me but to the Logos. Hegel claims to give the first full account of nonpersonal thinking's actualization out of lower forms of thinking in his system of science.

We resist this insight for practical reasons, since we want to hold on to specific desires that define us as conscious individuals. The preface argues that philosophy has no place for this sort of individuality, and if we mean to participate in this pure science, we will have to learn to leave the practical, erotic self behind and embrace the deeper work of selfhood in general. Though we will never cease to be conscious individuals at one level, it is also possible to set these concerns aside while we think in another way. The impersonal callousness which marks so many philosophical discussions and "thought experiments" might seem like an example of this. Imagine two moral philosophers talking casually about human beings strapped to train tracks (i.e., the "trolley problem"), you will get the idea of what I mean here. But this callousness results from a formalistic attempt to simply ignore the practical self rather than the more difficult speculative task of contextualizing and embedding the activity of practical self in a much wider, ultimately nonpersonal and nonpractical activity of Geist (i.e., making thoughts "fluid").

Without the preface, we may not be properly prepared for what philosophy will demand of us and we may find the ultimate trajectory of the *Phenomenology* confusing or disappointing. If we were hoping to *empower* consciousness in its mastery over objects, we will not be pleased by a book that ultimately deflates this intention and dissolves individuated consciousness as the bearer of truth. To exact revenge on Hegel, we can then complain about how ridiculous and occult the very idea of Geist is, rejecting out of hand what we have not done the work to unpack. Much of Hegel's rocky reception makes perfect sense in the context of desire's attempt to protect itself from encroachment that would dissolve its ultimacy. Similar defenses are used against art and religion (which have a similar capacity to reveal the greater context of Geist). Even if Hegel is wrong here, it is worth testing the possibility that there is more to thinking than consciousness' ego-object disparity.

Selfhood as Self-Motion (§37)

In Aristotle's *Physics*, motion is discovered to be ontologically primary and self-evident while rest is found to be derivative. But we today, with Hobbes and other materialists, tend to assume rest is primary: "That when a thing lies still, unless somewhat else stir it, it will lie still for ever, is a truth that no man doubts of" (Leviathan I, ii). Aristotle's primacy of motion led to the conclusion that there must be self-motion, motions that are the cause of themselves. (To show this, Aristotle goes toe to toe with Parmenides and his disciple Zeno and dissects the paradoxes that supposedly demonstrate the Eleatic denial of motion.) Hobbes' account reaches the opposite conclusion, that nothing is truly self-moving. There is a great deal at stake in this ontological question and it hovers in the background of the 1807 preface without really being made clear.

Instead of saying, with common sense, that first there is something *then* it is negated, a phenomenology shows that to be something determinate always already implies the *activity* of negation has taken place. Parallel to Aristotle's account of motion, negation-motion is primary and a determination-resting is derivative. The result of a phenomenology is that negation is shown to be primary. This standpoint, from which negation is seen as prior to determinacy, is what Hegel calls "philosophy" or "science." Further, this inversion of determinacy and negation accounts for why natural consciousness or common sense encounters philosophy as a "violence" akin to "walking on its head." The primacy of negation appears strange to ordinary consciousness. Natural consciousness wonders: if I accept the primacy of negation, won't this throw me into a nihilism of pure flux? To answer this question, we must see how negation and motion are connected.

Paragraph 37 opens with the claim that negativity (with regard to consciousness) is the *Ungleicheit* [disparity, inequality, or non-sameness] between the modes of being-subject and being-object. So far I have been calling this their "disparity" or "tension." Hegel continues:

> It [the negative] can be viewed as the defect of both, though it is their soul, or what moves them; for this reason some of the ancients grasped the void as what moves [things], insofar as they conceived of what moves [things] as the *negative*, though they did not yet conceive the negative as the self. (W3:39, §37)

Here, several crucial thoughts are strung together in sequence. First, negativity is viewed by phenomenal consciousness as a mere defect. Things change and this appears to challenge our knowledge of them which seems to require constancy. The fundamental failure felt at the heart of phenomenal life is the failure of the "I" to mirror the objective world or the failure of the world to mirror the "I." We live in a hostile tension between subjectivity and objectivity where fantasies are frustrated and knowledge claims are dashed. The ongoing motion and change of things and of the ego itself do not seem to respect our fixed categories. In brief, being in a flow of continual change is perceived as a bad thing.

Motion would be impossible without resistance. If ego and object existed in harmonious equivalence, there would be no need to change, to grow, to develop. Each thing is only what it is as a result of tensions, changes, motions. What kind of aspect could a wholly perfect being even manifest? How could it be definite in any way or have any qualities, if each determinate quality is a privation of another, opposing determination? If determination is negation, a world free of this disparity or conflict would be a world free of all things, beings or motions, free also of their states of rest. It would be a worldless world. Vision is motion or change, hearing is change, touch is change, and even thinking (as we know it) changes as one thought replaces another.

Hegel calls on the atomist position that motion is caused by a void to clarify. Even in the atomist's simplified (and false) account of motion as the product of the interaction of atoms and void, we can see recognition that any account of motion relies on negation. Here we should note that Hegel is effectively comparing the German Idealist epistemological debate about subjects and objects with the ancient ontological debate about the cause of motion. This is much like what he did with mediation, comparing the German Idealist debate about mediation with the ancient debate about teleology or purposiveness, that is, the self-mediating. Through this comparison, the issues concerning consciousness look completely different. The problem of consciousness and difference is now a special case of the problem of being and motion. As a result, the goal is no longer to find a unifying principle that grounds knowledge of ego and object but to articulate *how movement between moments of consciousness is possible*, just as ancient philosophers wondered how motion in general was possible.

Most modern thinkers deny self-motion is possible or meaningful (often by way of denying "final causes"). On the other hand, self-motion was central to the thinking of Heraclitus, Plato, and, most explicitly, Aristotle. The word "*Selbstbewegung*" [self-motion or self-movement] appears nine times in the preface to the *Phenomenology of Spirit*. This is striking. Even without any further analysis, the recurrence of this word already announces that Hegel parts ways with a central dogma of the modern epistemological paradigm.

It is no wonder, then, that Hegel reports, at the end of the preface, that he expects to be misunderstood precisely because he claims "that through which science exists is the self-motion of the concept" (W3:65–6, §71). He goes on to note that this view is entirely opposed to the prevailing "views [*Vorstellungen*] in our time about the nature and shape of truth." The opposition here is between those who expect truth to be a fixed datum and those who recognize dynamic self-relation as the form of truth. Viewing truth as a kind of frozen, abiding law or essence correlates to the view that motion is not primary but derivative: first there are things, and then there are motions of those things. The atomist position suggests this by defining the condition for motion as void, absence. First there is something, a presence, and then, defined against this, there can be a void, an absence, the space beyond the limits or boundaries of this something. Only then can the something can move by acting against the void, by moving into it. Motion depends upon there being a fixed and stable something which will do the moving. This should be familiar. The common-sense view of motion aligns closely with the atomist view. Yet even this atomist view that fails to see the primacy of motion still recognizes that movement is negation.

Hegel's point is that a thorough presentation of movement as negation will reveal their primacy, thus showing the supposedly stable conditions of subjecthood and objecthood to be derivative. If we hold motion itself to be primary and (to take up one side) objectness or somethingness or determinateness to be produced by certain kinds of motions or activities, we will approach the whole question of being and selfhood differently. The being and selfhood of something cannot be traced to a stable condition before all motion that underlies motion. Such a state does not exist. There has always been motion, and somethingness is a consequence of motion rather than a condition for motion. This means that to grasp the somethingness of something is to grasp the motions by which that somethingness presents itself. This involves negation, grasping it in relation to what it is not (i.e., to other somethings) as a way to catch sight of the movement between them. The negation is what made it possible to be a something in the first place. This is why negativity is "absolute" (independent and ontologically primary).

Hegel makes yet another decisive move in the short passage quoted earlier. From the problem of consciousness, we are brought to the problem of motion; from the problem of motion, we are brought to the problem of selfhood. The atomists made negativity extrinsic, out there; "they did not yet conceive the negative as the self." Aristotle first makes it possible to conceive the negative as a self through what he calls "*dynamis*" or potency. A being is not just what it is doing but also what it is not doing yet *could* do. This is related to what I have been calling "internal tension" or a capacity for internal division into moments or non-actual parts.

When we discuss potency, we are discussing an inner tension between having and lacking, a negativity that *belongs* to the being in question, as opposed to the void which is always *outside* it. To change in a natural way, a thing must already contain the determinate lack of what it will become (as a potency for it). If a being does not already possess the end of the change in some respect, the being's change must happen to it by force, coming from outside.

Aristotle often relies on the premise that transitive motion cannot ground itself; it forms an infinite regress of causes. Self-motion is thus a necessary postulate if the whole is to be bounded, meaningful, knowable. The atomists deny an ultimate whole in favor of infinite regress. The introduction of the void (as the condition for motion) captures this well. For one thing to move, there must always be more emptiness somewhere to move into. We might think of Lucretius' famous javelin thought experiment: place him at the end of the universe and he will throw a javelin over the edge, proving there is yet more space. This results in seemingly distinct and meaningful parts (i.e., atoms) but a meaningless whole (i.e., a limitless universe governed by chance). On the other hand, the Eleatics deny any meaningful parts in favor of a fixed whole. All the parts with their apparent motions are illusory and only the fixed totality is meaningful. Aristotle's postulate of self-motion through activating potencies allows both the whole and the parts to be meaningful. Hegel hopes for something similar to Aristotle's profound mediation of part and whole in relation to the modern subject/object and freedom/determinism problems. A self must be whatever-can-account-for-itself as a source of its own motion and change. If the "I" or ego cannot do this, then the ego cannot be the proper characterization for the self. A phenomenology of Geist shows that neither ego nor object can be the self. Negativity better accounts for what really makes the subject a subject and the object an object, just as beginning from motion better accounts for rest (than beginning from rest accounts for motion).

As we have seen, in one short sentence from paragraph 37, Hegel brings us from epistemology (I-object) to physics (motion-rest) to metaphysics (*ousia* or selfhood). Beginning with the ego-object disparity that engrosses modern epistemology, we find our way back, through a phenomenology, to the primary philosophical question: what is it to be a something, to be a self? Philosophy seeks self-knowledge not merely in the sense of knowing one's ego-self but in the sense of knowing what selfhood itself is. Thus phenomenology is not philosophy, but because it is at least oriented toward the apparent self (consciousness), it can gradually open us up to the inquiry into the true self (negativity).

Again, I must reiterate that this claim that true selfhood can be found in negativity is contentless without a systematic study of actual negations. The argument I have been outlining is, at best, a way of highlighting some of what is at stake in the question about motion and selfhood. It does not count as an adequate presentation (and thus demonstration) of negativity's scope, power, and truth.

The Concept: Style and Substance

Hegel concludes paragraph 33 with an important final note. When thoughts become fluid they are what Hegel calls "concepts" [*Begriffe*]. What we call ordinary "thoughts" are I-posited, but "concepts" are self-positing self-movements of thinking. No longer the property of the limited ego-object field, these movements call out to each other and work to arrange themselves in an "organic whole," a system of science (W3:38, §33). To view this as "Hegel's system of science" is thus to precisely miss the point here and view system as I-posited rather than self-positing. Hegel, of course, wrote these books, delivered those lectures. Yet the relation between being and nothing or quantity and quality is not Hegel's thought, but its own concept.

The work of philosophy proper does not concern thoughts, but concepts. In the "Wastebook" of 1803–6, Hegel writes:

> We are no longer concerned so much with thinking. We have enough thinking, good and bad, beautiful and bold. Rather [we are concerned] with concepts. Insofar as each thought is immediately valid through itself, and concepts [*Begriffe*], on the contrary, must be made comprehensible [*begreiflich*], then the form of writing style is changed by this, [given] a perhaps embarrassingly effort-demanding appearance [*Aussehen*], as with Plato and Aristotle. (W2:558)

As we can see in paragraph 33, philosophy no longer needs to present the world in thoughts. This has already been done and we have plenty of available thoughts, groups of categories that contrast each other and offer analytical clarity and differentiation to the understanding. We have no shortage of analytical clarity available if we can accept this or that presupposition that the distinctions require to get off the ground. The work of fashioning a double for the sensed world in thought and words is ongoing, but it is being undertaken in many disciplines and discourses. We do not need to find words or images for dogs or concertos or anger or laws or courage. We moderns live in a world of thought, where all the things we encounter are saturated with thoughts "good and bad, beautiful and bold."

So we have thoughts. Concepts, on the other hand, demand more work than thoughts. They are not immediately recognizable or knowable "through themselves." Concepts [*Begriffe*] must be *made* comprehensible [*begreiflich*]. They must be made comprehensible through some special kind of presentation, some transformed "art of writing." As we have seen, Hegel's thinking returns to and revolves around this question of presentation or performance [*Darstellung*]. It is for this reason that asking about Hegel's style is not an idle question. How Hegel writes is very much the issue here because Hegel is trying to see if writing can change such that it supports the thinking of self-determining concepts, not just determinate thoughts. It is striking to me that Hegel mentions Plato and Aristotle as allies here. They are philosophers who, like Hegel, tried to stretch the available form of writing to accommodate more speculative and conceptual thinking.

Concepts, then, are not "immediately valid." They must be mediated, worked on, worked out, presented. A concept will never be expressible in a single word, image, thought, or even a single proposition or definition. A concept appears only as the active principle behind a long sequence of words or thoughts. We must be "made" to comprehend the concept through a special kind of presentation, a special art of writing. This art of writing will not create our capacity to think speculatively, which is natural or innate, but it will serve as an effective reminder. The right kind of writing will lead us back; it will allow us to recollect the speculative work.

To engage with concepts, writing must take on a "look" [*Aussehen*] that demands an "embarrassing" or "painful" [*peinlich*] amount of effort. The reader must work hard to keep a variety of thoughts in play and work to see the concept that emerges from the movement between them. The following chapters develop this theme of presenting concepts by exposing the limitations of two common ways of presenting philosophical thoughts that fail to actualize the concept within them: mathematics and propositions.

5

Philosophy Is Not Mathematical (§42–46)

But body gone he sleeps no more,
And till his intellect grows sure
That all's arranged in one clear view,
Pursues the thoughts that I pursue.

—W. B. Yeats, "The Man and the Echo"

For in [the mathematician's] thinking the natural bodies are separated from motion . . .

—Aristotle, *Physics* 193b34

In this chapter I examine Hegel's concerns about modeling philosophical method on mathematical method. This critique occurs within a broader critique of any philosophical method that attempts to exclude falsehood. The connection between these two concerns is easy to see in Descartes' *Discourse on Method*, where he praises the accuracy and certainty of mathematical demonstrations and takes them as inspiration for his own method for avoiding errors in philosophy. Even if mistakes are made as we learn mathematics, the presentation of demonstrations and proofs does not incorporate or recount those errors. Because mathematics concerns idealized and abstract objects rather than real existences, it does not need to incorporate falsehood or error. Philosophy, on the other hand, concerns the real, actual, and existent, and just as it must muddy its presentations with the peculiarities of empirical particulars, it must incorporate the entire genesis or coming to be of a content, including the negative, the false, the erroneous steps that are taken along the way.

In Praise of Falsehood

Hegel's choice to introduce a system of science through the illusory domain of phenomenal knowing raises a crucial question: why should we study illusions, errors or falsehoods at all? The answer is surprising: falsehood is part of the whole truth. In this and the next chapter we examine Hegel's criticism of the ways of thinking that cannot accept the false as part of the true, ways of thinking that strive for the ideal of simplicity, of atomic truth.

The interdependence of the true and the false is a recurring theme in Hegel's Jena writings. Several aphorisms from his Wastebook offer early observations about it.[1] The introduction to the *Phenomenology* opens with a well-known discussion of "the fear of error" as "fear of the truth."[2] And here, in the 1807 preface, Hegel returns to the subject of falsehood. The chief discussion of the interdependence of truth and falsity is found in paragraphs 38–47 and entails a discussion of mathematical truth as an ideal for philosophy and how it can lead us astray. Before we turn to those paragraphs, some general remarks about falsehood may be helpful.

Consider the following aphorism from the *Wastebook*:

> *To study* means coming to see as true what others have thought. But when [the student] then expects to be finished and done with it, as with something false, one does not get to know things at all. (W2:558)

We often treat true and false as exclusive categories. If something falls in one category it cannot fall in the other. This aphorism suggests an important practical consequence of this dominant attitude. If we treat truth and falsehood as mutually exclusive, *both* the true and the false will keep us from actual knowledge, from "getting to know things." If truth and falsehood are stopping points for our thinking, then both of them equally inhibit further questioning. Declarations of what is "true" or "false" often indicate thought-at-rest rather than thinking-at-work.

Hegel is suggesting in this aphorism that receiving a "fact" should be a beginning of inquiry not the end. The purpose of arithmetical exercises is not to produce correct answers (a calculator can do this) but to learn *how* to calculate. If we ask no further questions precisely because we have the correct answer, what good has correctness done us? The isolated correct fact operates just as a false one does: it keeps us from seeking knowledge in the interrelation of contents. This bars us from "getting to know things" because real, existent things are connected to each other. An isolated true proposition is thus *functionally* false. By contrast, the right flagrant falsehood may actually awaken our thinking into action. Awareness of an error may spur further investigation. As a result, the truth and falsity of individual propositions cannot be used as an indication of the liveliness of thinking or the health of inquiry.

Treating the true as simply true is just as damaging as treating the false as simply false. Even rock is altered over time through crystallization, metamorphism, erosion, and sedimentation. Because being involves becoming, opposed qualities and states are always held in tension together in what we call *motion*.[3] If our thinking is to unite itself with what is, then it must learn to think things in motion or as movements.

True and False: A Musical Analogy

No thing or content is simply false. Hegel writes, "Nor *is* there something false any more than there is something evil" (W3:40, §39). To be false is to be in a specific kind of relation. If the relation changes, the falseness too may vanish. To be true is to be in another kind of relation. True and false are thus like consonance and dissonance among notes. The note "C" is not simply euphonous (true) or cacophonous (false), but acquires these qualities in different situations, different relations. In music, a key offers the context in which each note appears with a different value. For the most part, being in accord with the key is being in accord with the whole. Likewise, being in tension with the key is being in tension with the whole.

The dynamic relation of tones offers a helpful way to think about the dynamic relation of thoughts. "Truth" occurs when a thought is in healthy relation to some whole. "Falsehood" thus names when some thought chafes against the whole. We fail to realize this because we often do not articulate for ourselves the whole that is the actual source of our judgment of truth or falsity. This will be a crucial point for Hegel in the paragraphs from 38 to 47.

Often the context for judging truth and falsehood is merely conventional. This means that it is so widespread as to be considered universal and necessary when it is actually arbitrary and contingent. As long as this context remains unexamined, claims of what is true and what is false will seem generally applicable rather than applying to a specific historical or cultural context. Often, we presume but do not make explicit the context for judgment and thus fail to recognize the rationale for accepting one claim and excluding another. Lacking this specific context, we presume (prematurely) that what appears false in *this* context is simply false in every context. Here it is vital to point out that while some contexts for thought contents are merely conventional, other contexts are necessary. It is inadequate to claim that truth is simply subjective and also inadequate to claim it is simply objective. We participate in many contexts at once and this leads to confusion when we assume that what holds in one holds for the other. In fact, sophists often use uncertainty in one arena to bring about general unease about the possibility of truth. The sophist wants to elide the difference between truth as relational and truth as merely relative.

The musical analogy can take us even further. Just as a melody requires some dissonance to produce more pleasing consonances, thinking requires the movement toward falsity (toward the parts) as part of the movement toward truth (toward wholeness). Thinking is a movement that requires tension between part and whole, between analytic *Verstand* (understanding) and comprehensive *Vernunft* (reason). Recall that in paragraph 32, Hegel dramatizes the work of *Verstand* as killing or breaking the whole into parts and *Vernunft* as surviving death by returning to a greater whole. When we represent thinking as determinative and decisive, we are highlighting only one part of its total work (*Verstand*). We do indeed break things apart and fix them in place to think them, but then, just as soon, they are unfixed as one thought yields to another in a pattern that gestures toward the life of the whole (*Vernunft*).

Failing to grapple with the full scope of thinking's activity, the conventional attitude toward truth and falsehood tries to create permanent landmarks among shifting sands. Looking for the wrong kinds of signs, clues, or markers, this attitude is tempted by relativism the moment its limited context collapses. Hegel offers us a way to take seriously the critique of truth we associate with postmodern thinkers, but instead of abandoning truth for social construction or relativism, he urges us on to a dynamic conception of the true-false relationship that will be rooted in the abiding nature of thinking itself. There is a pattern or rhythm to the way thinking moves and this can offer a kind of repose amid activity. We are not abandoned to ceaseless change that thwarts all reason. Just as meditation techniques concentrate on the calm shape of the moving breath to bring stability to a wandering mind, a system of science concentrates on the regular intervals of negativity to bring repose and order to the restless activity of thinking and being.

In an infamous passage that has vexed interpreters, Hegel calls the true a "bacchanalian whirl" (W3:46, §47). Drunkenness here is symbolic of a self-absorbed perspective. By noting with a double negative that "no member [*Glied*] is not drunk," Hegel is reminding us that each part is isolated from the others. But the parts are false if taken alone. If we look with the eyes of one participant in the bacchanalia, we see something distorted, drunken, false, chaotic. But if we look at the whole ritual, we see order emerge from chaos. In the great bacchanalia of truth, individuals lack proper perspective. Nevertheless, this very same ego-drunkenness also leads each part to abandon its isolated individuality as one by one, the members collapse, as the drunken collapse from continued drinking. Each member eventually "dissolves" its own individuality. This reveals "transparent and simple calm." The wild individuality of the drunken dance collapses into a deep, *collective* sleep. Rabid self-assertion leads to self-dissolution which leads to absorption in a greater self. This, Hegel indicates, is truth: not the exclusion of difference by clinging to one-sided sobriety and refusing to engage with the false, the partial or the particular, but indulging "drunken" differentiation to the point of collapse. Most importantly, truth comes by way of participation.

No single thought or content is true or false. Truthing is one kind of movement and falsing is another and thinking requires both. Thinking requires the interplay of self-assertion and self-negation, point and counterpoint. Though Hegel chooses the word "negativity" to express this, we might remember that negativity in this Hegelian sense always includes positivity, determination, or assertion. Hegel dismisses abstract negation and advocates determinate negation because the latter is not merely unspecified negation but assertion-through-negation.[4]

Contrasting Ancient and Modern Attitudes toward Error

Philosophers have not always feared error and envied the certainty of mathematics. Plato and Aristotle include impasses and mistakes and confusions in their representations of philosophical thinking as dialogue and as inquiry. Both thinkers also place mathematics in a subordinate position, a preparatory position, to philosophy. The third power on the divided line, *dianoia*, includes the sort of mathematical thinking that works from a given set of hypotheses toward a conclusion. But the highest activity of thinking, *noesis*, goes the other way. It questions the starting hypotheses and makes its way not toward a practical end but toward a beginning, a source (*Republic* 511b). Mathematics cannot work this way and provides little to no guidance for how to think noetically. Aristotle is even more insistent that we not confuse the goals of mathematics with those of philosophy. Mathematics, he notes, does not concern itself with material or natural motion—it abstracts from it—while philosophy always concerns what *is*—that is, what has form *and* material and is in motion.[5] Mathematical objects are pure entities of the imagination, while philosophy deals not with what can merely be imagined but with what *is*.

If we contrast this with Descartes' analytic method, Hobbes' and Spinoza's use of the *more geometrico* or even Locke's stated aim to clear the ground for scientists like Boyle and Newton, we can see that these early modern thinkers approach error and the relation between mathematics and philosophy quite differently.[6] We might mention that mathematics itself changed greatly from ancient Greek geometry to modern algebra.[7] It is not my purpose here to explore this vast historical problem but merely to note an outcome.

The most celebrated early modern thinkers view philosophical inquiry as playing catch up with the mathematically oriented natural sciences. Kant too lauds the natural sciences for not begging but commanding nature by means of clearly framed experiments (CPR Bxiii). It should be no surprise that his books aim to proceed experimentally by way of fixed definitions and their consequences.[8] Nothing like this direct, axiomatic approach can be found in the works of Plato or Aristotle. And nothing like it can be found in Hegel's books. Plato and Aristotle showcase the hypothesis questioning power of *noesis*. Hegel follows this ancient tradition, noting that "going forward is a *retreat* into the *ground*, toward the *original* and *true*." (W5:70)

We are now in a position to study more closely why the axiomatic approach is doomed to close off our access to speculative philosophy, the account not of thoughts but of thinking itself. Hegel's modern forebears trust too much in the fixed truth value of individual propositions. And this is a consequence of trying to imitate the way mathematical truth works by replacing angles and areas or integers and operators with subjects, predicates and copulas. To grasp the problem with propositional truth we must first explore the problem with mathematical truth. We will discover that mathematical construction and propositional logic both rely on arbitrary, fixed limits instead of self-governing activities that make limits only to surpass them.

Formalism and Mathematics

The general shape of Hegel's critique of mathematical truth as a model for philosophy has already been prepared by his critique of formalism. The critique of mathematical truth, like the critique of formalism, concerns its *externality*. The mathematical content is not allowed to develop itself internally. Instead, a form is imposed on it from outside. The parallel between these two critiques is not incidental. Formalism in philosophy increases as the direct result of adopting mathematical truth as its lodestar. Studying Hegel's history of philosophy lectures, we can observe a dramatic increase in cases of formalism after the early modern period, that is, after Galileo and Descartes make convincing arguments in favor of mathematical physics and against the teleological physics of the Aristotelian tradition.

Modern philosophers, in pursuing a single, correct *method* to apply to objects, increasingly disregard as untrustworthy the diverse presentations of the objects that are not produced through application of that method. Yet since these other ways the content shows itself also belong to it, early modern philosophy becomes increasingly reductive. This formalism mirrors the reductive abstraction of mathematical operations. When we solve for the travel time between two cities, we reduce the problem to simple abstract terms of rate and distance. This is perfectly adequate in mathematics because we are not aiming to know the thing itself but rather to have a general estimate, an abstraction that is like it. We often forget how much is ignored by such operations because we are accustomed to finding these mathematical abstractions *useful*. Further, we tend to confuse the useful and the true, or the useful and the real. But, and it is odd we need to remind ourselves of this, the world consists of much more than what is useful to us. If we want to know it *as it is*, even useful abstractions are obstacles to that goal.

In philosophy we are not content with mere abstractions, however useful they may be. We do not want a practically useful stand-in for the truth but rather the whole truth itself. A system of science does not reject mathematical physics altogether; it rather rejects the claim that mathematical physics offers the highest or best description of nature, the final frontier of truth. We will still pursue these mathematically rooted natural sciences, but they should be viewed as offering one-sided, abstract material for the more comprehensive vision of nature that emerges in a philosophical system of science.

What Is Construction?

To go beyond initial axioms and demonstrate a "new" geometrical relationship, Euclid relies on a procedure called construction. A construction is a set of instructions for drawing a particular figure. For example, one might be instructed to draw two perpendicular lines and then to draw a third line that bisects them both. The result is that we now have a figure, a triangle. Depending on what we are trying to prove, we may construct yet another figure in relation to the first: a circle, some squares, and so on. By considering relationships between lines, angles, and areas, we may arrive at any number of different demonstrations.

Hegel's example in §42 alludes to the Pythagorean theorem or some similar simple demonstration. He discusses a "right triangle" and how it does not "divide itself" into parts. Instead, the geometer constructs and then divides the triangle into distinct parts so that those parts can be compared to produce a "ratio." The result of the construction is that we can establish a fixed ratio between the sides of the triangle and its hypotenuse. For example, in Euclid's proof, we construct three squares, one on each side of the triangle. These squares are then divided in various ways to produce further triangles and parallelograms that can be used to calculate angles and areas. The end result is the demonstration of a ratio: the sum of the squares on the two sides equals the square on the hypotenuse.

How is this process of construction relevant to philosophical thinking? In Kant's *Critique of Pure Reason*, mathematical construction offers a model for how an *a priori*, pure concept could correspond to an a posteriori, empirical intuition. Kant notices that (1) human experience is unified but (2) the primary faculties responsible for this unity (sensation and understanding) are heterogeneous. It is unclear how sense and understanding could combine to form a single whole. When Kant tries to account for the production of experience out of its elements, he finds himself saddled with a capacity for spontaneity (understanding) on the one hand and a capacity for receptivity (sense) on the other. The central epistemological problem thus concerns how we bring these two heterogeneous faculties into conversation such that experience, which we already know to be unified, could result. Having an experience means that we apprehend three oranges, not the number three, the color orange, and the shape round.

A mathematical construction is an important clue here because, like Kant's schema, it offers a middle ground between pure concepts and empirical intuitions. Geometrical constructions are prominent examples of pure or *a priori* intuitions. The triangle and squares in Euclid's construction are not empirical (they are produced spontaneously not received, i.e. there are no triangles or squares in nature) and yet the fact that we can perform various *spatial* operations with them indicates they are nevertheless intuitions. If there are pure intuitions (as geometrical construction suggests), then perhaps we can get pure concepts to align with empirical intuitions by means of pure intuitions, special techniques that have a foot in abstract concepts and a foot in the spatial dimension that supposedly belongs to "real" world experience.

Material without Motion (§42–4)

What, then, is the problem with construction in philosophy? We might recall that in Plato's *Meno* a construction is used in the conversation with the slave boy as he tries to figure out what ratio exists between the side of a square and the side that square doubled. In that context, the mathematical exploration indicates that recollection is possible. It answers Meno's skeptical insistence that learning is impossible by offering an instance of learning. Hegel's situation, however, is different from Socrates'. Hegel is faced not with Meno's sophistical skepticism but with his modern predecessor's empirical optimism. Hegel has to show us that philosophical knowing is not as simple, analytic, and abstract as a mathematical demonstration. It is helpful to remember this context as we read. If Hegel found himself in Socrates' position, he might well appeal to construction as a starting point or as a clue (as Kant himself does in response to Hume's skepticism). Instead, on the other end of a long history of uses and abuses of geometry by philosophers, Hegel urges caution.

Hegel impresses on us just how violent (i.e., how indifferent to the original content) the procedure of construction is. He describes a triangle getting "ripped apart" with its sides "given over to other figures" (e.g., the squares in Euclid's construction), noting that the original figure is only "restored" at the end (W3:43, §43). Like Humpty Dumpty the triangle is shattered and reassembled bit by bit. It is worth noting that Hegel could raise the same general objection to Kant's analytic procedure in the first Critique. Kant takes thinking and rips it apart, hoping to show how each of the parts relate, one by one.

To say construction is violent is just to say that it lacks internal motivation or natural, organic, or genetic necessity. A construction adds new lines to form new figures or splits up its initial object with no account for *why* this or that addition or division is made. Indeed, a construction is just a set of instructions which, as Hegel writes, must be "blindly obeyed" (W3:43, §44). The procedure is thus experimental; it simply keeps trying new things until it arrives at the desired ratio. Though it arrives at a ratio in the end, the procedure itself is reasonless, conceptless. The demonstration is not the self-movement of the content but a subjective movement forced onto it by the geometer. A sign of this is that for any given ratio there exist countless ways of demonstrating it, with varying numbers of steps. By contrast, there is only one developmental sequence that leads from acorn to oak and it cannot skip the sapling stage.

Mathematical construction is thus nothing like the sort of philosophical thinking whereby a single content is studied intensively until it reveals a new content *from itself*. This revelation comes by contrasting what the content appears to be doing with what it is actually doing, or (if the content is a consciousness and can speak) what it says it is doing with what it really does. Because selfhood necessarily involves development which involves otherness and negation, any self-relating being can be studied in this immanent way. Philosophical thinking simply holds things accountable to the standards they present for themselves.

As with a teleological account of acorn and oak, a speculative-dialectical presentation will link up all the stages of development as necessary outcomes of the previous stages. Any deviations or extra steps observed in particulars— steps that belong not to the content's selfhood (which is inherently necessary and thus rational or intelligible) but to external contingencies—can be dropped from our final consideration. Some readers interpret the dropping of contingency as a willful imposition of Hegel's subjectivity, but it is just the opposite. Hegel's presentation hopes to show only what belongs necessarily to the content. By contrast, I may favor my own demonstration of the Pythagorean theorem over another person's simply because it is mine: the contingent, added steps are only defensible from a subjective point of view.

Philosophical thinking would not add on squares if it wanted to know the triangle; it would simply investigate the triangle's own genesis. This is, of course, impossible to do with mathematical objects because they are not living things or even part of the living world. Even rock changes over time, but mathematical objects remain inertly the same until *we* do something *to them*. This subjective imposition is the theme of the challenging discussion of "mathematical cognition" in §43 and §44.

Magnitude: The Conceptless Concept (§45–6)

Mathematics demands the active manipulation of its content. There is no losing oneself in the content or tarrying with the negative here. There is a subject (the mathematician) and an object (the figure or problem) and the former must mediate the latter. The problem will not solve itself if we leave it alone. Notice that this is not a problem unless we take mathematics as a model for philosophy, which concerns not abstract but actual (natural and second natural) content. In this case, mathematics will mislead us into thinking that truth is found externally, that is, through construction, not immanently, that is, through negativity or self-othering self-sameness. If modeled after mathematics, philosophy is thought to conduct experiments and make conjectures rather than gather up and recollect what is *already available* to know. Following mathematics, we might think that philosophy constructs the world according to models. Consider how Kant's second preface to the *Critique of Pure Reason* echoes Francis Bacon: nature will not give up its secrets until we wrest them from it. We can then contrast this with Hegel's insistence that we must give ourselves over to or "forget ourselves" in the *Sache*, the issue or content.

Now we can see why Hegel calls the purpose of all mathematical thinking, determining magnitudes, "conceptless." The mathematician's indifference to the content is tolerated in mathematics because the mathematician is only interested in magnitude or size-relation which is itself indifferent, unessential, lacking necessity. Hegel refers to magnitude as the "concept" of mathematics but then calls it "conceptless." Magnitude is the conceptless concept, the pure abstraction of body removed from life, nature, and motion. One example of this conceptless concept entering into popular consciousness is the comparison of "brain size" as if that told us something about thinking. On its own, magnitude is too abstract to be an indication of anything actual. Mathematics thus busies itself with "non-actuals" and never rises up to a consideration of the concrete, embodied, moving, living actuality of nature. (It is important to remember here that "concept" for Hegel is a synonym for organic development and self-motion.) Mathematics cannot return life to the abstract bodies it studies because the precision of its methods depends on the lifelessness of the content. If the content moved itself while we were moving it, we could not keep track of exactly what we had done to it and what it did to itself. We can choose either formalism (subjective imposition of form on content) or philosophy (allowing content to present its own form) but not both.

In paragraph 45, Hegel finally returns to the theme of paragraph 40 and compares the "non-actual" elements of a mathematical construction with "fixed, dead propositions" (W3:44, §45). Philosophers, mistaking the indifference and conceptlessness of mathematics for the supposed virtue of "objectivity," have sought to make philosophy equally "objective," which is to say, equally conceptless. This can be done by treating individual categories or contents as isolatable elements, like the bits and pieces of the "dismembered" triangle.

The irony here is that philosophers seeking objectivity through an imitation of mathematical procedure are actually privileging subjective manipulation. This is what it means to say that construction lacks inner necessity. What holds the steps together is the knower, not the content. This echoes §23 and looks ahead to §60, except that these paragraphs concern not numbers and figures but words.

6

Philosophy Is Not Propositional (§22–23, 38–41, 47–66)

I might have thrown poor words away
And been content to live.

—W. B. Yeats, "Words"

But it is not difficult to see that the way of asserting a proposition, adducing reasons for it, and in the same way refuting its opposite by reasons, is not the form in which truth can appear. (W3:47, §48)

Truth, just as it cannot be presented in a preface, cannot even be expressed in ordinary sentences taken one by one; nor can it emerge from a series of sentences if each of those sentences is taken to have a fixed value and truth is approached as their sum. This point is made repeatedly throughout the preface, appearing in paragraphs 20, 23, 40, 48, 50, and 60–6. For speculative thinking, all sentences, just like all views or positions, are one-sided. This means that learning to read philosophy involves learning to read holistically, taking the individual statements as moments in a single developing idea. Reading philosophy demands a special relationship to language. On the one hand, we take words very seriously and try to follow their precise meanings. On the other hand, we recognize that what is meant is always eluding expression and that language can never simply duplicate the whole activity of thinking.

Speculative philosophy maintains a close but critical relationship with language. Aristotle's inquiries often follow common understandings of words. However, Aristotle also notes that sometimes a word is lacking for a concept that has come into view through inquiry.[1] At these times we must invent or re-purpose words to stand-in for that concept. This illustrates Aristotle's interest in following the cues of natural language when they are available but also his willingness to go beyond it when necessary. Hegel follows this model.

Language often gives the "form" to thinking but does not ultimately govern it.[2] This means Hegel will extract lessons and implications from etymologies and usages, but insists that thinking is ultimately independent of language and that nonrepresentational conceptual thought can guide and call for change in the use of language, even as language guides and shapes it. This means that language is of the utmost importance for thinking and yet we must maintain a critical relationship between them as opposed to collapsing them (as we often see in the wake of Wittgenstein and Heidegger).

The Problem with Propositions (§23)

Hegel begins paragraph 23 remarking that the human need to grasp and express the being of being (or, in his words, to represent the "absolute" as "subject") has found expression in the following sentences: "God is the eternal, God is the moral world order, God is love, and so on" (W3:26, §23). What these sort of sentences get right is that they present the whole as independent, absolute, and as a self, as something self-relating, as "Subject." Love, for example, is something that is only conceivable as the action of some kind of self, something that has the independence and awareness to act on its own behalf. Though they are on the right track, these propositions do not actually communicate speculative truth. The words "God" and "eternal" do not have determinate values. We do not know what they mean. Even if we fix the values through definitions, we then undermine our own (speculative) purpose because we had hoped to express not some finite, definable content but the ultimate truth of all things. As a result, our consideration of the individual proposition "God is eternal" is either too empty (indeterminate) or too rigid (overdeterminate). A sign that we already know this is found in a joke within the *Hitchhiker's Guide to the Galaxy*. In that book, the ultimate answer to the ultimate question is the number 42. The humor of this joke depends on our common awareness that an overly fixed and determinate answer to an ultimate question is laughably inadequate.

What Hegel will suggest is that we need many sentences taken together to express the absolute as subject. Just as a person needs many actions to show his character, thinking needs to express many sides, many faces, to be seen in its full scope. We need, in fact, an entire system of science, a total presentation that arranges the content of philosophy from merely abstract being to absolute spirit. "Being" only has its proper meaning when it is put in its proper place. Knowing the proper place of being, however, is knowing being in relation to all other contents of the system. Even though being is the first content treated in the system, it is not properly grasped in its place *as first* until we have made it through to the last content and can look back and see the first in relation to the last. That collection of relations is its truth, not any given sentence from the being chapter of the *Logic*.

Hegel's insistence on our need for a system of science has struck many readers as advocating the very sort of rigid overdetermination of thinking that Hegel means for it to oppose. We hear the word "system" and think about fixed rules and inflexible order, the death of freedom and creativity. What Hegel actually aims to do with a systematic presentation, though, is to continually unsettle each content by reflecting it into the next. The system of science is not a series of positive claims (being is nothing, existence is quality, etc.) but a series of *deferrals*. We can only project a rough picture of the content that remains revisable as we read. With each negation, the shape of the whole emerges in relief.

This becomes clearer when we study Hegel's comments about propositions in the preface to the *Phenomenology*. No single proposition can do speculative work. Only the continual negation of propositions can hope to approach the speculative truths of a thinking that thinks itself. This is how negative theology works. God is not directly known by any proposition or any combination of propositions. God is the negation of the negations.

Hegel's critique of propositional truth is poorly understood by later philosophers. While many seem to grasp the fact that no individual proposition can communicate truth, this has led not to deeper commitment to transpropositional intelligibility but rather to doubts about the ultimate intelligibility of everything. The denial of propositional truth has ignited Nietzschean skepticism rather than Hegelian holism. This is an inevitable consequence of failing to grasp negativity as positive, one of the lessons Hegel is at pains to teach us in the preface. Just because individual propositions cannot be true does not mean we cannot express truth. It means we need a more broad-minded consideration of what it is that we are calling true.

Taken as a whole, paragraph 23 argues for why no individual proposition can successfully present substance as subject. Hegel's chief insight here concerns the subjectiveness of propositional knowledge:

> The subject is assumed as a fixed point to which, as support, the predicates are affixed by a movement belonging to the knower of this subject, and which is not regarded as belonging to the fixed point itself; yet it is only through this movement that the content could be represented as Subject. (W3:27, §23)

We might remember that Kant described human understanding as a faculty of judgments (i.e., propositions) and also the unifying condition for all experience as an "I think" that accompanies every judgment. Instead of expecting unity on the side of nature or the cosmos, in the Kantian account, unity is provided by the single point of view from which everything is apprehended. Hegel may be referring to something like the Kantian approach here when he highlights how every proposition, even "God is eternal," has an implicit "knower" which renders the actual proposition as follows: "I think God as eternal." Our hope was to present knowledge of God, but we actually managed to reveal only the movement of our own subjective thinking. While this may be satisfying to one who has, on Kant's advice, given up the expectation of rational knowledge of God, it does not satisfy the original intent of offering the proposition: expressing the absolute as subject. This shows only how an individual mind mediates the absolute, not how the absolute mediates itself.

Here we see the problem with formalism and mathematical truth repeated again in a new context. The problem, once again, is the externality of the guarantor of truth (the knower or framer of the proposition) from the occasion of truth (the content of the proposition). Once again we are treating truth as something constructed from without, not grown from within. This is an inevitable result of treating the sentence's subject (God) as "a fixed point." Because the content is treated as inflexible, we need to look elsewhere for the activity, the energy, that imparts growth and development. We need to look elsewhere for the movement that reveals a purposive activity. We find this outside the proposition in the "knower" of the proposition. The sentence may be fixed and dead but the person that framed it is living, moving, thinking. Instead of asking the speaker, "what kind of activity must God be such that this activity could be considered eternal," we ask, "what do you mean by your sentence?" We turn away from the content toward the speaker. In turning away from the absolute, we turn away from philosophy.

Teleology and Propositional Truth (§22)

Notice that Hegel's concern with propositions in paragraph 23 can now be seen to echo the problem of the previous paragraph, a problem with which, at first, it seems to have no obvious connection. In paragraph 22, Hegel detailed how early modern thinkers cast aside Aristotle's teleological approach to nature and, in so doing, lost the very concept of self-mediating activity. As a result, modern philosophers treated all mediation as violence, that is, as externally imposed.

This led to a romantic/pietist backlash that insisted on immediacy (since all mediation was wrongly thought to be distortion imposed by outside parties). It then falls to Hegel to remind us of what we have forgotten: examples of self-mediation are all around us. The system of science is largely the recollection of examples of self-mediating activity arranged in a developmental arc.

The only arena in which teleology was still allowed to operate for most modern thinkers is human action. Human beings have purposes but nothing else should be treated as inherently purposive. Notice that this problematic belief is mirrored exactly in the approach to propositions where we expect the meaning to come from the speaker of the sentence, not the content of the sentence itself. We expect meaning to be a human product. We thus treat language as a series of subjective inventions or constructions rather than as a medium in which we communicate the continual self-revelation of the world.

Most of the dialectical lessons learned in Hegel's *Phenomenology* concern standpoints that claim to be independent when they are, in fact, embedded. The whole book bristles with objections to the radical spontaneity of subjectivity. The human individual is not, on Hegel's thinking, the origin point for meaning, but rather a link in a chain, a wondrous link that, through self-study, can study the whole. We are born into already available meanings, both natural-biological and spiritual-habitual, and seek to understand ourselves and our world in tandem. What, then, must be done? Hegel has already implied it in the foregoing quoted passage: we cannot treat the subject of the proposition as a fixed point to which predicates are simply added. We must find a way to treat the content, the subject of the sentence, as a true subject, as a purposive activity that develops over time by generating and negating its own predicates. If we want to know God, for example, we should expect God's activity to appear in relief only through positing and negating many, many sentences.

We have entered so deeply into the modern prejudice of subjectivity or mentalism (even the so-called "physicalists" or "naturalists" among us) that all talk of a living, purposive world sounds like Neoplatonic world soul mysticism. We today easily recognize that non-minds exist; we simply deny they could be meaningfully purposive without human interpretation. Meaning is reserved as the prerogative of an individual human mind. "What does *it* mean?" translates to "what do *you* mean?"

And yet, the very fact of living is itself a kind of meaning. It is a kind of meaning that needs nothing added to it by human minds in order to be purposive and self-ordering in its own right. The acorn grows into an oak. To be alive is to be one's own meaning. This is something Aristotle tries to put into words. Even with all his advantages, it proves difficult work. We find Aristotle expressing himself in strange locutions about how the being of some individual being (*ousia*) is "the what-it-was-and-keeps-on-being" (*to ti en einai*). The very strain under which Aristotle puts language here is a sign that he stretches out toward a thinking that ordinary approaches to predication obscure. If the reader finds it strange that I should discuss Aristotle so much throughout this book, he need only re-read paragraph 22, where Hegel indicates his project can be understood as doing for "*das Subjekt*" (or the negativity common to being and thinking) what Aristotle did for nature.

Hegel recognizes the claim of life to be its own meaning. At the same time, he carries forward a modern project that seeks to understand human culture as the perfection of natural life. Hegel attempts to think human spiritual activity *on the basis of natural life*, to tell the story of how purposivity stretches from the formation of crystals into the founding of laws. Despite some appearances to the contrary, the system of science is an argument for the interdependence of nature and Geist. In place of the radical disjunction between natural determinism and moral freedom proposed by Kant, the system of science attempts to unfold their continuity. A study of purposive activity provides the common concern.

It is no wonder, then, that Kant approaches propositions and definitions as fixed and Hegel approaches them as fluid. Kant understands rational purposes to be the product of a radical act of human subjectivity. We make things mean what they mean to us. Hegel grasps rational purpose as something deeper, something that eludes and even uses human individuals as much as it submits to them. This need not be seen as extravagantly metaphysical or sinisterly totalitarian. It can be viewed, rather, as a humble acknowledgment that the human individual finds herself embedded in a rich natural and cultural world governed not by mere chance or subjective whim but by intelligible purposive necessity.

Anticipating the Absolute (§23)

Hegel tells us at the end of paragraph 23 that a proposition like "God is eternal" offers, at best, an "anticipation" of the absolute. This may be obvious. Who claims that single sentences express the nature of God or being or the absolute? But the problem goes deeper:

> This mere anticipation that the absolute is subject is not only not the actuality of this concept, it makes this [actuality] impossible; for it sets [the subject] as a fixed point, when it is self-movement. (W3:27, §23)

Sentences not only fail to capture the self-relation of self-relating beings, they cover this actuality over with an illusion of fixed categorial stability. Hearkening to the grammar of sentences we would never catch sight of the self-moving absolute. We learn to expect a dead universe into which motion is injected by some strange chance or some human act.

So we have a problem: the ordinary way we view the function of language is too fixed, too rigid, to mirror the self-moving soul, self-moving nature, or a self-moving God. But these are the absolutes we most want language to express. We cannot fix this problem with new names or new definitions or new observations about the properties of matter. Philosophical analysis of language and research in the physical sciences, two popular models for discovering truth in the twentieth century, are both barred from truth methodologically, according to Hegel, because they have no method by which to realize the self-movement of the concept. Both rely, in fact, on the now common ontological assumption that everything remains at rest until something *else* moves it.[3] As a result, the terms and objects we describe lie indifferently alongside one another and lack the account of natural or spiritual self-movement that would link them together.

The point of these remarks on the subjectivity of propositions becomes clear in the following paragraph. Hegel begins:

> Among the various consequences that flow from what has just been said, this one can be picked out, that knowing is only actual, and can only be presented [*dargestellt*], as science or as *system*; and more, that a so-called fundamental proposition or principle of philosophy, if true is also false, just because it is only a principle. (W3:27, §24)

This sentence arranges several crucial considerations in a constellation. Each theme of the present chapter (the interdependence of true and false, the critique of the mathematical-axiomatic approach to truth, and the problem with propositions) has hopefully contributed something to our understanding of what Hegel writes here. First, we can note that Hegel uses the words "science," "system," and "philosophy" interchangeably because philosophy should be science and science should be system. The reason for this is that only a system (not propositions or principles) can present or perform [*darstellen*] the work of making truth explicit, the work of knowing.

A system gives us another way to direct our attention, a way that allows individual propositions to appear as moments in the whole. Instead of asking of a sentence, "Is it true?" we should ask, "What part of the whole is this? Where in the whole does it fit?" We can ask this equally of so-called true and so-called false propositions and principles. Ptolemy's observations get a place in the whole just as Einstein's do.

The remedy to the conceptual rigor mortis imposed by anticipations of the absolute in propositions is what Hegel calls "system." In a system, the system itself becomes the subject instead of the speaker or writer. I think we are familiar with this from reading books. When one aims to read closely, the book as a whole must be the measure of each sentence, the testing ground of each claim. Neither my own personal preferences nor those of the author are to be privileged over the work taken as a whole. This, we might say, is systematic or scientific reading in Hegel's sense of those terms.

Because no writer invents the language they use, authorial intentions cannot be the deciding factor. The written work is already embedded in a communal practice of language that outstrips private intention. The whole point of writing a book is to write it well enough so that it can stand on its own and answer questions posed to it without authorial intervention. This may never succeed perfectly but it succeeds well enough to make books one of the most valuable ways we enter into dialogue with each other. To the extent that the author succeeds in writing a compelling work that holds together as a whole, it is no longer his or her work but equally the work of language itself, and thus of thinking itself. This work, I hope, is not seen as some spooky metaphysical oversoul but as the everyday interconnection of beings and thinkings.

When we read well, our trust is not in individual words, propositions, intentions, or mental states but rather in the self-relating activity of the content that self-organizes into a whole, "the self-moving concept."

Familiar Language: Dogmatism (§40)

Though Hegel highlights several "obstacles" to philosophical knowing, the chief obstacle to which he returns again and again is how we use language. This becomes clear in paragraph 40, where Hegel connects "dogmatism" (a general, pejorative term for the many varieties of unreflective thinking) with a certain theory of propositions.

Hegel sees dogmatism in everyday knowledge claims and in the study of philosophy. (W3:41, §40). We confront a problem when considering "Julius Caesar was born in July" or "a stadium is 176 meters long" just as we do when considering "God is eternal" or "the soul is immortal." None of these claims can be simply true just as such but each requires "reasons" that are only acquired through "the movement of self-consciousness," by which Hegel means (at least) "comparing many things" and "investigation." (W3:42, §41). Even as simple an item as Julius Caesar's birth date is relevant or significant only in a constellation of other claims. It is a moment in a movement of investigation, of thinking. Though Hegel acknowledges that when someone asks when Caesar was born we should not launch into a sermon on propositional truth but rather answer them "nicely"; the social exchange of conventionally accepted information is not what we mean by truth.

Here in paragraph 40, dogmatism is not a specific position or set of positions but a certain kind of rigid attitude that can take hold of any way of knowing at any time, whether ordinary or philosophical. Hegel's own examples of dogmatism are mathematical and historical "facts." The dogmatic attitude presumes that truth is found in a proposition that is "a fixed result" (W3:41, §40). To the question "when was Caesar born?" or "how many feet are in a stadium" there seems to be a fixed, simple, determinate answer. If we find ourselves looking for (and thus identifying truth with) this kind of fixed determinacy, we are thinking dogmatically. Why? We should first notice that these values are only determinate because we have constructed them as such. We invented the date system we will use to date Caesar and we invented the stadium as a measurement. Truths of this kind are determinate only because they were determined in advance by *arbitrary* limits. The proposition thus becomes a vehicle for tautologies that seem to add to our knowledge only because we have forgotten the arbitrary construction that lay at the root of the particular determination.

What such dogmatic truth ignores is what we might call context. The question of Caesar's birth must itself be part of another question, a broader context. Why do we want to know this? Given what concerns will this "fact" count as an adequate answer? Here we hit on a purpose, on a cause with life and movement and vitality, not just an arbitrarily fixed determination. Facts are always facts within living contexts; facts are always *for the sake of* purposes and thus are never atomic or independent. For one purpose, to say "July" may be enough, for another "100 BCE," for a third, "after Plato died," and so on. To treat these claims as facts as if they were context-independent is to treat them dogmatically. What really matters is not the "fact" as such but the wider field in which each proposition is only a moment, the purposive context in which it has its life, just as a heart is nothing but an inert lump without a living body (for the sake of which it is).

As we have seen in paragraph 23, we are all too prone to identify the purposive context of inquiry with conscious awareness of the individual inquirer. We tend to assume a person asks a question for their own purposes and reasons. We therefore overlook the possibility that the individual questioner is only a node, a transit point, in a broader cultural movement. The actual designs and purposes of a question often outstrip our individual understandings. Philosophical inquiry is often described as a pursuit of questions rather than answers for this reason. Our aim is to allow the actual question to emerge from behind the facade of a familiar question. Our aim is to allow the necessary to emerge instead of the arbitrary.

Predicate and Concept (§60)

As we saw in paragraph 23, when we try to employ the procedure of predication for philosophical content, it blocks the way to philosophy altogether. Decisive verdicts in grand philosophical lingo are "anticipations of the absolute" that offer only premature satisfactions. The object or content of philosophy is not a finite, sensible artifact known by its predicates but rather something Hegel calls "the concept" [*Der Begriff*]. Content is said to be "the concept" when it is *self-determining* content. As a result, the concept does not present an object or content in a fixed or final state but rather as its own coming-to-be or development [*werden*]:[4]

> Since the concept is the ownmost self of the object, which presents the object through *its own development* [*werden*], the object is not a resting subject that motionlessly carries accidents, but the self-moving concept that returns its determinations into itself. In this movement, every resting subject brings itself to collapse." (W3:57, §60)

If we were to object to a stranger's description of a friend based on a single encounter, we would do so because we do not take human beings to be finite objects, but rather ongoing activities, developing beings. I am still growing and changing, still showing the world who I am by presenting what I can be. No person is just the qualities they happen to display at any given moment in time. Nor is a person the simple sum of all qualities displayed throughout a lifetime. The human being is the activity responsible for each quality and thus the qualities are instructive only if taken as indications of or "moments" of an ongoing activity of being-a-self. This activity of being-a-self which both causes and collapses finite qualities is the concept.

Understanding of a human life demands not a *predicate* but a *story*. Novels, for example, do not simply predicate characters; rather they unfold their development or coming-to-be, thus allowing us to glimpse a single concept that drives growth and change. Good fiction is governed by the necessity of the concept of its characters. These expressions are thus closer to presenting the truth of human being (despite being fiction) than isolated predicative sentences about "real" or existent persons. Just as stories require patience because we must wait and see how the character unfolds and avoid premature judgment, so too philosophy requires patience. Philosophy hopes to tell the long story of thinking's self-development.

In Hegel's preface to the *Phenomenology*, we are on the hunt not for a method but for a manner of presentation [*Darstellung*] that is adequate to the concept, a performance that presents things not as static but as their own coming-to-be, in their own developmental movement. We are looking for the kind of presentation that dramatizes the subject that "brings itself to collapse" rather than the resting subject with its fixed predicates.

Räsonieren and *Begreifen*: Two Ways of Thinking (§59–60)

If the concept demands patience just as a long story demands patience, what can we offer the reader before they set out on the long journey of system, science, or philosophy? An anticipation of the absolute will, we saw, obstruct the journey. The premature certainty of decisive predicative sentences about grand subjects renders us unable to flex with the changing nature of the subject as it unfolds. Therefore what we can offer at the beginning is not certainty but *perplexity*. The right kind of puzzling statement, made at the outset, can ignite interest and entice the reader to set out on the long journey of inquiry. Hegel will explore this special kind of anticipation, this special kind of "speculative sentence" in the paragraphs from 61 through 66.

Before he mentions the speculative proposition by name, Hegel opposes two ways of thinking [*Denken*]: *Räsonieren* and *Begreifen*. The speculative proposition is meant as an illustration of the latter (and better) sort of thinking. Both *Räsonieren* and *Begreifen* are difficult to translate. I will leave them untranslated in order to prompt us to think in a new way without taking refuge in our available conceptions for what thinking is and how it works. *Räsonieren* comes to German by way of the French "*raison*" [reason] and has negative connotations in German (and for Hegel) of complaining, of reasoning with more detail than necessary, of argumentation or sophistical debate, of *rationalizing* events or circumstances. *Begreifen* is related to the word for concept, *Begriff*, and carries connotations of grasping, of fully comprehending, of realizing. Both are arguably words for "reasoning" but they stress two different ways of reasoning, two different ways of thinking. Just as Aristotle noted that sophistry and philosophy both concern being but are turned in opposite directions, *Räsonieren* and *Begreifen* can be treated as opposite styles of reasoning. Grasping the difference between them will illuminate the role the speculative proposition has to play in our search for truth.

We should not expect Hegel to define either *Räsonieren* or *Begreifen*. Nor does he. Ways of thinking cannot be defined; they must be presented. We have already seen why this is. At best, the single definition reveals something about the definer, not what is defined. Definition, like predication more generally, cannot capture a movement or an activity like thinking.[5] All it can do is note some fixed stations of the activity and, by reifying these, offer a one-sided picture of the development. Nevertheless, we can get some sense of how these different sorts of thinking move or work through examples.

The first difficulty we encounter in distinguishing these two different ways of thinking is that both seem to apprehend the true as the "subject." But each grasps the subject differently. Hegel has told us that "everything depends on grasping and expressing the true not only as substance but as subject" (W3:22–3, §17). But what does it mean to grasp and express something as subject? Does it mean to grasp and express the true as appearances for an ego? Or does it mean to grasp and express the true itself as a subject in its own right? Here we return to a theme we saw in paragraphs 23 (in relation to propositions) and 42 (in relation to mathematical proofs): grasping substance as subject often amounts to grasping the content in relation to the individual ego, not as the content's own self-relation.

What does it mean to grasp and express something other than oneself, one's own I, as a subject? Isn't the only access to being-a-subject that we have the immediate access each of us has to the "I think" as Descartes and Kant have suggested? If so, we align the term "subject" with the subjective. Hegel sees more deeply. He sees that being-an-I is a concept; it is a way of selfing, a kind of self-relation. And further, he sees that this concept, this way of relating oneself to oneself in an ongoing way, is manifestly at work in other living things. The concept is "self-like [*selbstisch*]" and refers to the meaningful motions of any whole that keeps being itself by changing (W3:39; §37). While we normally take the "I" as the paradigm for the subject, Hegel takes the concept as the paradigm for the subject and treats the I as one important example of this. It is through the concept that both "object" and "I" become what they are, and it is through the same concept that both are comprehended. This insight is what allows Hegel to move out of the shadow of the Kantian project which remained confined to subjective idealism. *Räsonieren* and *Begreifen* each apprehend the subject differently. The former apprehends the true as subjectivity, the latter, more broadly, as selfhood or self-relating activity.

We are introduced to *Räsonieren* as *Räsonnement* in paragraph 34. In that earlier paragraph, it is explicitly contrasted with proper method and science. We can thus connect it back to Hegel's plan for the preface, where he states he will give us a "general outline" and alert us to the "habits" of thinking that form an "impediment to philosophical knowing" (W3:22; §16). *Räsonnement* picks out objects of thought at random; it moves "back and forth," and it "tries to ground truth on the inferences and consequences of rigidly defined thoughts" (W3:38; §34). *Räsonieren* is both too fixed in its categories and too loose in its movement. The vital point here is that if the subject matter itself is inflexible, the individual mind must be the source of movement. *Räsonieren* is trapped by its fixed thoughts but *feels* free because it can move anywhere between them *at will*. *Räsonieren* composes its music without a key and thus can choose any note it wants at any time. But the result of such a procedure will not be music. *Räsonieren* mistakes license with freedom.

Räsonieren names subjective thinking, thinking that cannot get beyond itself. By contrast, *Begreifen* names thinking that loses itself in the selfing of what it thinks. Hegel describes *Räsonieren* as "freedom from all content and a sense of vanity [*Eitelkeit*] toward it" (W3:56; §58). *Räsonierendes Denken* is so sure of its own truth as an ego or I that its willful sense of self trumps all content that it thinks. Because *Räsonieren* is guided by the conscious aim of a human subject, it is prone to debate, to argumentative attacks on whatever gets in the way of its private, subjective goals. *Räsonieren* will avail itself of skeptical tropes or sophistical sidebars or empty formalisms because the means of thinking do not matter to it. It does not see that the means and end of thinking are the same: we think with the concept to reach the concept.

Begreifendes Denken is more difficult to observe. If we could see clearly what it is right away, our need for a system of science (and Hegel's books) would be greatly diminished. *Begreifen* is experienced by ordinary consciousness as a "*Gegenstoss*," a push or shove backward, a "counter-thrust" (W3:58, §60). Rather than give us a positive definition, Hegel introduces us to the better mode of thinking by negation. If we felt we could pinpoint *Begreifen*, it would become a fixed category of *Räsonieren*. Pinning things down is what *Räsonieren* does, just as a sophistical debater pins down an opponent's position in order to raise objections. By contrast, appreciating the dynamic movement of wholes is what *Begreifen* does, yet this appears to us, first and foremost, as an appetite for destruction, the destruction of all our fixed thoughts. *Begreifen* seems dead set on introducing confusion, even chaos, to our familiar categorial constellations. We must be careful to distinguish this from skepticism. Unlike the skeptic, the speculative thinker finds a new kind of intelligibility in the negations. Philosophers choose deliberately difficult language that perplexes us not into *ataraxia* but into further inquiry.

Hegel's Examples of Speculative Propositions (§62)

So what are these deliberately perplexing turns of phrase that help us enquire beyond the boundaries of propositional truth? Hegel calls them "speculative sentences." It may be helpful to reverse the order of presentation and consider Hegel's examples before we consider his general comments about the speculative proposition. Hegel gives two examples of the speculative proposition, but he says relatively little about how they are supposed to work. As a result, readers have drawn diverse conclusions from them.

The first example is "God is being." Hegel says only that "being" here is not a "predicate" but an "essence" and thus "God" ceases to be a "fixed subject" (W3:59; §62). I take Hegel to mean the following: "God is being" calls the assumption that God is *a being* into question. To be a fixed, predicable subject, God must be *a* being. If God's essence is rather being itself, God cannot be *a* being and the firm ground of predication is lost. When we say, "God is eternal" (the chief example of the ordinary proposition used in paragraph 23), we assume that God is an eternal being. We do not assume, for example, that God is eternity itself. The latter would be, on this argument, a speculative proposition. Not incidentally, ordinary predication is thus responsible for the religiously popular but philosophically disputed notion that God is a person, that is, a being that loves, gets angry, and so on.

Notice that in Hegel's other example, "the actual is the universal," he indicates that the proposition would not be speculative without the second "the" (W3:60; §62). If the sentence were "The actual is universal," we would have an ordinary proposition rather than a speculative one. Why? Because "universal" can function both as a property or predicate and also as a substance or subject (i.e., something that has or comprehends predicates and so is not a predicate itself).

The addition of "the" indicates we are talking about the universal as subject, not universality as a predicate. In both cases, the question we hoped to answer through the predicate meets only a further, deeper question. The question "what is God?" becomes the question "what is being?" and the question "what is the actual?" becomes the question "what is the universal?"

We begin with something we feel that we half understand (God) and the speculative move takes us to something we do not understand at all (being). By destroying our half-understood "fixed subject," the speculative move frees us up to immerse ourselves in the content without prejudice, without artificial limitations on what can be known.

We are hampered in our quest for truth by the inherited prejudice that God is *a* being. As long as we take God to be a being, we will expect certain ways of thinking about beings to apply to God. We will expect God to be a subject that bears predicates, for example, and then we will seek out the applicable predicates. When this procedure fails we will prematurely conclude that either (1) God is an incoherent thought of a being that does not follow the rules of beings or (2) God exceeds all human knowledge. Both of these turn out to make use of presumed knowledge (that God is *a* being) which leads to the rejection of knowledge as such. The first leads to a premature rejection of God, religion, Geist, the infinite, the absolute, and thus philosophy. Atheism, here, is not just the rejection of God, it is the rejection of the human spirit in relation to wholeness; it is a rejection of reason itself. But theism that claims God is unknowable (based on a premature grasp of what knowing is) leads to the same place. Our inherited, prejudicial "knowledge" that God is *a* being turns out to be "knowledge" that destroys the possibility of knowing. Such artificially fixed "knowledge" in every case ends with the denial of reason, knowledge of the absolute, and thus, ends with the rejection of philosophy itself. Such denials are the norm in our time as they were in Hegel's time as they were in Plato's time. No age has seen rational thinking predominate over familiar prejudice. Plato's Socrates says that the Athenians hope to put him to death in the hopes of sparing themselves the trouble of accounting for their knowledge and their lives (*Apology* 39c). Common sense aims to spare itself the hard work of philosophy by holding to the beliefs which point toward the impossibility of truth and philosophy. The speculative proposition "God is being" destroys the prejudice that God is a being. In doing so, it perplexes us and makes us think twice about how we talk and think about God. In the perplexity of the speculative proposition, we are freed up to think again.

Yet we do not *feel* freed by the speculative proposition. Instead, the customary freedom of subjective thinking feels "checked." Reading philosophy, we encounter "unfamiliar obstructions [*ungewohnten Hemmen*]" (W3:60; §63). Normally, we feel "free" to think whatever we please on the "firm objective ground" of some fixed categories. The loss of this ground feels not like a liberation from prejudice but like an inhibition by unfamiliar obstructions. Grasping "being" as such now stands in the way of understanding God. If "God is being," then we must inquire into the being of being. The new subject staring at us in the predicate position of the speculative proposition appears to us as an obstacle. Hegel goes on to say that these unfamiliar obstructions to thinking's customary, free-roaming pursuit of its own agenda are the source of complaints about "the incomprehensibility of philosophical writings" (W3:60; §63).

When we lose our "firm objective ground," we experience the free fall of thinking, the weightlessness of thinking, the true freedom of thinking. Thinking has not been inhibited or lost at all. What has been lost is artificial clarity, prejudicial fixity. But if this is all we lose, why do we react so negatively to confusion, perplexity, impasse, speculation, philosophy? What we lose in the speculative proposition is the ego, the subjective agenda that we bring to thinking. We lose *Räsonieren* and are immersed in *Begreifen*, in thinking for its own sake. This is an experience Hegel associates with the "floating center" of poetry and music.

Overcoming Dogmatism: Speculative Rhythm (§61)

In his brief discussion of the speculative proposition, Hegel describes the relationship between thinking and language as a tension between the "unity of the concept" and the "form of proposition" (W3:59; §61). This is a theme throughout the preface. The concept is "self-like" [*selbstisch*] (W3:39; §37). To be self-like is to assert oneself by negation, to be oneself by becoming other, to grow, mature, expand, to self-overcome, and yet to hold on to the driving unity of self despite constant change. Though difficult to articulate and to think, this self-like-ness is nevertheless easy to be since we all do this all the time as we eat, digest, breathe, sense, imagine, think, and act.

Propositions are not self-like; each designates an independent unit of meaning, not an ongoing, developing, self-relating movement. Concept and proposition are thus in conflict because the unity of the concept is not static or passive unity by fixed arrangement but turbulent unity. In later work, Hegel will note that "unity" is an inadequate word for the concept's activity because it suggests calm identity rather than dynamic process.[6]

Hegel is clear that speculative thought cannot be expressed in propositions.[7] The proposition, taken at face value, fails to communicate the fluidity and wholeness of thinking. That said, the rhythm born from tension between the fixity of propositions and the flow of thinking is precisely what makes the proposition a workable means for the expression of the concept. The key to reading philosophy is to recognize what emerges from the tension between sentences and selfhood. What emerges from this productive tension is what Hegel calls a "floating center." Hegel writes:

> This conflict between the general form of the proposition and the unity of the concept which destroys it is similar to the conflict that occurs in rhythm between meter and accent. Rhythm results from the floating center and the unification of the two. (W3:59; §61)

Hegel is to be thinking of poetry or metered verse here. Our speech is accented in certain conventional ways. At the same time, metrical forms expect stresses on certain beats. If the accents demanded by our "natural" speech conflict with the metrical form, a tense movement called rhythm emerges. For example, "To **be**/ or **not**/ to **be,** / **that** is /the **ques**tion:" is a line of iambic pentameter verse. Thus we expect five iambic feet. An iamb is a two-syllable foot with stress on the second syllable. As I have scanned it, the first three feet in the pentameter line are clearly iambs, the natural language accent, and the metrical stress align. But the foot "that is" is not clear: in normal speech today we are more likely to stress the first rather than the second syllable, resulting in a trochee (stressed, unstressed), not an iamb. We experience a pull toward accenting both "that" and "is" in the fourth foot. This double pull, the pull of accent against the pull of meter, creates tension or rhythm. This is what makes poetry interesting rather than predictable.

The line can be scanned in other ways, of course. The general point here is that this line of iambic pentameter gets its unique rhythm from a "floating center," a tension between how the poetic meter invites us to stress syllables and how normal speech does. Hegel is not arguing that there is a final decision to be made in the experience of rhythm but that rhythm is precisely this experience of floating, of suspending that final dogmatic judgment. Without this floating center, a poem becomes either doggerel (the metrical inflexibility of nursery rhymes, limericks, or light verse) or prosaic (completely natural and unpoetic accented speech without any hint of metrical tension).

The rhythm of poetry subverts *both* the stiff artifice of the merely formal meter and the arbitrary way accented syllables occur in natural speech. This is poetry: neither the form nor the words, but the experience of "floating" that emerges between form and word. Hegel's point is that rhythm is the product of *preserving* the tension between meter and accent, and disappears wherever one predominates over the other. This is one way to understand *Aufhebung*, the mutual cancellation that preserves the "floating center."

In music, the tonal center for a musical key provides the value to each note. The movements between the notes only become meaningful movements if some key is established, if some tonal center is found. Yet if the tonal center is too obvious and the musical piece too predictable, it quickly loses its dynamic quality, its life. There must be a center, but not a rigid or fixed center. Likewise, a rhythmic center in poetry must be flexible enough to accommodate natural speech but yet make it more *dynamic*. Even free verse manages this by creating its own temporary expectations of meter to subvert for the sake of rhythm. Hegel's remark about the floating center invites obvious comparison to the negativity of selfhood found in living beings that is thematized throughout the preface. Poetry and music imitate the floating quality of living selfhood, the quality of tension that drives developmental movement.

The So-Called Dialectic

It may be worthwhile to pause here and note that this "floating center" excludes any notion that "Hegel's dialectic" is a matter of thesis-antithesis-synthesis. Speculative thinking moves by a speculative rhythm which has a floating center, an *unresolved unity*, not a firm synthesis or fixed end point. To end in a clear synthesis of two clear contraries is, in fact, dogmatism. Every moment in the presentation of a system of science includes the tension of thesis and antithesis in itself, and thus there are no properly atomic thesis or antithesis moments. As in a fractal, each moment is a microcosm of the conceptual tension expressed throughout the whole. There are simply no fixed parts in a system of science that can be opposed to other fixed parts to produce some third fixed part. Rather each "part" is opposed inwardly to itself. Each part is an inwardly tensed, living moment. The whole that is arranged out of them offers stability and repose only because it comprehends every intelligible case, not because it bases them all on some fixed principle or foundation. I suggested this previously by calling the system a series of deferrals.

We may recall the blossom and the bud from the second paragraph of the preface: the blossom and bud cannot be combined or synthesized because they do not coexist in time. One replaces the other. Each moment may nevertheless be said to contain the other as a potency (though in different respects) and thus each moment contains polarity and unity. The meaningful difference between blossom and bud is due not to some schematic role it plays but to the degree to which the floating center has become manifest. If we do not differentiate between potencies and their full activity, the content of a system of science is actually the same at every stage. The content appears different only because it articulates itself by degrees. We privilege later developments in a system of science because they articulate more expressly what is present but hidden in previous moments. In the *Science of Logic*, we begin with "being" and we never add to it any "new" subject matter; rather we re-express the whole of being in increasingly articulate ways.

The method is thus not separate from the content. The oppositional movement we ascribe to the so-called dialectical method is actually present in every "object" method treats. It is not our method applied to the objects; it is the object's own being mirrored in our thinking of it. Just as Spinoza argued that method is nothing other than the true idea itself and not some second order reflection on the idea, the speculative method here is merely observation of the negativity charging each presumed moment, the very power that makes it appear and also the power that makes it collapse.

Coming back to paragraph 61, what Hegel calls the "speculative" or "philosophical" proposition is a sentence in which tension between subject and predicate is preserved because the predicate is another independent subject in its own right and cannot just be subordinated to the grammatical subject. It cannot be synthesized. This destroys the rigid operation of predication and communicates a new kind of subject, the subject as "floating center" resulting from the tension between subject-subject and predicate-subject: "So, in the philosophical proposition the identity of subject and predicate should not destroy the difference between them which the form of the proposition expresses, but their unity should emerge as a harmony" (W3:59; §61). "Harmony" (and not synthesis) is the word for the stability within instability of a moving world that expresses its truth as absolute negativity. But harmony, as Heraclitus teaches, involves preserving opposition.

Speculative thinking is musical thinking, thinking that is at home in tensions that form ongoing harmonies and expanding, self-overcoming wholes. What becomes so natural to our listening proves continually confounding to our understanding. No listener holds on to a single note as a fixed and inflexible standard when its time is through. He lets them each go to grasp the moving whole. Likewise, in poetry, each separate accent gives way to the emergent rhythm. Speculative thinking turns toward the whole developing movement rather than the isolated accented moments. The accent of each moment is not ignored; each matters. But these accents matter collectively only, not each as independent from the others.

The "notes" of philosophical thinking are not just individual words but entire propositions. It takes a proposition to express a relation. Yet the relations expressed in propositions are not simply additive. They can be subtractive, contrastive, contrapuntal, harmonizing, and so on. Some propositions that are technically or literally false prepare us for a recognition beyond the propositions that is true. Hegel's image of a floating center captures how the individual propositions in a philosophical exposition demarcate extremes and the work of thinking takes place *between* them. Though Hegel discusses a special propositional form (S is S instead of S is P) that accomplishes this floating within a single proposition, it is more likely that we will encounter standard propositions in his work and that the floating center will be found between them. There are certainly speculative propositions in his work and in the work of other philosophers. Aristotle's discussion of the God as "thinking thinking thinking" is a canonical example. Nevertheless these speculative propositions are not the brick and mortar out of which philosophical texts are composed. It is important to bring the arguments about the speculative proposition together with everything else Hegel writes about propositions in the 1807 preface. When we do this, we may notice that Hegel's advice about how to treat standard propositions mirrors the work of the specialized speculative proposition. A floating center is often achieved by holding standard propositions loosely in one's thinking and allowing a more expansive relation to emerge between them.

So much of what we do in the academic study of the history of philosophy involves reminding readers that single propositions should not be taken out of context. We aim to correct the overly simplistic cultural transmission of "Plato's Forms" and "Descartes' Dualism" and to attune readers to the subtlety and complexity of the texts and the music of their arguments. We remind readers to consider propositions like notes whose values change depending on position rather than like numbers with fixed values. We aim to open back up a dialogue where opinion has calcified. This is an impulse guided by speculative thinking which sees beyond fixed oppositions to the rhythmic movement of a governing activity.

7

Philosophy Is Not Personal (§67–72)

Those men that in their writings are most wise,
Own nothing but their blind, stupefied hearts.
—W. B. Yeats, "Ego Dominus Tuus"

We have seen how prefaces, edification, formalism, phenomenology, mathematics, historical analysis, and propositional truth can masquerade as philosophical thinking. Each offers a different set of restrictions on what kind of content philosophy can consider and how it should consider that content. Each fails to observe that philosophy is open inquiry: an autonomous, self-determining thinking about thinking that cannot be limited in advance. In this chapter, we turn to discuss the simplest and most prevalent mistake we make with regard to philosophy, a mistake that lies at the root of many others. Instead of treating philosophy as a self-determining intersubjective activity, we treat it as a product of individual persons or individual minds. For Hegel it is essential to the development of philosophical thinking that it develop past any personal, individual or idiosyncratic starting points. Merleau-Ponty captures this well: "philosophy actualizes itself by destroying itself as an isolated philosophy" (*The Phenomenology of Perception*, 521).

The History of Philosophy Is Impersonal

In the introduction to his *Lectures on the History of Philosophy*, Hegel contrasts philosophical history with the more familiar kind of history, which he calls "political history." Political history, he reminds us, concerns the individual characters of the major players and will take note of the particular "temperament, genius and passions" that belong to them. These temperaments prove important to understanding the events themselves. The history of philosophy concerns something else altogether:

> but here [in the history of philosophy] what is brought forth is all the more admirable the less its attribution and merit depend on the particular individual;

by contrast, the more it belongs to free thinking, to the general character of the human as human, the more this idiosyncrasy-less thinking is itself the productive subject. (W18:20)

The history of philosophy is not the story of Socrates, Plotinus, or Descartes but the story of human thinking itself. Without a personality to tie it down, thinking will be free, without arbitrary and contingent restrictions. It will be free to consider itself not just in this or that opinion laid down by a so-called philosopher under the conditions of a certain individual life but insofar as it works through all human life and activity. In a properly philosophical history of philosophy, thinking will be free to consider itself as a *trans-subjective and intersubjective activity*. As such, this free thinking is not a consequence of human individuality and personality but rather the "productive subject" that makes individuality possible.

Philosophy is not just lacking an individual and subjective character. Rather, it is felt as a need that goes *against* the drive toward individuality and its accompanying practical interests. Philosophy "exists only as an inner necessity that is stronger than the subject" and we pursue it "without rest" until we satisfy "the pressures [*Drange*] of reason" rather than our own private interests (W8:38). This may sound severe or old-fashioned, but Hegel is reminding us that humans need philosophy precisely because to be human is to seek truth, to reach out beyond our myopic individuality into the wider shared space of nature, habit, language, social-political life, art, religion, and, ultimately, knowledge. The drive to know guides us, eventually, toward the need to know knowing, that is, to philosophy as science.

Human Nature (§69)

The final paragraphs of the 1807 preface make explicit the account of human nature that undergirds a host of arguments made in the preface. Our "humanity," Hegel writes, consists in "pressing on [*aufdringen*] to agreement [*Übereinkunft*] with one another" (W3:65, §69). Hegel's verb choice is significant: *aufdringen* conveys necessity, compulsion, and constant activity. What we are, he suggests, is an inalienable drive toward *Übereinkunft*: agreement, concord, literally, coming together. It is our nature to seek knowing through sharing.[1]

Hegel is not just insisting that we are social animals. He is not just indicating that our self-fulfillment will require cities, laws, cultures, histories. The upshot here is wider than a social-political reading of Hegel suggests. "Pressing on to agreement" here means that our nature is to reach beyond subjective thinking toward thinking as such. Our fulfillment requires that the idiosyncratic experience of thinking expand to the point where it can recognize itself in the thinking of others and, eventually, in all genuine thinking.

For Hegel, humans are thinkers. Our need for philosophy concerns our need to recognize ourselves not only in the outer world of determinate things but also in the inner world of pure thinking. Indeed, we must "win thinking as an object" because human beings find their "unadulterated selfhood is thinking" (W8:55, Enz §11). So there is a need to think about thinking or to recognize ourselves at work in our thinking, to recognize thinking as our own doing. Without philosophy we remain passive in relation to the activity of thought. We inherit thoughts and concepts and also arrangements of them, connections between them that must be worked over, explored, tested, and finally comprehended. Without this working over of the spiritual inheritance of thought, we will not recognize ourselves in thought and thus fail to realize our own selves in and as thinking, missing out on the human being's deepest sense of self.

Our humanity appears only in what Hegel calls an "achieved commonality [*Gemeinsamkeit*] of consciousness [*Bewusstsein*]."[2] Miller's translation "community of minds" unnecessarily narrows the range of interpretation here. The word *Gemeinsamkeit* could mean "community" but more often simply means "similarity" or "commonality." The point is not that we will build a working community with many diverse, plural minds but that my thinking will become indistinguishable from your thinking to the extent that it is philosophical thinking. Philosophy actualizes the human drive to have thinking in common. To call this the nature of humanity is therefore to assert that philosophy, the thinking of thinking as a single, common whole, is at the root of all that is distinctively human like complex languages, cities, ethics, art, religion, and so on. These things are only possible if diverse acts of thinking are held together by aiming toward a single, common thinking.

The first lesson learned in the *Phenomenology of Spirit* is that words are always universal. Well before Wittgenstein, Hegel argued there can be no private language. The moment we say "this," regardless of any private intention, we have uttered the "universal this" (W3:85, §97). The uniqueness presumed to belong to a passing subjective experience cannot be represented in language. This is an early clue that personal or private impressions do not have what Hegel calls "*Wirklichkeit*" or effective actuality. If such impressions have any value at all, it is not a *human* value. We are not human by virtue of the idiosyncrasy of our impressions.

We should recall that in §4, Hegel championed the Aristotelian account of experience rather than the Lockean: human experience of the world begins with universals and proceeds from there to particulars and not the other way around. At first, Aristotle notes, children call all men father and *then* they learn to distinguish each.[3] The particular is what stands out from the universal and thus relies on it. Universality is not an abstraction born of many instances blurred together but an active, actual source of particularity and individuality. Universality is the basic condition of intuition: we see things first as a whole.

This has powerful consequences for Hegel's thinking. If we begin with the whole, whenever we find ourselves alienated from the whole, we can still have confidence that we can press on toward it. On a Lockean account that presumes that particulars precede universals, where the world consists of atomic individuals related into kinds only by mental abstractions, the drive to communion and communication is more difficult to justify. On the atomic view, communication in words or universal terms is always a betrayal of the underlying atomism of reality.

Philosophy must become a science, we learned in paragraph 5, simply because it is its "nature" or "inner necessity" to do so. This is another way of stating the claim from §69 that human being itself is constituted by the pursuit of a community of knowing. Knowing anything at all presupposes and aims at a collective state of knowing, a *Wissenschaft* or science. In German, the "schaft" suffix turns nouns into collective groups (e.g., *Mannschaft* or *Brüderschaft*). *Wissen* naturally becomes *Wissenschaft*. All human knowing entails sharing knowing and, eventually, aims at knowing-in-common or science.

At the end of the preface, Hegel indicates that these seemingly separate strands (knowing, thinking, universality, language, science, consciousness, community) follow directly from our human nature. We speak to be heard, write to be read, act to be known. But too often we think that this self we are presenting for others is already particular, determinate, personal. Too often we presume that we are sharing something that *already has determinate being*. In fact, Hegel is suggesting that the act of sharing itself is our human selfhood. The human self is not a *thing shared* or presented in words and actions but the *act* of presenting itself. This is one important face of self-relating negativity: pressing on to agreement without rest, seeking science.

Hegel thus does not require that perfect agreement be achieved and does not theorize some end where all knowing has become common and everything becomes static and human nature can collapse or disappear. He is situating the Kantian imperative to bring philosophy to the status of a science within the long-standing human quest to achieve a common, shared consciousness. The drive as well as the activity is what interests Hegel, and a more perfect expression of the drive to share knowing will not destroy it but rather will invigorate it.

Here it is interesting to note that many philosophers hope and expect their projects to be carried on by others after their deaths. Kant's critical project was just an overture for the larger metaphysical project he did not have time to articulate, but hoped his students would continue to develop. Like Kant, Hegel hopes his system will invigorate and sustain philosophical activity into the future. We can view philosophy as a cult of personality and philosophers as cult leaders who want disciples to adopt their idiosyncratic perspective, or we can view philosophy as a science and view philosophers as servants of thinking whose aim is to leave thinking on better footing than they found it.

Thinking that falls short of a system of science is likely to view works of philosophy as the personal projects of individuals and not the common labor of human being pressing on toward agreement with itself *through* these different expressions. At the end of the preface, we finally consider two obstacles to philosophy that lay bare what was implicit in the formalisms that often pass for philosophy. The attitudes Hegel will call "common sense" and "genius" offer an easy way out for anyone who, tiring of the human work of pressing on to agreement, prefers the illusion that the opinions he has thus far borrowed from the human whole are in fact his own.

The Subjectivity of *Räsonieren* (§58–9)

If human nature consists in "pressing on to agreement" with one another, then persuasive argument can be a means to that end. But Hegel makes it clear that by "agreement" he does not mean one person compelling another to agree with his opinion. Rather, human interlocutors come together when both parties forget their private interests so they can meet on the middle ground of the content itself, the *Sache selbst*. When, in a philosophy classroom, we submit to the text as a common ground and work together to exposit it rather than our private views, we are practicing for this sort of thinking.

The chief problem that speculative philosophy faces is that its proper content is found only in the movement of the concept. This means that the true content of philosophy is selfhood or the activity of self-relation. But just as we saw in Chapter 5 that Geist is not itself a phenomenon (even though it is a *source* of phenomenal appearances), "selfhood" does not correspond to any image in the imagination [*Vorstellung*]. As Hegel points out in paragraph 58, the work of selfhood is often expressed in abstract-sounding words and phrases like "being-in-itself" and "being-for-itself." These phrases can easily be misunderstood as an abstract negation of content rather than as a means of patient inquiry into it. Hegel's readers may think he is dissolving the concrete world of physical stuff into a ghostly realm of empty phrases that serve only to win arguments against his philosophical opponents. And so, just like that, dialectic would become eristic, philosophy would become what Hegel calls "*Räsonieren*" or rationalizing.

Philosophy confronts us with the challenge of thinking selfing activity itself, not just its expressions. Traditionally this has been understood as inquiry into God (the active self of the cosmos) and the soul (the active self of some individual entity). This inquiry is not satisfied by the giving of examples (e.g., "God is what makes the sun shine which makes this grass grow" and "the soul is the cause of the tabby cat sleeping and waking"). Faced with the challenge of thinking self-determining acts themselves, most readers of philosophy will flee to one of two sides, taking refuge either in overly determinate images or in overly indeterminate thoughts. The first refuge Hegel associates here with imagination and, later, with common sense. Hegel associates the second refuge with "*Räsonieren*" or rationalization here and, later, with genius. Turning from thoughts to images should be familiar by now, but Hegel feels compelled to say more about *Räsonieren*, how it operates and how it keeps us from philosophy.

To use argument as a way of achieving "freedom from content" is what Hegel calls "*Räsonieren*." (W3:56, PS §58). This is something like the misuse of reason we call "rationalization" in English. When we say that a person rationalizes something, we mean that he offers reasons and arguments as a personal consolation rather than as a way of understanding the subject matter. Every argument given by a rationalizer is not about the content but about himself. To rationalize is to flatter one's own opinion in the face of contrary evidence, to search for any justification, no matter how remote from the topic at hand. Typically, this justification as well as consolation takes the form of a skeptical destruction of opposing views.

The rationalizer cannot give content-rich reasons for the opinion he favors, since what is of interest to him is not the content itself but merely the fact that the thought is *his*. We often hold casual political views in this way, knowing nothing about the policy details or consequences but fighting bitterly for what we perceive to be our own. We focus on tearing down the other available opinions, aiming for an agnostic state that favors no content and thus makes the mere fact that a view is mine as good a reason to hold it as any. All content thus becomes mere "reflection into the empty I, the vanity of its own knowing" (W3:56, PS §58).

This brings us to the relevant point for our current concern. *Räsonieren* takes things personally; it sees no reasons but personal reasons. But personhood here is highly abstract: it is the "empty I" or the mere fact of mine-ness, not the positive content of a particular personality. This "empty I" has often paraded itself as the supreme philosophical content: it can appear as Descartes' Cogito or as Kant's Transcendental Unity of Apperception. It is important to recognize how sophisticated this form of skeptical egotism can be. The rationalizer has lifted himself up out of the confines of the imagination and its familiar representations. He has recognized that thought is a fluid, dynamic process, an engine of continual content destruction. But he has not seen the generative side of this destructive power.

Hegel will recognize this "empty I" as a crucial stage in the birth of Geist out of nature.[4] But this "empty I," so crucial in liberating us from the familiar representations in the imagination, can block the road to any substantial development of content in philosophy. Descartes must arbitrarily import content into his empty I, appealing to innate ideas. Kant skeptically undermines the very possibility of giving a positive account of God and the soul. The transcendental idealist cannot account for selfhood or self-relation as anything other than the "empty I." Seeking the universal self, modern philosophers ended up privileging the arbitrary power of pure subjectivity.

Like a messenger who runs off before hearing the whole message, *Räsonieren* capitalizes on the power of *Verstand* (understanding) without waiting to witness the work of *Vernunft* (reason). And so it mistakenly thinks that the "empty I" is the source and wellspring of all negativity. It mistakenly thinks that thinking is a process that belongs to individual minds and merely serves their personal ends, whatever they may be. Chiefly, it misunderstands negativity as something we intentionally choose (and thus control) rather than as what we *are*. *Räsonieren* remains aloof from its own negativity. It treats thinking as if it were a mere instrument when it is a way of life.

For human beings, thinking is like the water in which a fish swims. It seems absurd for the fish to believe she owns the water, and yet, the water she swims through is always the water that touches only her body. Thinking, as I encounter it, is always my thinking. But it is mine only in that it passes through me. If I attend to it, I can see that just as words call to one another and generate sentences I had no prior conscious intention of writing, thoughts call to one another, summon and dismiss one another. We do not create thinking and its complex internal relationships; we merely present it. We present thinking with the hope that it will call to thoughts in others and that together we can "press on to agreement" in the content itself.

In Hegel's terms, rationalizing thinking involves abstract negation ("no") while speculative or conceptual thinking involves determinate negation ("not this"). Rationalizing thus cannot make any positive use of its skeptical argumentation. To get a new content, it must simply pick it at random because the negation of the previous content was not pregnant with any relations or associations that might lead to a new thought. *Räsonieren* is negative, but it "never gets its own negativity as a content" (W3:57, §59) By contrast, speculative thinking or genuine philosophy refuses to impose subjective preference for this or that argument onto the content. Philosophical thinking demands patient inquiry, not debate.

Hegel's critique of *Räsonieren* is not a critique of argument itself. It is a critique of a certain subjective use of argument. It is a critique of the attitude that we are the *masters* of arguments and can employ them to serve our will.

Misology (§70)

The final paragraphs of the preface foreground a conflict that has been nascent throughout. Hegel opens paragraph 67 noting that "the study of philosophy" is hindered not only by the argumentative *Räsonieren* discussed in §58–60 but also by the refusal to argue that takes "already made truths" for granted (W3:62, §67). Hegel then discusses this misology, the refusal of argument, in two forms: the appeal to common sense and the appeal to genius or inspiration. Both forms misapprehend thinking as a private affair and distrust rational argument precisely because it works toward universal assent. Both attitudes believe themselves to be defending the sanctity of humanity, which they take to reside in private impressions and feelings, against encroachment by a dehumanizing juggernaut called "Reason."

These recent trends in German "philosophy" (advocacy for common sense and genius) mirror long-standing worries in modern philosophy. Among early modern philosophers a similar anxiety was directed toward scholasticism and, by extension, the whole tradition of philosophy up to the seventeenth century. If Aristotle's arguments could keep us from using our own eyes to discover that the earth actually revolved around the sun for over a millennium, what other harms had so-called rational argument worked?

The epistemic attitudes here called "genius" and "common sense" openly espouse that thinking is a personal matter, though in opposite ways. The former insists that only special individuals are gifted with truth or insight (and thus it cannot be taught or demonstrated by argument). The latter insists that common-sense insight is available to everyone but because the true meaning of common-sense platitudes is felt "in the heart," it cannot be communicated by argument. Common sense relies on a pre-established harmony of sentiment. In other words, both attitudes reject the communication and sharing of knowing. They reject *Wissenschaft*, science in the Hegelian sense.

We might think that Hegel's critique of these two positions is merely a historical artifact of his time. At the opening of the nineteenth century, the Scottish common-sense school exerted continued influence in Germany while Romanticism trumpeted genius. Viewed historically, these attitudes opposed one another. Schelling, for example, can be found criticizing common sense while he lobbies for genius. Hegel's insight is that these seemingly opposed attitudes are guilty of the same crime. Insight into their commonality also helps us see that Hegel's concern here is more conceptual than historical. Indeed, the root problem is still with us even if it does not take these exact forms. It is still a constant temptation to view thinking as something private, something that belongs to individuals. Scientistic explanations are regularly given for how each of us has a unique collection of neurons and neural paths and, by extension, a private host of thoughts.

By insisting against this personalism that philosophy must be a science, Hegel advocates for collective knowing, for an account of thinking as a shared activity. This is a fundamental epistemic split. On the one side, we have all those who argue (or refuse to argue) that private meanings are coherent in themselves and thus that all communication is an imperfect, lossy transmission of personal thoughts, percepts, and feelings. On the other side, we have all those who argue that private meaning is incoherent and that shared communication, whatever form it might take, is the condition for the possibility of meaning in the first place. Hegel makes it clear in this preface that he favors the latter view. As he closes the argument against those who will not argue, Hegel appeals to communication, persuasion, or "pressing on to agreement with one another" as the "root of humanity itself" (W3:65, §69). Misology tramples on this root.

Still, Hegel recognizes that we cannot decide this issue in advance. The *Phenomenology* begins with sense certainty so that we can experience the failure of private meaning firsthand. Here in the preface, however, Hegel cannot rely on any shared dialectical experience. All Hegel can do here is offer

The Perils of Genius (§70)

First, Hegel confronts genius or poetic inspiration as a source of knowledge. He does not say much, though what he does say should remind us of his critique of formalism, especially paragraph 53. What genius passes off as "direct revelations from heaven" are in fact arbitrary combinations of images in the "imagination" that lack the "concept" or the organic interrelation of thoughts developed through attention to self-moving content. Hegel notes these monstrous assemblages are "neither poetry nor philosophy"; they are caught in some illegitimate in-between state. The problem with such monsters is that they have no nature, no concept, no inner necessity to express that drives them onward, and thus they can appeal to either philosophy or poetry whenever it suits them. A story has a narrative arc and argument has purposive order. Genius dispenses with both, claiming they limit its freedom of association. But since the genius' product lacks internal logic, we must simply wait for him to add another item to the list. Ultimately, genius is barren and can produce nothing but stillbirths. If the arbitrary sequence of images appeals to us, it is because it flatters some prejudices we already hold and dresses them up in colorful ways.

The organic metaphors of Hegel's preface do a great deal of heavy lifting and can easily seem like cheap polemics: my thinking is living; my opponent's thinking is dead. To look more deeply at the relation between genius and life, we can turn to one of Hegel's Wastebook aphorisms:

> The truth of science is a quiet light, illuminating and joyous to all, like a warmth in which everything sprouts and thrives, [one that allows] inner riches to articulate themselves throughout the whole of life. The *flash of thought* [*Gedankenblitz*] is the Capaneus who imitates this heavenly fire in an inferior and evanescent way, a formal and destructive way, and is incapable of sustaining life. (W2:545)

This aphorism plants a seed for the whole 1807 preface. Here Hegel pits quiet, life-giving *thinking* against flashy individual *thoughts*. He pits philosophy (the fluid activity of thinking) against its doppelgängers (positions of thought).

The contrast Hegel stresses between the truth of science on the one hand and the flash of thought on the other may not be immediately obvious, in part because of his reference to the lesser-known mythological figure, Capaneus. Capaneus, known to us through Aeschylus' *Seven Against Thebes*, is the epitome of human arrogance. Large and strong, he declares that even Zeus cannot stop him from invading the city. Zeus does indeed stop him, killing him with a lightning bolt. Hegel's aphorism contains a pun on this lightning bolt [*Blitz*] that killed Capaneus, and the flash of thought or moment of the genius' inspiration [*Gedankenblitz*].

In this grisly image, inspiration is the temporary illumination that, at the same time, kills or destroys what it illuminates. The flash of thought kills what it illuminates because it fixes in place the ongoing movement of thinking that is its source. The flash of thought puts itself forward as a divine inspiration rather than as a moment in a process of thinking. It cuts itself off from its own genesis. It rejects its roots. It thereby hides the process of thinking from view and denies all others access to its genesis. This sort of "genius" is esoteric, self-centered, and deceptive. By contrast, the truth of science is not a bright light, but a soft glow that suffuses everything with continuous life-giving warmth. True science links results to the processes that bring them about. Often, this process reveals what we already know and simply *reorders it in a way that makes it more generative.* We often prefer genius because it is flashy, exciting, disorienting, and piecemeal: it allows us to ignore the interconnected truths that we prefer not to order into our lives.

Hegel thus puts a distinctive spin on the metaphor of illumination. While Socrates' cave image in Plato's *Republic* contrasts the life-giving sun with the shadow-producing cave fire, Hegel contrasts a life-giving "quiet light" with a destructive lightning bolt that imitates the "heavenly fire." But Hegel never uses the word "sun." The light of the truth of science is not the unapproachably bright light of the sun but a diffuse glow, the sun mediated by a cloudy day. It is not pure unalloyed immediacy that represents truth here but rather the slow revelation of developing, self-mediating illumination. The immediate flash of thought, on the other hand, is unbearably bright. Socrates' image presents the mediation of light by way of fire and shadow as distortion. Hegel, by contrast, considers the immediacy, the unfiltered brightness of the lightning flash of inspiration, as misleading. He favors the fully mediated light and warmth that suffuses every part equally.

This aphorism contrasts the arrogance, evanescence, and lifelessness of individual genius with the broad, continuous, life-giving work of many people for the sake of collective knowing or *Wissenschaft*. The individual's moment of inspiration may be exciting, bright, flashy, but it sustains nothing, feeds nothing, develops nothing. The collective work of science is slow, comparatively dim, and comparatively dull, but in its steady light an idea becomes the property of the whole community not just geniuses with flashes of insight. Each member can grow the idea from its seed because the "code" is open source and not hidden behind a claim divine inspiration.

In philosophy the goal is not to approach the naked truth alone, Icarus-like, but to inquire and converse together. We labor together in the gentle light of *werdendes Wissen*, becoming knowing. Immediate knowing must rely on individual revelation and is therefore fundamentally hostile to the slow-built consensus of developing truth. This reliance on individual revelation is tantamount to rejecting humanity itself, which Hegel locates in "*die Gemeinsamkeit der Bewusstsein*" [the commonality of consciousness] (W3:65, §43).

Romantic Immediatism is a form of heroic individualism and is fated to experience the tragic hero's reversal of fortunes. The revelation of genius, exciting at first, soon misses the mark on account of its own pride. Such personal revelations cannot be joined up with the projects of other consciousnesses except by dominating them.

System and Genius

The reception of Hegel's 1807 preface involves this irony: Hegel's defense of the impersonal has been widely received as a personal attack. One standard interpretation of the preface is that Hegel wrote this preface to criticize his friend Schelling and distance himself from his way of thinking.

As we have seen, the turn toward science, philosophy, and system is a turn away from the personal justifications (and polemics) on offer in prefaces, explanations, and individual propositions. Philosophy turns away from these and toward the general act of thinking itself, the rhythm of thinking that makes human collectivity possible. Hegel argues that such a thinking held in common can only come to know itself through the self-elaboration of thinking, thinking unfolding itself on its own terms. This amounts to losing ourselves in thinking itself which will turn out to be our innermost self, though at first, it feels like we are abandoning the self we know. This means that to raise ourselves to the universality of knowledge, we must, as Hegel says, "lose ourselves in the exposition" (W3:18; §10).

Hegel contrasts this self-discovery through self-loss with the prefatory explanation, which "grasps after an Other yet remains much more preoccupied with itself" (W3:13; §3). Prefaces offer a poignant example of a writing style that seems to make knowledge common or universal, but really does the opposite. Prefaces turn truth into a subjective possession of the author. The universal or general truth of their work is recast in the contingent terms of their personal aims and historical context. This is the ironic reversal of explanation that recurs in "Force and the Understanding." Explanations appear to be about something else, but are really narcissistic affairs.

The view Hegel opposes here can be found in many of his contemporaries. As Schelling puts it in the fifth of the *Philosophical Letters*,

> Every system bears the stamp of individuality on the face of it because no system can be completed otherwise than practically, that is, subjectively. The more closely a philosophy approaches its system, the more essentially freedom and individuality partake of it and the less it can claim universal validity [*Allgemeingültigkeit*].[5]

This, Schelling goes on to say, is why there will always be conflict between multiple opposed systems of dogmatism and criticism and why no system of philosophy will ever be complete.

Hegel might agree that this assertion of subjectivity can indeed be seen in philosophical writings, but to attend to it over the argument is to miss the common activity of thinking that brings us together with each other and with the thinkers of the past. In a lecture on Schelling's philosophy given in 1826, Hegel remarks:

> Since the presupposition of philosophy [for Schelling] is that the subject has an immediate intuition of this identity of the subjective and the objective, philosophy thus appears as an artistic talent or genius in individuals that comes only to "Sunday's children." By its very nature, however, philosophy can become universal, for its soil is thinking, the universal, and that is the very thing that makes us all human.[6]

This recalls us to paragraph 70 in the preface to the *Phenomenology* where Hegel has opposed philosophy as genius with philosophy as the universality of knowledge. For Hegel, a properly immanent philosophical system does not, as Schelling argues, "bear the stamp of individuality." Isolated propositions do, prefaces do, explanations do, but a system is precisely the form of expression that no longer bears the stamp of individuality. Hegel writes:

> A philosophizing *without system* cannot be scientific; insofar as this sort of philosophizing expresses more of a subjective disposition, it is contingent

according to its content. A content has its justification only as a moment of the whole, without this it is an ungrounded presupposition or a subjective assurance. (W8:59–60, Enz §14)

What does this mean, that a content has its justification only as a moment of the whole? A system turns us toward the activity of development itself, not its intermittent results. As adults we differ in many ways but we share a common developmental path of growth in body and soul from infancy to childhood to adolescence to adulthood that points toward a single activity of self-unfolding human being. For example, height may differ from person to person, but that we grow taller and at some point stop, this is something we all share. Hegel is not claiming that all opinions will be shared in some utopia of same-mindedness but rather that the philosophical system aims to make access to knowing universal. Because it begins with what is immediate and proceeds step by step (or negation by negation), Hegel's system demands not talent, not genius, but patience.

The Critic and the Public (§71)

Hegel predicts that his work would be misread and he tells us how. He predicts that the "self-movement of the concept" will be misunderstood. This has proven to be true. Broadly, Hegel's readers often miss the "self-movement" aspect of his recollective, systematic approach. Hegel is not a totalist or a completist thinker, but a developmental thinker. He may seem to be emphasizing that we gather everything up in an encyclopedic manner, but his actual procedure is to gather only what is necessary to catch sight of the stages of development of the content in question so that we can see its principle of self-development, its concept. Hegel is not doing violence to individual positions by highlighting how they are moments or stages in a larger development; he is giving them life. He is connecting them up with a larger, shared activity through a common principle of self-development.

As he closes his preface, Hegel calls out the critics of philosophy books for plying the public with premature judgments of complex works. In order to render a verdict on a new philosophy book for a newspaper or journal, philosophy critics reduce the work of philosophy to a shadow of its true self, committing all the offenses of pseudo-philosophy. Hegel knows the critics will misrepresent his book because it involves the "labor of the concept," an approach that is opposed to summary criticism, that is, the philosophy critic's job. A book review cannot judge a work immanently after years of proper study; it must make a cursory judgment from the outside by comparing it to other recently published works. But this may not be the proper context for the work in question.

This paragraph gives us evidence that Hegel wants his book to be judged against the standard of the long-standing tradition of speculative thought, not the recent fads of German philosophy. The mention of Plato's *Parmenides* and Aristotle's speculative depth are not only acknowledgments of other great works that critics have misunderstood but are works that also involve the "labor of the concept." As Hegel noted in §22, Aristotle's teleological vision, his recognition of nature as purposive, is also a recognition that natural beings are self-moving and self-mediating. What Hegel refers to as "speculative depth" is, in part, the capacity to see, with Aristotle, immanent causes, purposes, sources of self-motion. (The superficial view of nature attends to transitive causes: X causes Y, and Y causes Z. All causes remain outside of each other and thus can purport to "explain" one another without revealing anything essential about each other.) The "labor of the concept" is to philosophy what purposive self-motion is to an animal. To grasp animal life with speculative depth, we consider the immanent purpose to which all its organs and activities are directed (e.g., sexual reproduction). To grasp philosophy with speculative depth, we must likewise grasp its immanent self-moving purpose, the labor of the concept: for thinking to become knowing. Philosophy is "the peculiar mode of thinking . . . by which thinking [denken] becomes knowing [erkennen]" (W8:42, Enz §2). Hegel says of the *Phenomenology*: "This book presents the coming into being of knowing" (W3:593).

Notice that the task of the philosopher is to present thinking *becoming* knowing, not to present knowledge. The critic differs from the philosopher precisely here, because the critic treats books as finished, discrete units of knowledge to be compared and judged, not as participants in an ongoing, living act of thinking. The question for the philosopher is not whether Hegel is "right" about this or that claim but whether the work done in Hegel's book contributes to thinking becoming knowing. Aristotle reminds us that "it is right to feel gratitude not only to those whose opinion one shares, but even those whose pronouncements were more superficial, for they too contributed something, for before us they exercised the energetic habit of thinking" (Met. 993b11–15). Aristotle and Hegel are both often taken to task for how they appropriate and distort the views of their predecessors. They are often seen as not maintaining the appropriate boundaries between the various positions like the critic or academic might. Hegel and Aristotle are accused of turning everything into their position. But what if the point here is precisely that speculative philosophy sees through the discrete individuality of positions and recovers an underlying energetic habit of thought? According to the speculative approach, the history of philosophy is not a series of discrete units or viewpoints but an ongoing habit of thinking. This history is the becoming knowing of thinking.

Thus the critic's chief mistake is to presume that philosophy is the work of individuals and, consequently, that each position can be clearly individuated. The critic reviews a book of philosophy as if it were a book of opinion to be compared and contrasted with other opinions. This leads him to believe he has a grasp on the book only when he is able to identify it as a discrete position. To the critic, one understands Hegel when one can say how he compares and contrasts with Kant. But as philosophers our concern should be to lose ourselves in the content, in the question. For example: "What is triplicity? Does thinking move in threes? Why do we posit contraries in order to then think some third thing that mediates the contraries in some way?" The difference in Kant's use of triplicity (three term thinking) and Hegel's use is of interest not to define the position of each thinker but for the larger task of thinking triplicity itself.

To the critic, Hegel contrasts a general public whose response to a new philosophy book is quite different. Instead of casting premature judgment and blaming the author for anything they do not understand, the general reader assumes it is his own fault when he doesn't understand a book. This is precisely what we should do, so long as it does not discourage us from pressing on and trying, nevertheless, to understand the book. The general reader is still in touch with a human response of genuine perplexity that the critic's role as "expert" has obscured. This perplexity is necessary to pursue philosophical thinking. Unfortunately, the general reader is easily swayed by expert critics who destroy this perplexity by casting judgment. By addressing this problem with critics, Hegel hopes to reach his more open-minded general readers and inoculate them against the critic's summary judgments.

The End of the Preface (§72)

If we look at the final paragraph of the preface, we see that Hegel applies the claim he makes about "humanity" in general to his own case. His goal, he tells us, was merely to take part in the push toward knowledge present around him. Little can be expected of a single individual's efforts, he tells us, because the work of science is collective. We today tend to view the natural sciences this way, as the product of thousands of nameless individuals working in laboratories all around the world. But we tend to view the work of philosophy as taking place in the flashes of brilliance from singular minds. We cultivate myths of genius about Kant or Wittgenstein by talking about strange personal habits. Philosophy then becomes the clash of great personalities and their worldviews. Hegel is telling us that we are getting philosophy all wrong.

Those who interpret Hegel's project as one of titanic personal ambition, as an arrogant bid to complete philosophy once and for all, must be tempted to read this closing self-effacement as false humility. But Hegel's conclusion follows from his arguments so far. Hegel's own book is just a small contribution to the much greater work of philosophy as a whole precisely because it explicitly relies on those works and incorporates them. Hegel argues that his work involves the transgenerational effort of knowing to know itself. It is important to notice that this vital difference would be difficult to discern from the outset and could only become clear as we experience the system itself and see whether it effectively incorporates other efforts or not.

Hegel has a reputation for overweening arrogance. After all, he was impudent enough to think he could tell the whole story of philosophy in a single system of science. But we can look at this from the opposite direction: Hegel claims to do nothing more than bring together the thinking of others. Hegel's individual contribution (if we must talk this way) is to locate the ground on which the great conversation of the history of philosophy could be *presented* as one whole. And this groundless ground, we know by now, he calls "negativity." But Hegel did not invent negativity. He just reminds us of how pervasive it is. Hegel is asking his critics to read his work as a contribution to philosophy rather than as a creation of a new philosophy. His preface has, from start to finish, demanded we look toward the continuity of philosophy as a single activity.

Hegel's self-effacing admission comes right after he has lamented what he expects to be a poor reception for his book in the previous paragraph. What he reminds his would-be critic is that his book is only one skein in the tapestry of philosophy and cannot be expected to carry out the entirety of that work alone. Hegel invokes the centuries of misreading that Plato's *Parmenides* and Aristotle's more difficult works have endured, reminding us that a bad reception is not the end of the road for a book of philosophy.

The final paragraph is not, then, a throwaway paragraph or a merely rhetorical bid for the reader's sympathy. Hegel lets us know that he applies what he has been saying about "forgetting oneself in the *Sache*" to himself, to his own case, to this book. From Bacon to Kant, modern philosophers are keen to announce the novelty of their projects. Hegel, however, does the opposite. He does suggest he is writing in a pregnant moment, a "birth time," but he does not consider himself the catalyst of this renewal; he is only a participant (W3:18, §11). Each of the negations we have studied in the preface lead to and support the self-effacement of the final paragraph. In the preface's closing moment, Hegel insists: listen not to me, but to the *Logos*.

Conclusion

Notes toward Negation

Where everything that meets the eye,
Flowers and grass and cloudless sky,
Resemble forms that are or seem
When sleepers wake and yet still dream.

—W. B. Yeats, "Under Ben Bulben"

The Preface as Negation

I have foregrounded the substantive negations that take place in the 1807 preface. Philosophy is not explanation. Philosophy is not edification. Philosophy is not formalism. Philosophy is not phenomenology. Philosophy is not mathematical. Philosophy is not propositional. Philosophy is not personal.

I recognize that there is a good reason why other commentators have chosen to focus on the positive claims found in the preface. The preface is loaded with helpful clues about Hegel's system of science. These clues account for much of the preface's content. Yet I maintain that the status of these clues is strictly promissory. They need to be followed up with demonstrations that do not take place in the 1807 preface itself. The only adequate demonstration for most of them is the entire system of science taken as a whole. This makes them difficult claims to exposit and assess. If we like the sound of these claims, perhaps this is an encouragement to read the *Encyclopedia*. Even so, it is much more reliable to proceed into the system of science with a genuine interest in the questions and contents of philosophy rather than an interest in what Hegel thinks. As I have tried to show, the preface is not just a series of bold promises. It is also a collection of circumspect warnings. It warns us away from many bad habits that thinkers can easily fall into as they pursue philosophy. Admittedly, one might want still more of an argument as to why philosophers should not explain, edify, formalize, phenomenologize, mathematize, propositionalize, or personalize than Hegel offers. My efforts in this book have been directed at bringing out as much of the argument as I can from the textual basis provided. If we do not expend some effort, these warnings can become fine print that we fly past on the way to a more meaty paragraph about what Hegel "really" thinks. I myself began to take these warnings more seriously when I noticed many of the bad habits of pseudo-philosophy that Hegel describes are still with us.

Patience and Negation

Hegel's books are famously difficult. In large part, this is because Hegel's presentation of philosophy emphasizes the work of negation or negativity. As negative theology approaches the description of God by way of negations (God is not a body, God is not temporal, etc.), Hegel approaches the knowledge of the activity of knowing by way of negations (knowing is not this known, not this way of knowing, etc.). Negation itself is not new to philosophy but Hegel develops its role in thinking beyond any previous use. To grasp the truth in negations is to grasp it indirectly. This relentless indirection makes Hegel's books both longer and more confusing than most, if not all, other books in the already challenging philosophical canon.

The choice to foreground negativity impacts every aspect of Hegel's philosophical style, even its most basic parts. Hegel's central vocabulary—composed of common German words like *Geist* (spirit), *Begriff* (concept), *Denken* (thinking), and *Wissenschaft* (science)—remains difficult to define even after two centuries of scholarship because Hegel uses words in evolving ways as each book progresses and the negations pile up. In lieu of defining Geist, Hegel offers the *Encyclopedia*'s philosophy of Geist, a dense tour of human self-expression lasting hundreds of pages (and covering thousands of years). To grasp the proper range of *Begriff*, we read the whole third section of the *Science of Logic* (again, hundreds of pages). Hegel works hard to express the full range of a concept, foiling any attempt to use a narrow range of the concept's meaning in a tidy definition. Hegel's books do not offer clear definitions and fixed categories; instead, they attempt to describe movements, dynamic happenings, by negating the fixed stopping points we ordinarily use as atomic units of meaning.

Hegel's books change our sense of the pace of thinking. In place of clear, efficient arguments beginning from a few (presumptuous) axioms, we learn the "patience and hard work of the negative" (W3:24, §23). Once enough negations are gathered, the reader should find that she cannot return to the naive views she held opposed before undertaking this slow work of negation. The sign of success will be a new inability rather than a new power, namely, the inability to hold naive or reductive views. This may leave the reader with no view at all, no easily communicated, determinate position. This will often feel like a loss. Yet Hegel's books should also give the reader sufficient experience with the limitations of this sort of thinking so that she is glad to be rid of it. Hegel teaches us that philosophy is not about holding and defending positions but about the effort of thinking itself as it moves *through* positions.

This makes Hegel's project sound skeptical. How can this be, when, as Hegel himself says, his goal is to present a scientific system of philosophy? Is there a goal more positive (and less skeptical) than that? Here we can see the difficulty of interpreting Hegel in a nutshell: he is simultaneously one of the most skeptical and one of the most optimistic thinkers in the tradition. No single view should satisfy us and in this sense Hegel's work is profoundly skeptical and negative. At the same time, close study of all the relevant unsatisfying views should reveal the pattern, rhythm, or grammar of thinking itself, the power that flows through all the views like light suffuses a room without being bound to it or exhausted by it. The system is therefore not a large edifice constructed out of dozens of interlocking views; *it is the study of the power that animates these views*. In Hegel's system, we study not the static outcomes but the originating acts of human thinking. In other words, Hegel's thinking is negative with regard to determinate entities and positive with regard to fluid activities. Hegel's negations always reveal something positive. They do not leave us indifferent and unattached as strictly skeptical methods do. Rather, they give us a taste of the dynamic self-limiting process through which our limited and limiting views are formed and dissolved. A finite content, once negated carefully and determinately, reveals not a formless abyss but a formative activity.

Learning to recognize meaning as a dynamic process through the indirect path of negation takes practice and patience, but it is worth the effort because more direct approaches inevitably distort philosophy's rich content. The central contents of philosophy are unsuited to direct definition, as we discover early on in the Platonic dialogues. We cannot give a simple or clear answer to questions like "what is virtue?"or "what is being?" or "what is motion?" or "what is life?" or "what is thinking" or "what is the good?" or "what is philosophy?" These subjects are themselves dynamic and contain multitudes. Our task, then, is to inquire into them in such a way that this dynamism and these multitudes are not prematurely closed off.

Hegel proposes that articulation by means of determinate negations is the only possible approach that, precisely because it is slow and indirect, will not cut off the inquiry before it can gather into itself all the relevant considerations. Hegel's difficult writing sustains the perplexity of thinking-on-the-move. It allows us to feel the growing pains of a gradually deepening comprehension. Hegel's works are not massive, preplanned dogmatic structures but self-prolonging inquiries into how the same fundamental activity expresses itself through a wide variety of forms. Because we have no direct access to the pure activity, we must suffer its many forms in order to know it. If Hegel's prose seems contorted, dizzying, and strange, it may help to remember how many prejudices lurk in more familiar modes of expression. This is the chief lesson of the 1807 preface. Many of the methods we associate with philosophy rush ahead and pigeonhole contents before their full range of movement has been expressed. Negativity offers the slow and steady path that allows meaning to show itself.

Writing and Negation

It is worth noting that the problems Hegel discusses with prefatory writing relate to a more general problem of writing in the philosophical tradition. Hegel's prefaces, especially his first (1807) and last (1831), locate several reasons why it is difficult (if not impossible) to write philosophical thinking down in a book.

In addressing these obstacles, Hegel is participating in a long-standing tradition that goes back to Socrates. Plato's Socrates notes that an argument, once written down, "can neither defend itself nor come to its own aid" (*Phaedrus* 275e). The finality of the page misrepresents the fluid, living, plastic, exploratory nature of thinking as genuine inquiry. Aristotle's tone in his writings or lectures is routinely exploratory and open-ended, yet he is remembered as a great dogmatist, offering final verdicts on all manner of things. I would contend this is largely because his words appear to us in the form of fixed, printed books. Plato attempted to guard against such dogmatic finality through the extreme measure of writing only in the dialogue form and never speaking in his own voice and yet he is mostly remembered as a great dogmatist with a theory of forms and many other set opinions. Philosophers are often remembered for momentary conclusions they reached rather than the general spirit in which they worked.

Hegel is reputed to be an arch-dogmatist with the most infamously complete system in the history of philosophy. And yet, Hegel never finished a written exposition of the system. His *Encyclopedia* offers only an outline intended to be filled out by oral lectures to be given by Hegel himself. This allowed Hegel to continually revise or amend the written word through his live performance. In lecture he could nuance, retract, or amplify what he had written. While this is often viewed as an accident of circumstance, it dovetails suspiciously well with Socrates' concern that a written text cannot defend itself. Hegel's prefaces give ample evidence that he felt he was frequently misread. Whether intentionally or unintentionally, Hegel resisted finishing the written expression for a system of science.

Hegel worked in the outline-lecture hybrid until his death. Following his death, the system, composed as it was of written text and lecture, must be considered incomplete as it lacks an ongoing oral commentary from its author. Even with the inclusion of the *Zusätze* from student notes taken at the oral lectures, we are still dealing with an incomplete presentation. The *Zusätze* fix in place some comments made at one time or other and turn the living event of the lecture into yet another fixed text.

And yet, commentary on Hegel's system has not ceased. If, as Hegel has it in §72, the work of philosophy is not undertaken by individual geniuses but rather by discursive communities, then our latter-day commentary is not necessarily inferior to the commentary provided by the man himself. The texts are not philosophy, our ongoing thinking is.

The living work of thinking escapes the page. The awkward situation in which readers of philosophy thus find themselves can only be remedied by self-aware reading. The reader must struggle to restore the flexibility to concepts and relations that become rigid in their textual form. As Hegel notes, a "plastic discourse" requires a "plastic sense of apprehension and understanding."[1] Hegel goes on to worry that in the modern era we come to philosophical discourses already too invested in our own particular projects, and this hinders our ability to take philosophical writings up in a disinterested, exploratory spirit.

Hegel had hoped that dialectical presentation alone would secure this fluidity, openness, or plasticity, much as Plato might have hoped the dialogue form might spare him from the textual defenselessness Socrates underscored. Hegel found, however, that his work was received as if it had been written nondialectically (i.e., as a series of fixed claims.) The necessity of the movement of thinking was interpreted as the rigidity of a supposedly Hegelian Weltanschauung. Hegel tried to address this problem in his prefaces to limited success. Even the prefaces were interpreted as efforts to elaborate a Hegelian point of view, when their arguments point toward a need to overcome the very premise that philosophy is composed out of points of view.

As he notes in §60, what the reader is experiencing as a restriction (imputed to the "totalizing" Hegelian system) is not the fixity of the content but the absence of personal license or subjective caprice. When an author gives us a determinate or fixed view, we can experience our own freedom in negating it. If we can pigeonhole the author, we can liberate ourselves. Yet the freedom we gain is as empty and abstract as the rejection. Because Hegel aims to account for thinking as such, we find ourselves *within* this description of thinking rather than *against* it. Within Hegel's texts, we lose the capacity to fix the author's position and thus lose our own feeling of freedom to reject it. We cannot accept or reject what we cannot locate. We then experience this as being "trapped" in Hegel's position when we are in fact experiencing freedom from all fixed positions.

A more profound sense of freedom is found in sympathetic reading, not sympathy with an author as an individual but sympathy with the content of thinking itself, losing ourselves in the *Sache selbst*. This is the great reversal of thinking Hegel saw, a parallel to the great inversion of Christianity by which the first shall be last and the last shall be first: only by giving up our freedom to think whatever we want and submitting to the necessary movement of the content of thought do we win the true freedom of thinking itself.

Hegel's books foreground determinate negation because this is how thinking frees itself from fixity to become a pure activity of self-relation. What Hegel's books attempt to present is not our desires for the forms of thought but their own desires, drives, or natures. We should remember that Kant insisted on precisely the opposite procedure; he insisted that we should maintain tight personal control over the philosophical process, and we must constrain nature to answer questions of our devising, as a judge would do with a witness (CPR B xiii). By contrast, Hegel is asking us to let thinking flow, as a psychoanalyst would let an analysand free associate. Hegel, like the psychoanalyst, believes there is an underlying logic to the flow of thinking that will only reveal itself to us with wide exploration and patient recollection (W5:26). This is why his books are so long and torturous and why the interpretation of them should not aim to save us time but to remind us why the time is well spent.

Appendix
Hegel's 1807 Preface, Summary by Paragraph

In his own table of contents, Hegel divides the massive preface into the following eighteen sections:

Preface: On Scientific Knowing

   I. The element of the true is the concept and its true shape is scientific system: §5–6
  II. The current standpoint of spirit: §7–11
 III. The principle is not the completion, objections to formalism: §12–16
  IV. The absolute is Subject: §17
   V. What this [Subject] is: §18–25
  VI. The element of knowing: §26
 VII. The elevation of consciousness into that element is the Phenomenology of Spirit: §27–29
VIII. The transformation of the imagined and familiar into thoughts: §30–33
  IX. The transformation of thoughts into the concept: §34–36
   X. The degree to which the Phen. of Spirit is negative or contains the false: §37–39
  XI. Historical and mathematical truth: §40–46
 XII. The nature of philosophical truth and its method: §47–49
XIII. Against schematizing formalism: §50–56
 XIV. The demands of a study of Philosophy: §57–58
  XV. Argumentative thinking in its negative attitude: §59
 XVI. Argumentative thinking in its positive attitude, its subject §60–66
XVII. Natural philosophizing as common sense and as genius §67–69
XVIII. Conclusion, the relationship of an author to the public: §70–72

Note that in paragraph 16 of the 1807 Preface, Hegel begrudgingly acknowledges the "usefulness" of a "rough picture" of his way of presenting philosophy, aided by remarks about those views that "obstruct" access to the presentation. Sections I, IV–X, XII, and XIV deal with this "rough picture" of philosophy, while sections

II, III, and XI, XIII and XV–XVIII deal with "forms of thought" that obstruct philosophical knowing: formalism (III and XIII), history and mathematics (XI), argumentative thinking [*Räsonieren*] (XV–XVI), and finally, common sense and poetic genius (XVII). According to Hegel's own way of breaking down the preface, he weaves back and forth between the "rough picture" of philosophy and the obstructions to it.

Preface: On Scientific Knowing

1. Prefaces. Prefaces explain only the general aims and results of the books they preface. This seems like a promising short-cut to the truth, since a statement of aims might seem to offer the universals that include all the particulars of the exposition. But if the truth of a result follows from the process by which it came about, it cannot be given apart from that process.
2. Prefaces. Another problem: prefaces emphasize the differences between philosophical works rather than the continuity of the whole philosophical tradition. Prefatory summaries invite us to think about philosophy as if it consisted of discrete positions to accept or reject. But these so-called positions are only moments in a single developmental process we call philosophy.[1]
3. Prefaces. Looking at their aims and results only, it is easy to take a bird's eye view and separate philosophical positions from each other and judge them. One should, however, lose oneself in each view, yielding to the movement that works through all philosophical viewpoints (i.e., thinking).
4. Education. *Bildung* [education/formation/cultivation] begins by transforming substantial life into thought. Reminder to empiricists: education must begin with the general idea, then apprehend concrete differences within it (the particular), then pass judgment about their relation.[2] Reminder to idealists: a speculative grasp of life as a whole must include the experience of life in its various particular and empirical forms.[3] Development involves the reciprocal mediation of universal and particular.

I. The Element of the True Is the Concept and Its True Shape Is Scientific System

5. Science. The natural impulse of knowing [*Wissen*] is to become comprehensive, collective knowing, that is, science [*Wissenschaft*]. To

know even just one thing will require a presentation of the whole (a system of science). True science unites two sources of justification: an intrinsic source derived from the nature of knowing itself and an extrinsic source derived from a study the shapes knowing has taken. We can show (in this preface) that now is an opportune time to account for knowing as a whole.

6. Concept. The truth of any content is found only in the study of that content's activity of self-development, that is, the concept [*Begriff*] (see §34). This goes against the prevailing conviction that the element of truth is not the complex stages of self-development but something simple and immediate like intuition, feeling, faith, or poetic inspiration.

II. The Current Standpoint of Spirit

7. The current standpoint. We have already passed through and beyond all the ways of grounding knowledge: in pure thought, in faith, in reconciliation with God, and in self-reflection. These four stages can be correlated with classical Greek thinking, Judaic thinking, Christian thinking, and modern European thinking. In the wake of the Enlightenment, conscious of the failure to ground knowledge once and for all, we turn away from the step-by-step development of thinking and search for an immediate intuition. In this troubled state, we view philosophy as palliative edification, not healing truth.

8. The current standpoint. Immediate knowing turns against empiricism and common sense, demanding we turn from practical business toward an intuition of the infinite. This imperative reminds us of the spiritual focus of medieval culture, but without the rich content.[4] The modern, practical, empirical mindset has been so successful in replacing the spiritual that the romantic's call for a return to an empty, bare feeling of spirituality is still perceived as a gain.

9. Edification. If philosophy aims only to be edifying, it will flatter whatever prejudices are ascendent, be they empirical or spiritual. But philosophy should be science, that is, patient and comprehensive knowing according to immanent necessity.

10. Superficial depth. As knowers, we are not satisfied by the epistemic extremism that lists between the purely practical (empty breadth) and the purely spiritual (empty depth). Immediate knowing associates system, science, and concept with the empirical/finite/determinate and accuses

systematic philosophy of being superficial. But intensity without content (immediate knowing) is no less superficial than an indifferent sum of finite differences (empiricism). Superficiality arises from a refusal to fully engage with and be transformed by what one studies.

11. The current standpoint. The decline of culture into frivolity and boredom is not simply negative (see §7); it is also a sign of gestation and rebirth.

III. The Principle Is Not the Completion, Objections to Formalism:

12. Concept v. system. We have the *concept* of science but not the full presentation of a *system* of science. We have the potential for, but not the full activity of, science. Formalism mistakes the potency for the actuality. The concept is the principle of self-movement, but not the actualized, whole cycle of self-movement returned to itself (i.e., system).

13. Elitism v. universal access. Immediate knowing offers the whole development of thinking "veiled in its simplicity." The past moments are still present in memory but have not been connected up and thought through as a whole. This means that knowledge at present is "esoteric" not "exoteric." To allow universal accessibility, the simple immediacy must mediate itself.

14. Empiricism v. immediate knowing. We are caught between incomplete but articulate empirical sciences and complete but inarticulate immediate knowing. Immediate knowing seems to have the upper hand (in relation to truth, which is the whole) and invites us to give up articulate, discursive science altogether. Yet it would be premature to give up science as such just because our empirical sciences are narrow and incomplete.

15. On formalism. As formalism, immediate knowing offers a single formula that can string together all the results that the empirical sciences have discovered in diverse ways. A pseudo-system is thus produced through the mechanical repetition of a formula externally applied to contents already discovered by other sciences. For formalism, the means of discovery and of organization are not the same. By contrast, a true system is produced organically by allowing content to change itself internally, producing the whole out of itself.

16. Formalism v. system. Though immediate knowing condemns formalism, it winds up touting an abstract universality that it applies as a formula, the so-called "principle of identity" or "A = A." All content is swallowed up by this undifferentiated or abstract version of the absolute. Formalism will

reappear in philosophy again and again until we have a system of science, a system that takes us through a *self-developing* whole. Hegel now tells us that he will sketch a rough picture of his book and also draw attention to ways of thinking that are obstacles to grasping it. These two tasks direct the rest of the preface.

IV. The Absolute Is Subject

17. Substance and subject. We can distinguish true, speculative science from three other views: (1) prioritizing abstract substance (e.g., Spinoza), (2) prioritizing abstract subject (e.g., Kant), and (3) prioritizing the abstract intellectual intuition of their union (e.g., Schelling). Position 1 can make no transition from being to thinking (usually because it reduces thinking to being and denies the freedom of thinking (e.g., materialism). Position 2 can make no transition from thinking to being (usually because it holds that thinking is free and being/nature is determined (e.g., dualism). While intellectual intuition (position 3) claims to solve this problem of transition, it can only assert the abstract or indeterminate union of substance and subject; it cannot develop this since the very premise of an immediate intellectual intuition forbids mediation and development. This cannot work because all human knowledge is mediated. With the failure of position 3, we realize we need a concrete account of how substance and subject interact and develop. In this account, non-self-relating being (substance) will be grasped and expressed as self-relating being or selfhood (Subject).

V. What This [Subject] Is

18. Negativity. To be anything at all is to become oneself by means of self-othering (negativity). This paragraph features a dense barrage of speculative content aimed at revealing truth (both for being and for thinking) as self-relation through negation. All the sentences together form a compound chain of speculative propositions: living substance = being = subject = movement of self-positing = mediation of becoming-other with itself = pure simple negativity = division of the simple = oppositional doubling = negation of indifferent difference and its opposite = self-restoring sameness = reflection of being-other into

itself = the circular movement whereby something becomes itself. We must grasp "substance" (being) as "subject" (self-relation) as "negativity" (self-othering). Hegel compares this to a circle because a circle comes back to itself only by going away from itself.[5]

19. The life of God. God is not just pure, removed self-contemplation. God lives in and through creating life. The restless movement of life demands *expression* through self-alienation and return to self. God lives in the hard work of self-othering or the negative. Even God requires mediation or rather *is* by self-mediating. This suggests a new way of thinking about mediation.

20. Mediation. The absolute is result or end but the result, properly grasped, is all the developmental work that made the result come about (i.e., mediations). Words taken alone without experience do not count as knowledge. The absolute is self-mediating rather than immediate.

21. Mediation by the self. Those that reject mediation in philosophy do not grasp it properly. True mediation is not an adulteration of some pure truth by something foreign to it but the self-unfolding development we witness so clearly in living things. The purpose of the human embryo is to become a reasoning adult. The otherness of these two contents, the embryo (being/matter) and reason (thinking/mind), is overcome through the self-mediation of the content itself (the activity of being human).

22. Reason is purposive activity. Philosophers (e.g., the British empiricists) have recently raised the study of purposeless, mechanical nature over the study of thinking (treated as mere subjective psychology) and discredited the study of purposes in nature altogether. But just as mediation is self-mediation, purpose names the activity of each self toward itself. Thus what Hegel means by "subject" is what Aristotle meant by identifying "nature" with "purposive activity." Purposes highlight activity, unrest, self-overcoming not tranquil or static essences.

23. The limits of propositions. The proposition "God is eternal" seems to make a transition from substance to subject, or to give content to the absolute. The proposition seems to unfold a substantial content (eternal) from a subject (God), but it does not. The subject "God" is taken as a fixed point to which the predicate "eternal" is attached *by the speaker*. The holding together of "God" and "eternal" is not taking place within the concept of God itself but in the mind of the speaker who

merely anticipates and asserts the connection. Worse still, because the proposition assumes the subject as fixed, it can prevent us from seeing the subject in and as movement.

24. The need for system. A proposition, taken alone, is only a principle, true in some respects, false in others. A principle is only a beginning. The principle is refuted not by offering a new counter-principle out of the blue but by developing the original principle into another related principle. This movement is both negative (with respect to the first principle) and positive (with respect to the second). In one way, a single principle can be seen as a beginning or source. But in another way, the principle, taken alone, is not the source of anything without the movement of negation and development which is the true source of the system.

25. Geist. That we need a system to express the true (not just a proposition) indicates that the true requires a comprehensive knowledge that includes both the knower and the known in an exposition of knowing as activity. The system of science is not only a study of "human being" (Geist as for-itself) nor only of "the I" (Geist as in-itself) but is a study of all the major shapes and deeds of thinking (Geist as in-and-for-itself).[6] The aim of science is to present Geist, but to present Geist is to become Geist (because Geist is self-knowing knowing).

VI. The Element of Knowing

26. Thinking.[7] Thinking is the element of Geist, its "soil." Thinking is the activity by which we recognize ourselves in what is other. Thinking through something involves making it one's own, finding oneself in it and it within oneself. Thinking is being that is reflected into itself. Philosophy requires that we already dwell comfortably in and are aware of ourselves as thinking (not just as perceiving or imagining). But thinking only perfects itself by doing philosophy, that is, through self-aware thinking for its own sake. Many people think without being aware that they think, without thinking about thinking. One therefore has a right to demand proof that our human essence or nature is thinking. The *Phenomenology of Spirit* provides the "ladder" to this standpoint, that is, to philosophy. Thinking exists first as immediate certainty which opposes itself to its object and this must be transformed gradually into self-aware knowing.

VII. The Elevation of Consciousness into That Element Is the Phen. of Spirit

27. Phenomenology. The *Phenomenology of Spirit* describes the coming-to-be of science/philosophy, not its foundation. It shows how thinking about thinking (Geist/spirit) develops by degrees out of phenomenal absorption or natural consciousness or modes of knowing that privilege immediacy/sensation/imagination over dynamic, relational thinking.
28. Education. The *Phenomenology* is not about the *Bildung* [formative education or cultivation] of single individuals but about the universal process of *Bildung* itself. A modern individual must pass through ancient and medieval learning on her way to grasping modern developments, but these past studies will have the status of exercises. They involve a survey of already acquired possessions and are not treated as living pursuits. Yet from a philosophical point of view, the past moments are still living; they are constitutive aspects of a single activity: the self-becoming of thinking. Because the *Phenomenology* is about universal not particular *Bildung*, it will not be experienced as a book of historical exercises, but as an active self-reckoning of thinking with itself.
29. Education. To grasp what thinking is, we must go through the whole course of its development out of its immediate absorption in sensory consciousness. Each shape of consciousness along the way is a complete way of viewing the world and we should immerse ourselves in it. We moderns are able to know knowing not just because there are records of the past but because all the past moments are present implicitly in the present moment and can be unfolded from it and toward it. Knowing is not learning anew but recollecting.

VIII. The Transformation of the Imagined and Familiar into Thoughts

30. Recollection. We are in a position to recollect our whole intellectual development now because we have "sublated existence." We are no longer actively engaged in the struggle to rise out of our particular existence and become thinking beings—this has been accomplished. The rise of immediate knowing is the sign of this accomplishment. Ethical thoughts that took centuries to cultivate now appear in one's conscience as an immediate certainty. Immediate knowing has absorbed (but not recollected upon) the stages of development by which sensuous

consciousness becomes rational thinking. The task of a system of science, then, is to present, unpack, work through, and make explicit that development so that we do not just assume that we are thinking but can demonstrate ourselves as thinking by thinking through the coming into being of thinking itself.

31. Familiarity as the chief obstacle to speculative thinking. Many common "philosophical" terms have become familiar and thus we have stopped dynamically thinking through them when we use them: subject/object, God/nature, understanding/sensation. These pairs form fixed poles and we move back and forth between them superficially, accomplishing nothing because we have assumed already what we need to prove, namely that there is a real distinction between subject and object, or God and nature, or understanding and sensation. As long as we remain with familiar jargon and the prejudices they bring with them, the only measure of truth is majority agreement.

32. Understanding, part I: analysis. Thinking, in the mode of understanding, proceeds by analysis. Analysis takes a familiar, concrete representation (e.g., a sense object) and breaks it up into thinkable parts. These divided-up parts are thoughts [*Gedanken*], not representations [*Vorstellungen*]. These intelligible parts, thoughts, are non-actual [*unwirklich*] and not concrete and do not correspond to any specific objects of experience (as representations do). Nevertheless they are an essential moment of the whole. Why? Because it is only by dividing itself within itself that something concrete can move itself (as opposed to being moved or carried along by something else). Inner division is a condition for self-motion. Thus all concrete self-moving things must contain the non-actual, temporary divisions or differences that are not real or permanent differences. Likewise, understanding's analytic divisions into non-actual parts make the self-movement of thinking possible. The understanding's power to hold fast to these parts as if they were independent and real, even though they are temporary and non-actual, is the motor of thinking, "the monstrous power of the negative." The original whole is still present, as a negative trace, in every abstraction or internal division made by the understanding. By finding the negative wholeness presupposed by the negative analysis, we recover life in death, or actuality in non-actuality, or concrete wholeness in abstract parts.

33. Contrasting ancient and modern education. Ancient philosophy transformed every aspect of concrete existence available as a sensuous

representation into something abstract and thinkable (e.g., Socrates' hunt for the form or *Eidos* of each sort of thing). Thinking recognized itself in these universals in a way it could not recognize itself in the more familiar existences and representations. In modern times, however, the familiar is not the sensuous representation but the abstract universals produced through reflection. Moderns are raised on the abstract categories of natural science, business, law, religion, and philosophy. Accordingly, modern education must be directed *against* these abstractions of the understanding and toward concepts, grasping not the abstract category but the self-moving activity from which the category is abstracted. This means that the fixed categories of many already discovered arts and sciences must be made fluid again, put into question again. If we attend to the process of discovery as well as the result, we will grasp the self-moving selfhood of thinking and grasp the activity itself, not just its abstract products. What we have then are not fixed abstract universals but "spiritually essential ways of being" [*geistige Wesenheiten*].

IX. The Transformation of Thoughts into the Concept

34. From contingent thought to necessary concept. Philosophy is often practiced in a casual way. It begins from some fixed distinction and proceeds to relate it to some other fixed distinctions. By contrast, the nature of science is to find what is self-moving, that is, the concept. We seek what moves itself, breaking through the fixed distinctions to a developmental activity.
35. The limited scope of this book. The *Phenomenology of Spirit* is a science of consciousness, spirit's first shape. It is not the science of spirit in its totality. A phenomenology follows the whole range of movements from immediate consciousness to the self-aware thinking that finally recognizes the need for a system of science or a comprehensive expression of its total range and power as logic, nature, and spirit (i.e., thinking, living, and acting).
36. Consciousness. Consciousness is the first stage of awareness. Consciousness contains two moments: knowing and its negative, the known, or objectness. These two moments appear as opposed in every shape consciousness takes because it cannot yet see how they are two sides of a single activity. Experience is the movement by which consciousness becomes other to itself and returns to

itself. A phenomenology depicts a wild ride, a series of shapes and transformations that are often surprising because they happen to consciousness without its anticipating them.

X. The Degree to Which the Phenomenology of Spirit Is Negative or Contains the False

37. From phenomenology to logic. By pitting a fictitious pure ego against a fictitious pure object, consciousness strives for clarity concerning an opposition that does not exist. The truth of consciousness is not found in either knower or known, but in the disparity between these two or in the *act* of distinguishing something. Actual consciousness is the negation of both the fantasy of a pure subject and the fantasy of a pure object. Both fantasies are dispelled any time something is known because these supposedly separate powers (thinking and being) are always found together in experience. Ancient Atomists were right that the negative is a moving principle but wrong that the negative must be a void. Consciousness persists through various shapes until it can see that the negation of pure ego and pure object is its own doing, not the doing of some power outside it. The concept is "self-like" and beings and thoughts are both moments of selfhood. When consciousness grasps this, it transitions from phenomenology, the study of appearance, into logic, the study of thinking.
38. Why study the false? If a phenomenology or study of experience presents only the way spirit appears from outside, not its inner truth, why bother with it? Why not skip to a study of logic which better describes what spirit actually is, that is, self-aware thinking? In skipping consciousness we would skip the false. The false is valuable but this value is difficult to appreciate if one's thinking is influenced by the error-averse standards of mathematics. As a result, we should address the various views that discourage engagement with the false.
39. True and false. We take "true" and "false" as exclusive terms, as if we could take up one and avoid the other. This distinction true/false is better grasped as "self" and "other." The true is the substance or self; the false is the negation or other. But a living self changes to remain itself; it is by nature negative and self-othering. There is nothing purely false (wholly other) and nothing purely true (wholly without otherness). Our goal is not the unity of true/false, thinking/being, subject/object, infinite/finite

but the collapse of these fixed distinctions, which reveals a fluid self-relating movement.

XI. Historical and Mathematical Truth

40. Dogmatism. Now that we have seen the problem with maintaining a fixed truth separated off from falsehood, we can define "dogmatism" as the belief in this illusion of fixed truth. The preferred medium of dogmatism is the proposition (cf. §23). Propositions can be used to state particulars or tautologies (i.e., historical or mathematical "truths"), but they cannot encompass philosophical or speculative truths (cf. §61–62).
41. Historical truth. Even simple historical particulars like the year of Caesar's birth are meaningless without having some reasons for knowing it. These reasons cannot be known in the same propositional way and will require knowing more than historical facts.
42. Mathematical truth. Just as with historical truth, to know a mathematical result one must know the reasons for the result. If someone has simply memorized a proof, this does not count as mathematical reasoning because this person does not know the reasons for each step. Further, even if one does know the reasons for each step, in mathematics the steps are not essential to the result. Many different proofs could be given for the same result and this does not impact the result. This means that the movement of mathematical proof does not belong to the content itself but to the knower, the person doing the proof. Mathematical knowing is not concerned with essence (e.g., with the question "what is triangle?") but rather with abstract existences, the properties of this right triangle or that obtuse triangle. Philosophical knowing is (or should be) different; it concerns *both* existence and essence. Philosophical knowing treats essence and existence as two sides of a single movement.
43. The limitations of mathematics. Mathematical knowing also makes use of negation/falsehood. However, in mathematical knowing, the procedure is analytic and is not initiated by the mathematical object itself. In geometry, for example, *we* take a triangle apart (it does not sunder itself) and *we* consider its angles independently in a series of different figures. Still, even mathematics, which seems so much about strictly positive truth, makes use of the false and the negative; it divides figures into parts to analyze them.

44. The limitations of mathematics. Mathematical construction is arbitrary. Mathematics makes use of constructions in order to carry out its proofs. There is no reason why we should construct a figure of this sort rather than that sort, if both can serve to highlight the same point. We are given no justification or reasoning for the construction, but simply told to draw it. The value of the construction is only apparent after the proof is finished and we can look back and see why we needed it (e.g., why we needed to draw a parallelogram or inscribe a triangle in a circle).

45. The limitations of mathematics. The purpose of mathematical knowing is to describe magnitude, the indifferent amount of space or number. Both materials through which magnitude is expressed are non-actual abstractions. The actual world we sense (and think) is neither abstractly spatial nor numbered. Mathematics is a kind of formalism. Formalism progresses by establishing superficial equalities and cannot grasp life or self-movement. As a result the material or content generates nothing out of itself and we cannot follow its development; we must force it to change by manipulating it in some way. For this reason, mathematical knowing cannot grasp constitutive infinity (i.e., life, self-movement, thinking).

46. The limitations of mathematics. Pure mathematics considers only space, not time. Applied mathematics (physics) deals with time, but derives its understanding of time empirically, by observing sense objects in motion. The physicist does not consider the way in which time and space are actually conditions for any empirical intuition at all and thus cannot be derived from intuitions. The various laws of force (those governing free fall, equilibrium, gravitation, magnetism, electricity, etc.) are empirically derived but treated as if they were derived from the nature of space and time. Grasped philosophically, time is the "existence" of the concept; it is the way negativity expresses itself to intuition as constant differentiation, unrest, and change. The nature of time is becoming always another and another now (self-othering). In mathematics, however, this self-othering difference inherent to time (the now) is reduced to the indifferent, external unit, the point. This degrades self-motion to externally caused transitive motion. Aristotelian physics has become Newtonian mechanics.

XII. The Nature of Philosophical Truth and Its Method

47. Philosophical truth. Philosophy does not study or gather up empirical contingencies or "unessential determinations." Unessential determinations

are determined or caused by something outside and distinct from the thing determined/caused. Essential determinations are self-determining. To be self-determining, a movement must incorporate negativity or otherness into itself. Philosophy is not misled by the temporary appearance but grasps the whole movement in which each successive moment appears. The "bacchanalian revel" (at the level of moments) is at the same time a calm "repose" (at the level of the whole) because the claim to absoluteness made by each moment (which resists seeing itself as part of the whole) necessarily collapses. The perspective of the whole is achieved in recollection.

48. The limits of a preface. We cannot say more *about* the method of the self-determining concept (philosophy as speculative science) than we have already. The full exposition of this concept is logic (and is found in the *Science of Logic*). Because philosophical method is inseparable from content, no methodology can be given in advance. The aim of philosophy is not to give a revolutionary method for *using* thinking in some new way but rather to make explicit what thinking itself already is.

49. Method. As seekers of truth (which is self-determining or concept), we must reject the external style of argumentative debate and formalism. This does not force us to accept immediate knowing. Even though immediate knowing, like philosophy, rejects external methods, it also (wrongly) rejects all method, all science. The modern philosopher has been presenting us with a false dichotomy: either external method or no method at all. True science, which studies self-determining movements, is neither indifferent to content (like argumentative debate and formalism) nor indifferent to form (like immediate knowing).

XIII. Against Schematizing Formalism

50. Triplicity. The concept may be said to have three key moments but this triplicity has been taken up as a mere formula by Kant (who rediscovered the form of triplicity) and those that came after him. Kant calls the mediating "third" to the otherwise incommensurable powers of sensibility and understanding a "schema." Schematic thinking approaches triplicity not as a movement out of and then returning into self but as a bridging of two foreign elements. Those after Kant are formalistic schematizers because they too privilege two separate elements needing to be bridged by some special third thing, a schema. The third principle that bridges the

two incommensurate principles (subject/object, finite/infinite, etc.) in the latest formalism is usually some pseudo-scientific idea like "polarity."

51. Construction. Formalism introduces a "constructed" third thought as a bridge between two opposed thoughts. Formalism thereby establishes superficial analogies between disparate things. For the formalistic idealist, mind and matter are unified only by relating both to a common third thing, for example, excitability/electricity. For the truly speculative thinker, however, the unity of thinking and being is established not quickly and superficially through some third thing but by patiently attending to the movement of thinking and of being until they each show the differences which kept them apart to collapse (cf. §39, 47). Formalism can produce "systems" of the whole universe very quickly, a sign of its superficiality.

52. Formalism, necessary. Formalistic idealism cannot be avoided. It is a necessary stage that occurs when knowledge and science have progressed far enough, when the connection between the universal whole and the determinate parts seems within easy reach. Formalism's hasty completion indicates how much we desire a complete speculative system of science.

53. Self-developing content. Formalism forces its elements together by superficial analogies; it arranges pre-existing elements together in a flashy new way. It does not develop any content out of itself but rather takes content from other sciences. The task of science is to develop all content from a single starting point without adding or forcing new content. Self-moving beings already exhibit this form of self-othering-self-sameness required for this sort of comprehensive knowledge or science. Self-moving beings must become other than themselves in order to move themselves. To move itself to a new place, a being must be aware of itself in one place and yet desire to be in another place. The being is thus split into the self-as-is and the self-as-potency. A desire takes the present condition of the self as an object and negates it. The self becomes a content to itself in this way; it distances itself from itself in order to move itself; it makes itself into its own moment. Knowing that immerses itself in what it studies will eventually return to itself because being (what is known) *is* by returning-to-itself.

54. Being is thinking. To be an independent something ("substance") is to be self-moving ("subject"). Each independent being continues to be only by having some self it holds on to: "*Sichselbstgleichheit*" (sameness to itself). But self-sameness is a "pure abstraction." To be *self-sameness in*

general is not to be any one self in particular. Thinking can think any particular thought without ceasing to be thinking in general. This pure, "simple oneness" of *being relating to itself in general* is the essence of the activity we call thinking. Thinking can think all kinds of things without ceasing to be thinking, just as being can be all kinds of things without ceasing to be being. As such, being and thinking are both pure Self-sameness [*Sichselbstgleichheit*]. Self-sameness is pure in the sense that it is not one single content in particular. This means that it loses itself completely in each content yet when the content dissolves it is not lost itself. In becoming its content, thinking will never be at the mercy of each determinateness (each specific thought) and likewise, being is not limited by or exhausted by determinate beings. They will use determinate content rather than be used by it (this is the "cunning of reason"). Determinate contents are modifications of thinking/being, not the other way around. Thinking/being remains restfully self-same even as determinate beings and thoughts arise and pass away.

55. Understanding, part II; being and thinking, part II. There is another way of describing how being is thinking. To exist, something must be determinate. When we say something exists (*Dasein*), we mean it *is there* (*Da-sein*) as opposed to being somewhere else, anywhere, or nowhere. An existing being *is* in some particular, determinate way. Even a thought, in order to *exist*, must be a determinate thought distinct from some other thought. The understanding, then, as the power of differentiating and distinguishing things, is a *source of determinations* and, thus, of *existence*. Understanding determines "substance" as some determinate being or other, that is, an existence. This insight is found in ancient Greek thinking. Anaxagoras says that the way things are was caused by intellect, *Nous*, which *separated things out* according to kinds. Socrates hypothesizes that the being of something is best reflected in the intelligible kind (*eidos/idea*), a specific determination (this not that) which appears in thinking and speech. In these cases, existing (being of some kind) and being intelligible (determinable by the understanding) coincide. But there is a problem with the Greek view: kinds are simple and self-same and therefore seem fixed and permanent. But as we saw in the last paragraph, self-sameness is not motionless permanence but is always at work negating otherness. At first glance, simple existence seems to be defined by something outside it and against it. But the otherness of being, just like the otherness of thinking, is an otherness that a being or existence

produces from itself in order to move itself. The simplicity that belongs to existing kinds is the simplicity we saw before as the nature of thinking: it is the simplicity of abstraction, of not being any one of its moments in particular because it is capable of negating them all. Thinking is potentially any thought; existing is potentially any moment that belongs to some kind of existence. Self-sameness is possible only when self-moving is possible and self-moving is only possible if a being can differentiate itself from itself inwardly. "Thinking" is what we call this power of inward self-differentiation. Thinking/Being involves keeping alive many inner potencies at once even while actually being at work in some particular way. "Understanding" is what we name the movement of negation and differentiation in thinking. But if understanding is grasped not just as negation/differentiation but as a necessary part of being-a-self, as part of *becoming*, it becomes reason, the broader movement in which the fixed qualities arise and dissolve.

56. Speculative thinking. The unity of being and thinking can be said another way: whatever is, in order to be, must be "the concept of itself." A "logical necessity" structures all existing and all knowing according to a common triple rhythm, self-other-return to self. There is an inner necessity to self-movement that can structure our thinking in the same way that it structures being, according to the triple rhythm thus making thinking "speculative." This necessity is "logical" because it is inward and deals with the non-actual parts and potencies. All living things already treat themselves as abstractions. They are already "analyzing" and "logicizing" themselves. No being simply sits still in mute appreciation of its own permanence and fixity; all life suspends its own present determinateness in order to determine itself in new ways. This suspension is how being turns itself into thinking, how it turns itself into logical content. Speculative logic is the "inner" logic of all kinds of self-movement, including life and cognition.

XIV. The Demands of a Study of Philosophy:

57. Scientific method immerses itself in its content and allows the content to move itself by its own rhythm. The presentation of the true nature of this method is "speculative philosophy." This preface can only offer an anticipatory assurance of the truth of this method. But nothing we currently have, no prejudices or immediate convictions, can oppose

it because they are also just assurances. We should expect that the unfamiliar (and speculative philosophy is unfamiliar) will be either rejected before it is explored or applauded without investigation. In either case, we spare ourselves the burden of spending time with it. This preserves the status quo and protects the imagined freedom of thought we have under our present epistemic regime.

58. Speculative method is wrongly assumed (by the understanding) to be something new, something alien. It is actually at work in all thinking/being already. Our work is to recognize this. This sounds easy but it takes strenuous effort and patience. We must attend to all the variations of pure self-movement (e.g., being-it-itself, being-for-itself, self-identity), the moving souls at work in every kind of being and thinking that make each distinctively what they are and yet unite them all by the common rhythm of self-movement. Two different habits of thinking are both opposed to this speculative turn. First, the imagination resists attending to self-motion because it is too caught up in the evidence of sensation to see the inner self-differentiations required for self-motion. The imagination flatly denies self-motion, assuming that all motion is caused transitively by physical forces. On the opposite side, argumentative reasoning [*Räsonieren*] is so removed from experience and so enamored of its own capacity to give meaning to things that it sees no reason to give up its freedom (the freedom to determine content according to its subjective caprice rather than according to the content's own self-movement). Yet even the refusal of speculative thinking is an essential moment of thinking and cannot hold off from speculative philosophy forever.

XV. Argumentative Thinking in Its Negative Attitude

59. Räsonieren, side one. Argumentative reasoning has two sides, a negative side and a positive side. Both are obstacles to accepting comprehensive/speculative thinking. First, argumentative reasoning "adopts a negative attitude toward the content it apprehends." Content is not to be studied but merely refuted. Neither the content nor the argument by which it is refuted is of any real interest, both are a means to an end: *asserting one's power over the new content.* This *feels* like the freedom and power of thinking but it is only a negative freedom or license. Investing in the content and caring about it seems to rob this sort of thinking of this

negative freedom. The fear of losing this freedom becomes an obstacle to speculative thinking which "loses itself" in its content. Another sign of the emptiness of this freedom is that when it negates something, this is a dead end. The negation does not reveal anything about the content. Argumentative reasoning's interest was solely in itself, in defending its empty right to refute any content it chooses (and thus defend any position arbitrarily). Argumentative reasoning defends this license, but it never questions it or seeks to grasp how it operates. It does not grasp its own negativity as a content.

XVI. Argumentative Thinking in Its Positive Attitude, Its Subject

60. Räsonieren, side two. Second, when argumentative reasoning takes content up positively it does so by taking its subject as a passive basis for predication, not as a self-determining self. The subject of a conventional proposition does not generate the predicate. The predicate is simply added to it and the subject is treated as a passive container to hold the predicate. Standard predicative propositions appeal to argumentative reasoning because (see §23) the movement of predication is not the self-movement of the content but actually the subjective movement of the knower who is asserting a connection between subject and predicate. Thus predication is, for argumentative reasoning, a form of vanity or self-absorption [*Eitelkeit*] on the part of the thinker: seeing our own desired connections between things presented as independent facts. Having described both sides of argumentative reasoning, we can now turn to the philosophical procedure used to disrupt this vain, sophistical thinking. Our main target is the predicative proposition which was the supporting basis for argumentative reasoning. If we disrupt this, we shake the ground on which it stands. Predicates normally give a satisfying finite determinateness to the inert subject they describe. If, however, the predicate were to express not just some quality or other but the very being, substance, or essence of the subject, the subject is no longer a passive container to hold it. The predicate is not merely placed inside the subject container, rather the subject is destabilized by presenting another subject in the predicate position. The subject then passes over into this new content which does not simply add to it, but puts it into continual motion. We cannot simply move on from the original subject, but are forced back into questions

about it. A typical proposition like "the salt is white" concludes all inquiry on the subject, while a speculative proposition like "God is being" opens inquiry.

61. The speculative proposition, form. The previously described sentence that causes a disruption of predication, the "counter-thrust" against predication, can be called a "speculative proposition." This sort of sentence suggests that subject and predicate are functionally "identical" and it is unclear which one is the bearer of qualities and which one is the quality. The resulting disruption of expectation is like what happens when we read poetry. Complex rhythms result from the conflict between accent (where the stress falls in natural speech) and meter (the expected stress in the poetic form, e.g., an iambic stresses the first syllable of each foot). Rhythm cannot result from a perfect match of natural and metrical stress (this sounds mechanical or sing-song) but only from stretching their relationship without breaking it. This gives us a feeling for the "floating center," the dynamic movement back and forth between accent and meter. Similarly, in the speculative or philosophical proposition, the equal status or independence of subject and predicate does not completely eliminate the difference imposed between them by the form of the predicative sentence itself. Philosophical thinking depends on the resulting tension between the unity of its concepts and the differences forced between them by various forms of expression. Here the propositional form which subordinates the second term to the first implies difference between them. At the same time, the terms themselves appear to be conceptually equivalent (e.g., God and being are both substances). The speculative proposition expresses both unity and difference; it expresses "harmony."

62. The speculative proposition, examples. If we compare the proposition "God is being" with the proposition "God is a being," we can see that the first is speculative while the second is predicative. "Being as such" is not a predicate or quality of God; it is a term just as substantial as the term "God." The question "what is God?" now becomes the question "what is being?" The first term is swallowed up by the second, not rendered more determinate and fixed. Thinking "feels itself checked" by the loss of the subject inside the philosophical predicate. Instead of determining something, thinking has encountered a question. It cannot argue from a determinate point of view on the content (as *Räsonieren* does) but has lost any personal or subjective view on the content (God/being) and is

now absorbed in, lost in questions about that content. Or if one is not absorbed in questions about the content, one is at least confused by the proposition and "faced with the demand" that one inquire more into what might be meant by "God is being." We can also compare "the actual is the universal" to the proposition "the actual is universal." The first is speculative because "the universal" is another independent subject; the second is predicative because "universal" is used here as an adjective. The speculative proposition shakes our objective basis for argument or debate and opens us up to dialectic or inquiry.

63. The speculative proposition, reading. Because philosophical writing still employs many normal sentences, readers assume these work (as ordinary propositions seem to) by establishing determinate qualities in fixed subjects. When no clear determination emerges from reading a philosophical sentence, the reader feels his expectation betrayed and accuses the philosopher of being needlessly obscure. Readers of philosophy experience an "unfamiliar obstruction" and have to re-read sentences multiple times. But this circling back to the same sentence is not really an obstruction to thinking, circling back is the true movement of thinking and it is also the true movement of being (i.e., living/growing/selfing).

64. The speculative proposition, plasticity. Speculative thinking (philosophy) and argumentative reasoning (debate) should not be mixed. The former grasps essential movement of selfhood and the latter argues from fixed predicates, which are incidental. We should not use the same word sometimes as an infinite subject and other times as a finite predicate. If philosophy attempts to advance by fixed predications, it won't be "plastic" or flexible enough to follow the self-movement of the subject. If one is unable to tell the difference between the essential and the incidental, philosophical thinking is not possible.

65. The speculative proposition, its limited application. The action of the speculative proposition is helpful to consider, but it is not the basis of speculative method. Non-speculative thinking is also valuable to speculation and the speculative proposition cannot capture this relationship. The speculative proposition only helps to reveal speculative thinking in an immediate way. Because the speculative proposition only *inhibits* predicative thinking, it does not reform or transform it. True speculative method allows non-speculative thinking to express itself and run its course dialectically. This means that non-speculative claims

are allowed and presented but always shown to be unable to answer the speculative questions they purport to answer. Many philosophical works contain speculative propositions, but few actually observe the stages of the speculative insight in and through existence. We must combine outward-directed (attempts at) proof with inward-directed dialectic. If we show how existence negates itself, we incorporate the non-speculative interest in proving existences with the speculative interest in the self-movement of the whole.

66. The speculative proposition in relation to system. Dialectical expositions make use of ordinary propositions. As a result, the tension between the non-speculative expression and the speculative content returns again and again. Just as each premise of a proof must itself be proven, each proposition requires another proposition. Proof is a merely external way of knowing and it works by arbitrarily picking a fixed subject to prove. This method cannot be used to present speculative thinking, but individual propositions can be used. Because dialectical movement is about the truth and self-sameness of being/thinking with itself (cf. §54), no proposition in a dialectical movement ever becomes the true subject of the inquiry. When we typically think of "a self," we think of a self that appears to the senses and imagination or of the proper name. Proper names (e.g. "God") should be avoided in a dialectical exposition because they do not express the self speculatively. Names give an illusion of fixity to a selfhood that is essentially movement. Even if a speculative truth is asserted of some proper-named subject, the truth then loses its inner dialectical movement (which made it true) and becomes a fixed predicate. This results in mere edification, dressing up prejudices in profound sounding words (cf. §7, 9, 19, 55). This makes the fact that we must use propositions even more dangerous and misleading. How one treats those propositions makes all the difference. Proceeding in a wholly dialectical way means never taking any individual claim as true just as such.

67. Misology. The study of philosophy is not only hindered by sophistry but also by misology (i.e., not just by self-absorbed argumentative reasoning (§58–64) but also by a self-absorbed dismissal of all argument). The prevailing confidence in immediate knowing (cf. §7 ff.) inclines people toward misology. This has also led to the widespread belief that philosophy is a native ability and requires no training or practice. This belief is just misology in disguise.

XVII. Natural Philosophizing as Common Sense and as Genius

68. Against genius. Philosophy requires the work and practice of coming to terms with the long development of knowing. Instead of this hard work, people prefer more "natural" approaches: immediate knowing and healthy common sense. Immediate knowing is neither able to understand a single abstract proposition nor grasp connections between many propositions. This ignorance it fancies as an advantage, as a sign that it is "natural" and uncorrupted by the long history of philosophical errors. Because of this, immediate knowing has recently been drawn to intuitive poetic utterances as a replacement for dialectical inquiry. The result is neither poetic nor philosophical.
69. Against common sense. On the other side, common sense offers another outlet for "natural" philosophizing. It offers only trivial truths, the prevailing opinions of the day. When attacked, it falls back on an appeal to conscience and knowing things in one's heart. But the point of knowing is to make things explicit, not just leave them on the inside. Common sense accuses educated reason of sophistry whenever the latter presents arguments against it, insisting the basis for decision is not thinking but feeling. In this way, common sense destroys the possibility of the very thing that makes us human: community with others through shared knowing.

XVIII. Conclusion, the Relationship of an Author to the Public

70. Against common sense and genius. Common sense, aided by prefaces and popular critical assessments of philosophical systems, can easily fabricate a road to something that has the look of a science. Immediate knowing does not require any road for it goes nowhere. But neither can reveal the "source of being" itself (self-movement/negativity). Only by patiently attending to "work of the concept" can we discover a common universal knowing that is neither poetic vagueness nor popular opinion dressed up. This universal knowing is not knowledge as the private possession of an uncommon genius, but a mature, developed truth that can be possessed by all patient, educated people.
71. The reception of speculative science. Truth is found in what remains self-same-through-otherness, that is, the "self-moving concept." This is different from and even opposed to the prevailing views of truth, all

of which hold truth to be external to and separate from the knowing of truth in some way. As a result, we do not expect this system of science to be kindly received. But often Plato's writing has been valued more for its obscure myths than its patient dialectical inquiries (e.g., the *Parmenides*). Alternately, there have also been times in which people appreciated Plato's and Aristotle's speculative depth. One can therefore hope that the speculative science of self-moving essences may one day be accepted. We can also hope for a good reception of this work by the public at large, even if certain critics (who are entrenched in their views) are not kind to it. The general public is more educated than ever and less and less likely to accept a critic's opinion over their own.

72. Science is the work of many not one. Truth expresses itself and hardly needs a spokesperson. Science/philosophy is the collective undertaking of all human beings and does not arise from private interests, personal needs, or practical aims. An individual does more for truth by forgetting his or her personal interests and working patiently for universal knowledge in whatever way he or she can.

Notes

Introduction

1 Compare W3:20, §14 and W8:36.
2 Hermann Glockner calls it "the most important of all Hegel texts." This and other eulogies are quoted on the first page of Kaufmann's 1965 translation of the preface. By contrast, Robert Solomon describes it as "nasty, defensive, arrogant, and, ultimately, misleading." (Solomon 1985, 242) Additionally, we ought to consider the critical appraisal implied by omission: many prominent Hegel scholars simply do not talk about the prefaces. Graduate courses on the *Phenomenology* often skip the preface altogether. Likewise, many published commentaries on the *Phenomenology* skip the preface and begin with the introduction.
3 H. S. Harris' *Hegel's Ladder* offers the most detailed discussion of Hegel's intellectual context as it relates to each paragraph of the preface. For a quicker overview of Hegel's intellectual milieu, see Marx 1988. I have also benefitted from discussions of the preface in Schacht 1975, Lauer 1993, Rosen 2000, Siep 2000/2014, Yovel 2005, Asmuth 2007, Verene 2007 and Collins 2013.
4 See Solomon 1985, 237–8, Lauer 1993, 301, Harris 1997, 32, Schacht 1975, 41, Verene 2007, 1, Yovel 2005, ix, Siep 2000, 55–6.
5 See §67–70.
6 These twelve conclusions can be traced to the following paragraphs respectively: §3, 5, 9, 16, 48, 45, 20, 58, 63, 13, 69, 72.
7 This dilemma is seen throughout the preface in the oppositions Hegel sets up between immediate knowing and empiricism. See especially the crucial §48.
8 As an example, we might consider the substantial impact that William Harvey's scientific work on the circulation of blood had on Descartes's thought. He devotes the whole of the fifth part of his *Discourse on Method* to a discussion of it and its implications.
9 Two prominent examples of books that attempt to describe "Hegel's method" are Pinkard 1988 and Forster 1993. In the same vein, Clark Butler (2011) has written a book with the revealing title: *The Dialectical Method: A Treatise Hegel Never Wrote*. It is helpful to notice that 1) Hegel did not write treatises and 2) Hegel certainly never wrote a treatise on method.
10 William Maker was perhaps the first to argue in a pointed way that Hegel does not have a method in our usual senses of that word (Maker 1994, 99–100). Stephen

Houlgate offers a good, brief overview of the issue, favoring the no method camp himself (Houlgate 2006, 32–5). Richard Dien Winfield has written extensively on Hegel's "presuppositionless" logic and the inseparability of method from content (e.g. Winfield 2014 94–7). Glenn Magee also notes that attempts to formalize Hegel's dialectic are "misguided" (Magee 2010, 74, 214). K. R. Dove's "Hegel's Phenomenological Method" is also worth consulting.

11 As initial evidence, consider Bacon's preface to the *New Organon* and Descartes' *Rules for the Direction of the Mind* and parts 1 and 2 of Descartes' *Discourse on Method*.

12 As Angelica Nuzzo writes "For Hegel progress is made by staying where one is, not by looking away, aiming at something else" (Nuzzo 2005, 198).

13 On anatomy and history as contrasting examples that show more interest in practical "results" than insightful "reasons," see §1 and §41.

14 The word *Selbstbewegung*, self-movement, appears nine times in the 1807 preface (§19, 23, 33, 45, 46, 51, 55, 58 and 71).

15 See Enz §166 Zusatz, where Hegel compares plant growth and the act of concluding or making a judgment. See also Hanh 2007, 9–52, for a detailed treatment of Hegel's conception of organic life in its relation to logic.

16 W5:82–3. This movement is similar to the opening realization of the *Phenomenology* that immediate intuition ("Sensory Certainty") cannot say what it means, i.e. the thought of pure being is empty.

17 What does Hegel mean here? Hegel's final preface (the 1831 preface to the *Science of Logic*) closes with a similar warning and it spells out the details more clearly. There he notes that his book will be misread because most readers will not distance themselves from their practical interests enough to approach thinking in a non-instrumental way.

Chapter 1

1 These three claims are found at W5:13, W13:13, and W7:12 respectively.

2 W3:68, §73. Even within the *Phenomenology*, many sections begin by addressing a familiar prejudice about the topic.

3 Kierkegaard (mocking Hegel and his multiple beginnings that seem to announce that beginning is impossible) invents playful replacements for the preface such as "preliminary expectoration" and "exordium."

4 *Physics* 184a16–18.

5 Compare Hegel's second paragraph with what Aristotle says (Met. 993b1–15): "It is just to feel gratitude, not only toward those whose opinions one shares, but also toward those whose expressions were superficial; for they also contributed something by exercising the habit of thinking before us." This should help us

make sense of why Aristotle always includes the "things said" even if he compares some previous thinkers' thinking to drunken or lisped speech. In the study of philosophy we are not just acquiring correct arguments and opinions but exercising our human capacity for thinking. Hegel and Aristotle are often criticized for their treatment of predecessors since they seem to make them into stair steps to their own views. But the alternatives fail to put one's thinking in tension and dialogue with the thinking of the past altogether. To simply respect past views as independent monads may look more kind, but actually avoids engaging them from one's present standpoint.

6   Compare Kant's technical terms invented for special use: *transzendental, Apperzeption, Noumena, Paralogismen, Antinomien, Architektonik*, etc.
7   Aristotle, *Metaphysics* 982b12–20. Apparent impasses are a stopping point for common sense but the beginning of philosophy. Common sense is guided by prevailing opinions and if there is a conflict in the prevailing opinions it has no higher court of appeal. Philosophy is explicitly not bound by prevailing opinions and so philosophical thinking can make a distinction that clears up the impasse, though it must at the same time give up the prevailing opinions which failed to make the distinction in the first place.
8   *Theaetetus* 155c–d.
9   See Aristotle, *Physics* 206a12–14.
10 Though it is premature to explore it now, it may be at least mentioned here that Hegel notices something missed by many moderns that is at the root of so many impasses. In addition to mediation and immediacy, he also recognizes a third thing: self-mediation. My main discussion of this is in Chapter 4.
11 The most influential works of modern philosophy, despite their disagreements about what counts as epistemically fundamental, all advocate stripping thought back to simple, immediate beginnings. Descartes' *Mediations* make this case clearly, and argue that simple ideas like "I think" and "God" and even "Wax" have epistemic privileges over, for example, bodies and the perception of bodies. Spinoza's *Ethics* begins with fundamental axioms that privilege infinite substance and work, on the model of geometry, toward certain demonstrations concerning finite things. Locke's *Essay* argues against innate ideas, yet still aims to privilege certain immediate sensations as the building blocks of reflection. Hume's *Enquiry*, despite advancing mitigated skepticism, seems confident enough that impressions must be the sources of ideas and count as epistemically basic. All of these books begin by identifying the building blocks of knowledge. Hegel's books do not work this way.
12 Knowledge, for most modern philosophers, is not something natural, not an organic development. It is, rather, something wrested from an unwilling nature.
13 It is worth mentioning that a great deal of interesting work has been done on the question of whether Hegel's system is really "presuppositionless" or "without foundation." See Maker's *Philosophy without Foundations*, Winfield's *Hegel and the*

Future of Systematic Philosophy, Houlgate's *The Opening of Hegel's Science of Logic*, and Collins's *Hegel's Phenomenology the Dialectical Justification of Philosophy's First Principles*.

14 For more on anticipation, see paragraph 23 (W3:27).

15 The difference between these words in German usage has been a subject of investigation, especially in biblical hermeneutics where the Bible's historicity is subject to special problems. See De Laurentiis 2010, 214–15 for an overview of Hegel's usage. See Barth 1963:45 for a classic formulation of the distinction and Dale:17 for a critical view of the distinction in relation to Hegel.

16 References for what I have just quoted are found, in order, at W3:65, 16, 57, 65, 39, 56, and 51.

17 The non-metaphysical Hegel interpretation made famous by Pippin's *Hegel's Idealism* has generated great interest and been championed by influential and accomplished scholars. Still, it remains a minority position among Hegel scholars generally due to plentiful textual evidence against it. That said, the goal of the non-metaphysical reading was never textual fidelity, but rather to produce a leaner Hegel that could integrate more effectively into a variety of contemporary discussions. On its own terms this interpretation has been quite successful, though it can mislead unwary readers who do not understand its limitations. For a recent book reflecting scholarly consensus in favor of a metaphysical reading of Hegel, consider the essays in *Hegel and Metaphysics* (De Gruyter 2016). Not represented in that volume is strong work in favor of a metaphysical interpretation by Bowman (*Hegel and the Metaphysics of Absolute Negativity*, 2013) and Kreines (*Reason in the World*, 2015).

18 See, for example: "Die Geschichte aber haben wir zu nehmen, wie sie ist; wir haben historisch, empirisch zu verfahren" (W12:22). This aligns with Aristotle's claim in the *Poetics* that history is of particulars (while philosophy and poetry are of the universal). Hegel does not dismiss the empirical (as some critics think) but sees it as a content that must be enriched with reasons and purposes to move from being merely *Historie* to becoming *Geschichte*. It is worth noting that *Historie* is used throughout the preface but *Geschichte* is not, while *Geschichte* is used in the body of the *Phenomenology*, while *Historie* is avoided.

19 See esp. paragraphs 14–16 and 51–53. Paragraph 53 is the most revealing, but also presupposes an understanding of several previous remarks.

20 Schlegel 1958, v. 18, 341.

Chapter 2

1 Immediately following the so-called "second position of thought," identified with empiricism and Kantian critical philosophy, Hegel positions a "third position of

thought" called "immediate knowing" and underscores how this position prepares the ground for a speculative system of science.
2 "*Geist* is not a resting [*ein Ruhendes*], but much more the absolutely restless, the pure activity, the negating or the ideality of all fixed determinations of the understanding— not abstract simply but in its simplicity at the same time a self-from-itself-differentiating." (*Enc* §378A).

Chapter 3

1 These prejudices are: (1) that falsehood should be excluded from presentations of the truth, (2) that mathematics offers the ideal paradigm for philosophy, (3) that philosophy is concerned with historical facts, (4) that mediating a content involves the imposition of a third element (e.g., Kant's schema) as bridge between two heterogeneous elements, (5) that philosophical thinking involves a freedom to determine content (*Räsonieren*), (6) that philosophy must align with common sense, and (7) that the form of truth is the proposition.
2 There is a good account of this biographical episode in Terry Pinkard's Hegel biography (Pinkard 2001, 256–7).
3 Hegel refers to "external connection," "external schemas," and "external constructions" as signs of formalism: W3:21, W3:55, W10:69, W20:412, W20:445, W20:450.
4 See Jonathan Beere *Doing and Being* and Kosman *The Activity of Being* for two distinct but complementary discussions of being as *energeia* or activity in Aristotle's *Metaphysics*.
5 Alfredo Ferrarin has argued that Aristotle's *energeia* and Hegel's *Subjekt* are related but ultimately very different conceptions (pp. 15–27). But both are ways of talking about the same ontological performance: selfhood. Ferrarin presumes that *Tätigkeit* must be incomplete *energeia* (i.e., *kinesis*) and thus the activity of the subject being itself (selfing) cannot be *energeia*. But it is also possible that while motions toward a kind of selfhood will be *kinesis*, the ongoing activity of being-that-self will be *energeia*. In this case, *energeia* and *Subjekt* would name the same activity of selfing.
6 H. S. Harris offers a helpful overview of the intellectual history of the identity principle (1997, 51-3). Harris considers this attack on "A = A" to be primarily directed at Reinhold and Bardili, not Schelling. (For Harris's argument that Hegel did not in fact mean for his criticisms of formalism to be directed at Schelling, see Harris 1997, 126–7.) I do not think Hegel's attack is directed at individuals at all, but rather at "forms of thought." Naming names is useful if it helps us explore the form of thought under discussion. Hegel seems to feel that naming names is not helpful, since he does not do so. To attach a name to a criticism gives us a scape goat so that we can clear others (or ourselves) of the charge. But the point is precisely to recognize how our own thinking devolves into lazy formalism sometimes.

7 Harris argues that this example is likely drawn from Schelling's *System of Transcendental Idealism*. More, he argues that Hegel isn't simply dismissing the claim because he revives it in his own chapter "Force and the Understanding." See Harris 1997, 126–7.
8 I am referring to an aphorism from Hegel's Wastebook: "Just as we have had a poetic genius-period, so the present seems to be the philosophical genius-period. Take some carbon, oxygen, nitrogen and hydrogen kneaded together with each other and stuck to the pre-arranged content on the page with polarity etc., rockets fired into the air with a wooden tail of vanity, etc., they suppose that this presents the Empyrean. Thus Görres, Wagner and others. The crudest empirical fact with the formalism of elements and poles, embellished with reasonless analogies and drunken brainstorms" (W2:542).
9 The quoted words from this paragraph have appeared before with citations in the previous chapter, but for ease of reference I give them again here: "shape of life" (W7:28), "thing of the past" (W13:25), "inner necessity" (W3:14), "purposive activity" (W3:26), and "true is the whole" (W3:24).

Chapter 4

1 See Hegel's *Selbstanzeige*, the announcement for the book he sent the publisher after completing it in which he now calls it a "phenomenology" (W3:593). For discussion, see Harris 1997, 30–1.
2 The known usage of the word that likely brought it to Hegel's attention is in J. H. Lambert's *Neues Organon* (in: Lambert, J.H. *Philosophische Schriften*. 10 vol. Hildesheim, 1965. Vol. 1 and 2). Lambert's book is divided into sections like *Dianologie* or *Aletheologie* and *Phänomenologie* is the fourth section of that book.
3 "Luther made the Bible speak German, and you have done the same for Homer. . . . I wish to try to teach philosophy to speak German" (Hegel to Voss [*Letters*, 107]).
4 This question has been frequently debated. See the preface to Werner Marx's *Hegel's Phenomenology of Spirit* for an overview.
5 See Verene 2007, 9.
6 Beginning at least with Rudolf Haym in 1857, several readers have asserted that the *Phenomenology* is a Frankenstein's monster composed of multiple parts that do not fit together (see Harris 1997, 10 for a good discussion of this). But phenomenal knowing is itself a messy business that does not adequately distinguish between the conceptual, historical, imaginary, etc. The book beautifully reflects the motley nature of its subject.
7 A key moment in the *Republic* occurs at 533a when Socrates notes that Glaucon, who still relies on the imagination, will not be able to follow an account of dialectic because he would "no longer be seeing an image" but the truth itself.

8 Socrates shows the ambiguity of Hesiod's and Homer's verses on many occasions. One particularly salient set of examples can be found in the *Republic*, Book II.
9 See Ferrarin 2019 for substantial discussion of Hegel's critique of I-centered accounts of thinking.

Chapter 5

1 W2:548, 550, 558.
2 W3:69–70, §74.
3 A ripening apple will be neither all green nor all red; it will be slowly reddening. Even once wholly red, the apple will be working to maintain its redness, as if replacing it at each moment. All beings are on the way to something they are not already. More, their being-right-now is precisely this on-the-way-ness.
4 Our content is not just nothingness but "the nothingness of that from which it results" (W3:74, §79). Determinate negation bears the trace of what has been negated. Determinate negation is the "not this" while abstract negation is merely the "no" that says nothing about what it negates.
5 Cf. *Physics* 193b30 ff.
6 Hobbes remarks, with his characteristically sharp wit, that geometry is "the only science that it hath pleased God hitherto to bestow upon mankind" (*Leviathan* I.iv.12). Locke writes that "every one must not hope to be a Boyle, or a Sydenham; and in an Age that produces such Masters, as the Great Huygenius, and the incomparable Mr. Newton, with some other of that Strain; 'tis Ambition enough to be employed as an Under-Labourer in clearing Ground a little, and removing some of the Rubbish, that lies in the way to Knowledge" (Locke *Essay* 9–10).
7 Cf. Jacob Klein 1992.
8 When Kant defines intuition as a mode of immediate access to an object, this definition should stand for the rest of the book. When he turns to examine space, he does not engage the erroneous view (absolute space) until it collapses. He argues against it from the outset in favor of transcendental idealism (space as a form of intuition as opposed to an object). In short, Kant offers reasons why absolute space is untenable but does not evolve his own view out of it.

Chapter 6

1 Nic. Ethics 1110b25.
2 W5:20. For my argument that thinking and language are not coextensive for Hegel, see Davis (2016).

3 See Hobbes (1994, Chap. ii) for a clear formulation of this position.
4 On reading *"werden"* or becoming as *"Entwicklung"* or development, see *Enc* §161. As the concept develops throughout the course of logic, merely abstract becoming becomes (and is grasped as) concrete development.
5 It is worth recalling that Aristotle remarks that he cannot define *energeia* but can only offer analogies and examples of it (Met. 1048a35 ff).
6 W8:18.
7 "The speculative cannot be expressed as a proposition" (W19:397). See also ". . . a speculative determination cannot be expressed correctly in the form of such a proposition . . ." (W8:191, Enz §88).

Chapter 7

1 Hegel thus combines Aristotle's "definitions" of human being: humans are political animals and animals that have the *logos* (reasoning/speech). The *Phenomenology* teaches that the nature of consciousness itself is to seek cognition through recognition and recognition through reconciliation.
2 The Meiner critical edition does not emend "Bewußtseyn" to the plural "Bewusstsein[e]" as the Suhrkamp does.
   Compare GW9:lxxxvii with W3:65. I think Hegel's meaning here is even more striking in the singular.
3 Aristotle, *Physics* I.1.
4 See *Encyclopedia* §381 and Zusatz.
5 Schelling, *The Unconditional in Human Knowledge*, 170–1.
6 W20:428.

Conclusion

1 W5:31. For more on "plasticity" in Hegel's work, see Malabou 2005, 184–7.

Appendix

1 Compare Hegel's earlier statement in the *Difference* essay (1801) "Every philosophy is complete in itself, and like an authentic work of art, carries the totality within itself." (W2:19–20). This is Schelling's position, which Hegel abandons here.

2 Compare Aristotle *Physics* Bk 1, ch. 1.
3 Compare Hegel on Aristotle's thinking as both speculative and empirical: W19:172. Idealism should not blindly oppose materialism or empiricism, but incorporate it and raise its content to a higher meaning.
4 A comparison of Novalis' contentless *Hymnen an die Nacht* with Dante's content-rich *Divine Comedy* might serve to underscore this difference.
5 See Aristotle's arguments for why the first motion must be circular motion in *Physics* VIII.8–9. If the motion is to be unified and continuous, it is crucial that the movement away from some point also be movement toward it.
6 Notice Hegel mostly avoiding the words "subjective" and "objective" in this paragraph by developing a new nomenclature "in-itself" and "for-itself" designed to emphasize selfhood and relation and also designed to disrupt the usual associations of intense but merely personal (subjective) and publicly valid and neutral (objective). See also W3:71, where Hegel criticizes the unthinking use of "subjective" and "objective."
7 "*Das Denken*" plays an important role throughout Hegel's writings and implies more than consciousness or intuition or imagination. While Kant uses "think" in opposition to experience (we can "think" the ideas of reason but never experience them), Hegel aims to show that thinking is being and being is thinking. To qualify as "thinking," the awareness must be intelligible and communicable (*ENZ* §464). "Thinking steps forward again and again in these different parts of science, for this reason: because these parts are only different through the element and the form of opposition, thinking however is this center which is one and the same, to which the opposites return, as into their truth" (*ENZ* §467). To put thinking at the center of system is to put communicability, shared knowing, at the center.

Bibliography

Primary Texts

Aristotle. *Physica*. Ed. W. D. Ross. Oxford: Oxford University Press, 1951.
Aristotle. *De Anima*. Ed. W. D. Ross. Oxford: Oxford University Press, 1956.
Aristotle. *Metaphysica*. Ed. W. Jaeger. London: Oxford University Press, 1957.
Aristotle. *Ethica Nichomachea*. Ed. I. Bywater. Oxford: Oxford University Press, 1959.
Aristotle. *The Complete Works*. Ed. Jonathan Barnes. 2 vols. Princeton: Princeton University Press, 1984.
Descartes, Rene. *Oeuvres*. Ed. Charles Adam and Paul Tannery. Paris: Cerf, 1897–1913.
Diels, Hermann ed. *Die Fragmente der Vorsokratiker*. 7th ed. Berlin: Weidmann, 1954.
Fichte, J. G. *Fichtes Werke*. Ed. Immanuel Hermann Fichte. Berlin: de Gruyter, 1971.
Hegel, Georg Wilhelm Friedrich. *Gesammelte Werke*. Ed. Rheinisch-Westfälische Akademie der Wissenschaften. Hamburg: Meiner, 1968. [GW volume:page].
Hegel, Georg Wilhelm Friedrich. *Werke in zwanzig Bänden*. Ed. E. Moldenhauer and K. M. Michel. Frankfurt am Main: Suhrkamp, 1971. [W volume:page].
Hegel, Georg Wilhelm Friedrich. *Hegel: The Letters*. Trans. C. Butler and C. Seiler. Bloomington: Indiana University Press, 1985. [Letters].
Hegel, Georg Wilhelm Friedrich. *Vorlesungen: Ausgewiihlte Nachschriften und Manuskripte*. Ed. P. Garniron and W. Jaeschke. Hamburg: Meiner, 1989.
Hobbes, Thomas. *Leviathan*. Indianapolis: Hackett, 1994.
Jacobi, Friedrich Heinrich. *Werke*. Ed. Klaus Hammacher and Walter Jaeschke. Hamburg: Meiner, 1998.
Kant, Immanuel. *Gesammelte Schriften*. Akademie Ausgabe. Berlin: de Gruyter, 1900.
Locke, John. *Essay Concerning Human Understanding*. Oxford: Oxford University Press, 1975.
Lucretius. *On the Nature of Things*. Trans. W. Englert. Ed. M. F. Smith. Newburyport: Focus, 2003.
Merleau-Ponty, Maurice. *The Phenomenology of Perception*. Trans. D. Landes. Abingdon: Routledge, 2012.
Plato. *Complete Works*. Ed. John M. Cooper. Indianapolis: Hacket, 1997.
Schelling, Friedrich Wilhelm Joseph. *Sämmtliche Werke*. Ed. K. F. A. Schelling. Stuttgart and Augsburg: J. G. Cotta'scher Verlag, 1856.
Schelling, Friedrich Wilhelm Joseph. *The Unconditional in Human Knowledge*. Plainsboro: Associated University Press, 1980.
Schlegel, Friedrich. *Kritische Ausgabe*. Ed. E. Behler. Munich: F. Schöningh, 1958.

Seneca. *Selected Letters*. Trans. Fanham. Oxford: Oxford University Press, 2010.
Shakespeare, William. *Hamlet*. London: Bloomsbury, 2016.
Spinoza, Baruch. *Collected Works*. Trans. E. M. Curley. Princeton: Princeton University Press, 1985.

Secondary Texts on the Phenomenology and Its Preface

Asmuth, Christoph. "Negativität: Hegels Lösung der Systemfrage in der Vorrede der Phänomenologie des Geistes." *Synthesis Philosophica* 22, no. 1 (2007): 19–32.
Bonsiepen, Wolfgang. *Der Begriff der Negativität in den Jenaer Schriften Hegels*. Bonn: Bouvier, 1977.
Bonsiepen, Wolfgang. "Erste Zeitgenössische Rezensionen der Phänomenologie des Geistes." *Hegel-Studien* 14 (1979): 9–38.
Collins, Ardis. *Hegel's Phenomenology the Dialectical Justification of Philosophy's First Principles*. Montreal: McGill-Queen's University Press, 2013.
Dove, K. R. "Hegel's Phenomenological Method." *The Review of Metaphysics* 23, no. 4 (1970): 615–41.
Harris, H. S. *Hegel's Ladder*. Indianapolis: Hackett, 1997.
Hyppolite, Jean. "The Structure of Philosophic Language According to the 'Preface' to Hegel's 'Phenomenology of the Mind.'" In *The Structuralist Controversy*. Ed. R. Macksey and E. Donato, 157–69. Baltimore: Johns Hopkins Press, 1970.
Hyppolite, Jean. *Genesis and Structure of Hegel's Phenomenology of Spirit*. Evanston: Northwestern University Press, 1979.
Jamme, Christoph. "Platon, Hegel und der Mythos: Zu den Hintergründen eines Diktums aus der Vorrede zur 'Phänomenologie des Geistes.'" *Hegel-Studien* 15 (1980): 151–69.
Kaufmann, Walter. *Hegel: Texts and Commentary*. Notre Dame: Notre Dame University Press, 1977.
Lauer, Quentin. *A Reading of Hegel's Phenomenology of Spirit*. New York: Fordham University Press, 1993.
Marder, Michael. *Hegel's Energy*. Evanston: Northwestern University Press, 2021.
Marx, Werner. *Hegel's Phenomenology of Spirit: A Commentary Based on the Preface and Introduction*. Trans. Heath. Chicago: University of Chicago Press, 1988.
Sallis, John. "Hegel's Concept of Presentation." *Hegel-Studien* 12 (1977): 129–56.
Schacht, Richard. *Hegel and After*. Pittsburgh: University of Pittsburgh Press, 1975.
Siep, Ludwig. *Der Weg der Phänomenologie des Geistes*. Frankfurt: Suhrkamp, 2000.
Rosen, Michael. "The Preface to Hegel's Phenomenology of Spirit." 2000. Accessed at: https://scholar.harvard.edu/michaelrosen/publications/preface-hegels-phenomenology-spirit.
Solomon, Robert. *In the Spirit of Hegel*. Oxford: Oxford University Press, 1985.

Verene, Donald. *Hegel's Absolute*. Albany: SUNY Press, 2007.
Vieweg, Klaus and Wolfgang Welsch. *Hegels Phänomenologie des Geistes: Ein kooperativer Kommentar zu einem Schlüsselwerk der Moderne*. Frankfurt: Suhrkamp, 2008.
Yovel, Yirmiyahu. *Hegel's Preface to the Phenomenology of Spirit*. Princeton: Princeton University Press, 2005.

Other Secondary Texts

Barth, Karl. *Karl Barth's Table Talk*. Ed. John D. Godsey. Richmond: John Knox, 1963.
Beere, Jonathan. *Doing & Being: An Interpretation of Aristotle's Metaphysics IX*. Oxford: Oxford University Press, 2010.
Bouton, Christophe. "Hegel's Account of the Historicity of Philosophy." In *The Relevance of Hegel's Concept of Philosophy*. Ed. L. Illetterati and G. Miolli, 201–19. London: Bloomsbury, 2022.
Bowman, Brady. *Hegel and the Metaphysics of Absolute Negativity*. Oxford: Oxford University Press, 2013.
Dale, E. M. *Hegel, the End of History and the Future*. Cambridge: Cambridge University Press, 2014.
Davis, Andrew. "On the Limits of Language in a Hegelian Metaphysics." In *Hegel and Metaphysics*. Ed. A. De Laurentiis, 181–96. Berlin: De Gruyter, 2016.
De Laurentiis, Allegra. "Hegel's Interpretation of Aristotle's Psyche: A Qualified Defense." In *Hegel: New Directions*. Ed. K. Deligiorgi, 227–42. Montreal: McGill-Queen's University Press, 2006.
De Laurentiis, Allegra. "Universal Historiography and World History According to Hegel." In *Historiae Mundi: Studies in Universal History*. Ed. P. Liddel and A. Fear, 201–20. London: Duckworth, 2010.
Ferrarin, Alfredo. *Hegel and Aristotle*. Cambridge: Cambridge University Press, 2001.
Ferrarin, Alfredo. *Thinking and the I*. Evanston: Northwestern University Press, 2019.
Forster, Michael "Hegel's Dialectical Method." In *The Cambridge Companion to Hegel*. Ed. Beiser, 130–70. Cambridge: Cambridge University Press, 1993.
Hanh, Songsuk Susan. *Contradiction in Motion: Hegel's Organic Conception of Life and Value*. Ithaca: Cornell University Press, 2007.
Heidemann, Dietmar. "Hegel's Philosophy of Philosophy." In *The Relevance of Hegel's Concept of Philosophy*. Ed. L. Illetterati and G. Miolli, 37–53. London: Bloomsbury, 2022.
Houlgate, Stephen. "Hegel's Critique of Foundationalism in the 'Doctrine of Essence.'" In *German Philosophy since Kant*. Ed. A. O'hear, 24–45. Cambridge: Cambridge University Press, 1999.
Houlgate, Stephen. *The Opening of Hegel's Logic: From Being to Infinity*. West Lafayette: Purdue University Press, 2006.

Klein, Jacob. *Greek Mathematical Thought and the Origin of Algebra*. New York: Dover Publications, 1992.
Kosman, Aryeh. *The Activity of Being*. Cambridge: Harvard University Press, 2013.
Kreines, James. *Reason in the World*. Oxford: Oxford University Press, 2015.
Magee, Glenn. *The Hegel Dictionary*. London: Continuum, 2010.
Maker, William. *Philosophy without Foundations*. Albany: SUNY Press, 1994
Malabou, Catherine. *The Future of Hegel*. London: Routledge, 2005.
Nuzzo, Angelica. "The End of Hegel's Logic: Absolute Idea as Absolute Method." In *Hegel's Theory of the Subject*. Ed. D. Carlson, 187–205. Basingstroke: Palgrave Macmillan, 2005.
Pinkard, Terry. *Hegel's Dialectic: The Explanation of Possibility*. Philadelphia: Temple University Press, 1988.
Pinkard, Terry. *Hegel: A Biography*. Cambridge: Cambridge University Press, 2001.
Pippin, Robert. *Hegel's Idealism*. Cambridge: Cambridge University Press, 1989.
Pippin, Robert. *Hegel's Realm of Shadows*. Chicago: University of Chicago Press, 2018.
Sedgwick, Sally. "Hegel's Critique of Kant." In *A Companion to Kant*. Ed. Bird, 473–85. Oxford: Blackwell, 2006.
Sedgwick, Sally. *Hegel's Critique of Kant: From Dichotomy to Identity*. Oxford: Oxford University Press, 2012.
Stern, Robert. "Hegel's Doppelsatz: A Neutral Reading." *Journal of the History of Philosophy* 44, no. 2 (2006): 235–66.
Stone, Alison. *Petrified Intelligence*. Albany: SUNY Press, 2005.
Winfield, Richard. *Hegel and the Future of Systematic Philosophy*. London: Palgrave Macmillan, 2014.

Index

Absolute 42
absolute knowing 20
actuality [*Wirklichkeit*] 70–2, 96, 136–7, 153, 178, 183
Aeschylus *161*
ambiguity 22
anatomy 8, 12, 27–31, 46, 200
anticipating the absolute 24–6
Aristotle 15, 23, 70, 80, 105, 115–17, 124, 131, 135–6, 142, 150, 154, 165, 172, 180, 198
Aristotle's *Metaphysics* 2, 62, 83, 92–3, 200, 201, 203, 206
Aristotle's *Parts of Animals* 89
Aristotle's *Physics* 21, 32, 34, 78, 112, 119, 200, 201, 206, 207
Aristotle's *Poetics* 62, 202
atomism 112–15, 185

bacchanalian whirl [*bacchantische taumel*] 122, 188
Bacon, Francis 7, 11, 47, 83, 129, 167, 200
being 13–15, 28–30, 60, 70, 97, 132, 136, 149, 179
Bildung [education, formation]. *See* education
birth (of speculative science) 51, 82, 157, 168, 178
Bowman, Brady 202

Caesar 138–9, 186
Capaneus 160–1
categorical imperative 69
circle 74, 180
Collins, Ardis 199, 202
common sense 26–7, 112, 155, 158–60, 197
concept [*Begriff*] 15, 27–31, 67–8, 81, 100, 114, 116–17, 128–9, 140, 146–50, 177, 178
construction 24–5, 30, 67, 75, 77, 91, 103, 124–9, 135, 187, 189
counter-thrust [*Gegenstoss*] 143, 194
critics (of books) 164–6

Darstellung [presentation, performance]. *See* presentation (of philosophy)
De Laurentiis, Allegra 202
demonstration. *See* proof
Descartes, Rene 7, 11, 42, 43, 47, 69, 79, 83, 102–4, 119, 124, 125, 142, 157, 199–201
determinate negation 11, 78, 81, 112–14, 123, 156, 158, 171–2, 174, 191, 193, 205
dialectic 7, 11–13, 37, 45, 47, 92, 148–50, 156, 196, 199
difference 7, 14, 16, 30–4, 39, 48, 55, 57, 66, 73–5, 77, 78, 86, 93, 100, 106, 107, 113, 123, 178, 179, 183, 187, 189, 194, 195, 206
discursive knowledge 42–4, 178
dogmatism 27–31, 138–40, 186

education 49, 99–107, 176, 182
eidos [form, look] 184, 190
elitism 87, 178
empiricism 10, 30, 35, 46, 55–8, 74, 82, 177, 178, 199, 202, 207
empty I 73, 157, 192–3
end of history 61–3
energeia [effective actuality, being at work] 62, 70, 72, 203, 206
epistemology 54, 78, 79, 100, 113, 115, 126
esotericism 87, 91, 161, 178
Euclid 125–8
experiment (as method) 8, 53, 63, 73, 79, 124, 127, 128

falsehood 119–24
familiar [*Bekannte*] 1–3, 35, 55, 98–9, 138–40, 182–4
Ferrarin, Alfredo 203, 205
Fichte, Johann 22–3, 69
fluid thinking 16, 75, 93, 101, 103–7, 109, 111, 116, 136, 147, 157, 160, 171–3, 184, 186
formula 37, 67–84, 178, 188
Forster, Michael 199

foundation (of knowledge)   25, 26, 37, 45, 47, 58–60, 68, 81, 86, 88, 94, 101, 104, 148, 182, 201
freedom   3, 29, 42, 43, 48, 53, 74, 75, 80, 85, 86, 93, 115, 133, 136, 143, 145, 146, 156, 160, 163, 174, 179, 192, 193, 203
French Revolution   69

Galelei, Galilieo   42, 125
Geist [spirit]   29, 45, 58, 85–6, 108, 157, 181, 203
genius   158–64, 197
geometrical method [*more geometrico*]   9, 88, 94, 124, 127, 201, 205
Glockner, Hermann   199

Harris, H. S.   1, 199, 203, 204
Harvey, William   199
Hegel's *Differenzschrift*   204
Hegel's *Encyclopedia of Philosophical Science*   1, 11, 69, 101, 152, 153, 164, 165, 199, 200, 203, 206, 207
Hegel's *Lectures on Aesthetics*   21, 62, 200, 204
Hegel's *Lectures on the History of Philosophy*   69, 75, 76, 82, 94, 152, 203, 206
Hegel's *Philosophy of Right*   1, 11, 19, 60, 61, 83, 200, 204
Hegel's *Science of Logic*   1, 11, 12, 15, 21, 28, 57, 74, 77, 81, 87, 97, 99, 124, 133, 149, 170, 174, 200, 205, 206
Hegel's *Wastebook*   68, 116, 120, 160, 204, 205
Hegel's "Who Thinks Abstractly"   48
Heidegger, Martin   132
Heraclitus   7, 47, 111, 149, 168
history   12, 27, 50, 51, 61, 138–40, 151–2, 186, 202
Hobbes, Thomas   69, 78, 112, 124, 205, 206
Homer   63, 102, 204, 205
Houlgate, Stephen   200, 202
human nature   152–8, 163, 197
Hume, David   127, 201

imagination   60, 77, 89, 91–3, 97, 100, 101, 104, 107, 123, 156, 157, 160, 182, 192, 196, 204, 207
immediate knowing   4–5, 8–9, 41–4, 53–8, 160–4, 177–82

impasse [*aporia*]   23, 80, 123, 146, 201
infinite (as self-relation)   46, 58, 60, 187, 195
infinite regress   115
insight [*Einsicht*]   26, 44, 56, 65–6, 70, 81–2
intuition [*Anschauung*]   8, 12, 43, 55, 75, 79, 102, 126, 154, 163, 177, 179, 187, 200, 205, 207

Jacobi, Friedrich   53
judgment (logical)   37, 68, 69, 74, 111, 121, 134, 200

Kant, Immanuel   2, 7–9, 16, 22, 28–30, 47, 55, 62, 66, 69, 70, 75–80, 83, 87, 89–90, 100, 105, 110, 124–9, 134–6, 157, 166, 174, 188, 201–3, 205, 207
Kaufmann, Walter   199
Klein, Jacob   205
knot (epistemic) [*Hauptknote*]   52–4
Kreines, James   202

Lauer, Quentin   199
Locke, John   76, 79, 124, 154, 201, 205
Lucretius   115

magnitude   128–9, 187
Maker, William   199, 201
Malabou, Catharine   206
Marx, Werner   199, 204
method   3–4, 7–17, 40, 47, 78–81, 141, 149, 187–8, 192–6, 199, 200
misology   158–60, 196
music   88, 102, 121–3, 143, 146, 148–50
myth   6, 36, 73, 161, 198

Naturphilosophie   66, 75–7, 204
negativity   112–16, 169–74, 179–80
Newton, Isaac   80, 124, 187, 205
nihilism   45, 58–63
nominalism   69
non-actual [*nicht wirklich*]   106, 109, 115, 129, 183, 187, 191
nothingness   13–14, 68, 80, 116, 133, 205
Nuzzo, Angelica   200

objectivity   113, 129
ousia [substance, being]   92–3, 136
Owl of Minerva   59–61

patience 8, 25–7, 36, 39, 67, 80, 87, 92, 98, 103, 141, 156, 158, 164, 170, 171, 174, 177, 189, 192, 197, 198
phrenology 11, 84
Pinkard, Terry 199, 203
Pippin, Robert 202
plasticity 172, 173, 195, 206
Plato 2, 12, 14, 15, 26, 36, 92, 102, 116–17, 123, 124, 127, 145, 161, 165, 167, 171–3, 198
poetry 52, 63, 74, 146–9, 160, 176, 177, 194, 197, 202, 204
predicate 42, 124, 133, 135, 140–1, 144–6, 149, 193–6
presentation (of philosophy) 12–13, 20–1, 37–9, 117, 137, 141
presuppositionless thinking 87, 200, 201
private language 153
proof 6, 42, 80, 119, 126, 142, 181, 186, 187, 196
psychoanalysis 174

Räsonieren [argumentative rationalization] 141–6, 155–8, 192–4
reason (as purposive activity) 32, 83, 88, 134–8, 180
recollection [*Er-Innerung*] 8, 9, 24–7, 43, 45, 46, 50–4, 57–63, 80, 82, 95, 103, 104, 117, 127, 128, 135, 164, 174, 182–3, 188
reformation 69
rhythm 146–8
romanticism 52, 73, 76, 77, 135, 159, 162, 177

Sache Selbst [the main concern/the issue itself] 33–7
Schacht, Richard 199
Schelling, Friedrich 2, 65–9, 73, 75, 159, 162–4, 179, 203, 204, 206
Schlegel, Friedrich 37, 202
Schleiermacher, Friedrich 53
scholasticism 69, 102, 158
science 7–10, 37–9, 54, 154, 176–7
self-mediation 56–8, 180, 201
self-motion 112–16, 183
Seneca 68
Siep, Ludwig 199
skepticism 2, 6–8, 27, 52, 67, 82, 127, 133, 143, 144, 156–8, 171, 201

Solomon, Robert 199
sophistry 2, 44, 101, 122, 127, 142–4, 157, 193, 196, 197
speculative proposition 141–50, 193–6
Spinoza, Baruch 9, 16, 94, 124, 149, 179, 201
stoicism 32, 68
subjectivity 110, 113, 135–7, 143, 155–8, 163
substance (as subject) 26, 94, 133–4, 142, 179
system 41–5, 66, 88, 133, 136–8, 162–4, 169–74, 176–81

tautology 19, 34, 35, 139, 186
technical language 21–2, 150, 201
teleology 8, 55, 62, 125, 128, 134–6, 165
thinking 99–107, 207
time 105, 187
to ti en einai [what has been and keeps on being] 136
transcendental idealism 51, 77, 205

understanding (as analytic power) 99–102, 122, 124, 127, 183, 186
unity of being and thinking 148–50, 189–91
unity of form and content 10–13, 146–50

Verene, Donald 199, 204
Vernunft [reason]. *See* reason (as purposive activity)
Verstand [understanding]. *See* understanding (as analytic power)
violence (as opposite of nature) 70, 75, 93, 94, 112, 134, 164
void 112–15, 185
Vorstellung [imagination, representation]. *See* imagination

Winfield, Richard 200, 201
Wirklichkeit [actuality]. *See* actuality
Wissenschaft [science]. *See* science
Wittgenstein, Ludwig 132, 153, 167
wonder 23, 89, 113

Yeats, W. B. 19, 41, 65, 85, 119, 131, 151, 169
Yovel, Yirmiyahu 199

Zeno 112
Zeus 161

www.ingramcontent.com/pod-product-compliance
Lightning Source LLC
Chambersburg PA
CBHW062223300426
44115CB00012BA/2201